Excel

ADVANCED SKILLS

ENGLISH

YEAR 5

AGES 10–11

READING AND COMPREHENSION WORKBOOK

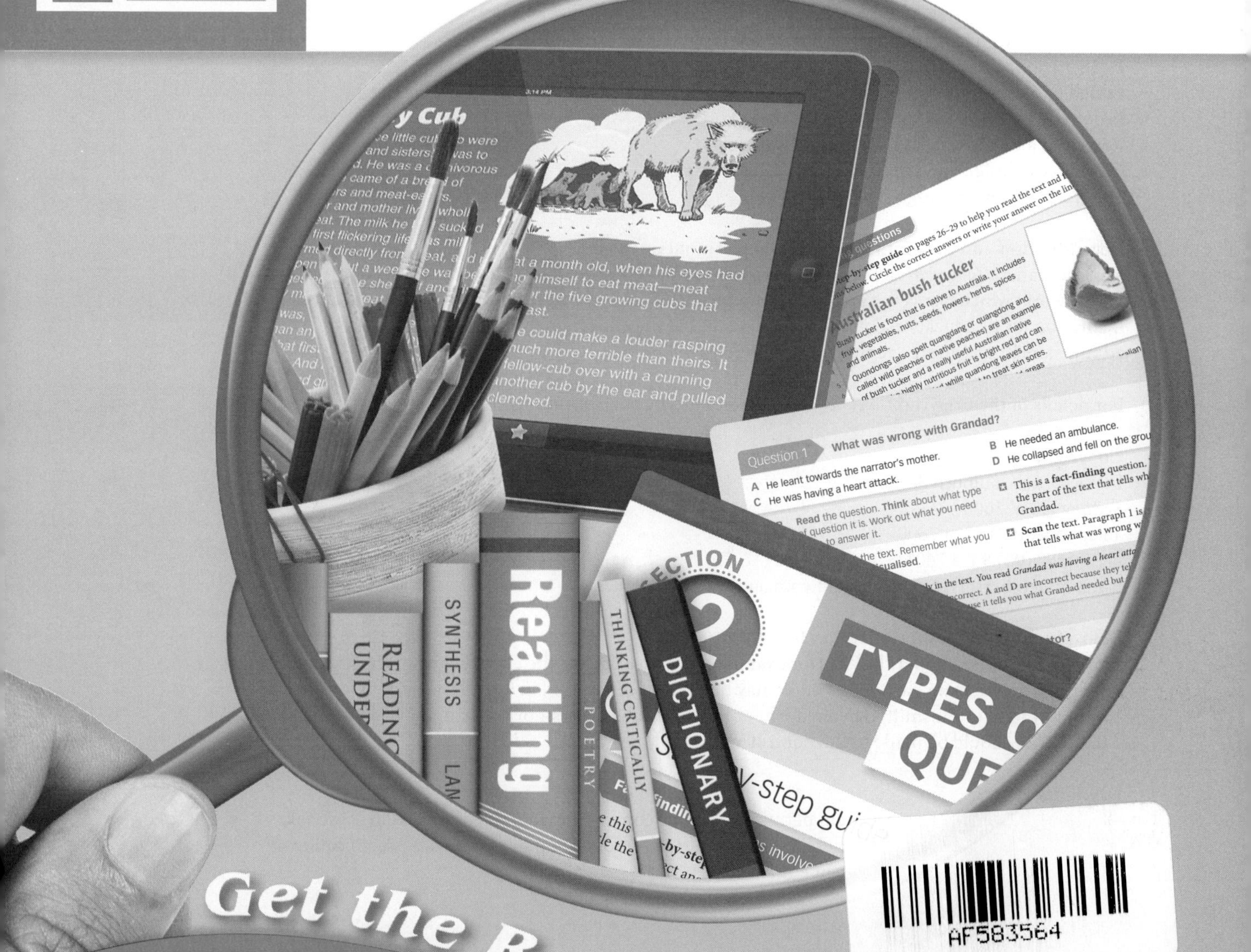

Get the Results You Want!

PASCAL PRESS

Tanya Dalgleish

Reprinted 2016 (twice), 2018, 2020 (twice), 2022

Updated in 2023 for the NSW Curriculum and Australian Curriculum Version 9.0 changes

ISBN 978 1 74125 454 9

Pascal Press
PO Box 250
Glebe NSW 2037
(02) 9198 1748
www.pascalpress.com.au

Publisher: Vivienne Joannou
Project editor: Mark Dixon
Edited by Leanne Howard
Proofread by Michele Croucher and Mark Dixon
Reviewed and answers checked by Glenda Walsh
Cover, page design and typesetting by DiZign Pty Ltd
Printed by Vivar Printing/Green Giant Press

CONTENTS

How to use this book

This book is designed to help students improve their reading comprehension skills and become more competent, reflective and critical readers.

It provides a step-by-step method of answering different types of comprehension questions, including those in standardised tests such as NAPLAN. Students are taught the strategies to read effectively.

The book is organised in four sections.

Section 1 Reading strategies

This section begins with a summary of the way the Step-by-step guide works for each type of comprehension question dealt with in this book. It defines the eight useful reading strategies frequently referred to. Once students have worked through Sections 1 and 2, they can use this guide to answer the mixed questions in Section 3.

Tips

- Make sure each student has ready access to the Step-by-step guide on page 4 as a useful reference when answering comprehension questions.
- Teach or revise the reading strategies of skimming and scanning, as well as ways to improve reading for understanding using the strategies of visualising, connecting, predicting, inferring, monitoring and judging (reading reflectively and critically).
- Have students complete the practice activities.

Section 2 Types of questions

This section deals with the five question types covered in the book. There is a chapter on each type: fact-finding, inferring, synthesis, language and judgement.

Each chapter begins with a sample reading text and step-by-step guide to reading that text and answering the particular comprehension questions.

There are five to six questions for each text. These are mostly multiple choice but at least one question per text requires a short written answer.

Tips

- Start with the chapter on fact-finding questions because these are usually the most straightforward questions to answer, depending on the complexity of the text. Judgement questions require higher-order thinking skills so they are dealt with last in the sequence here.
- Read and discuss the sample text at the beginning of the chapter. Point out the text's structure and language features. Discuss the content of the text and its purpose and audience.
- Talk to students about the type of question, how to identify it, what it's asking for and how to answer it. The Step-by-step guide makes clear to students the thought processes involved in reading with understanding.
- Discuss the strategies that competent readers use when reading a written text and answering comprehension questions.
- Discuss the answer explanations. These make it clear to students why their answers are correct or incorrect.

- Have students independently complete the comprehension tasks in each chapter.

Section 3 Bringing it all together

Mixed questions

This section provides 18 reading texts with mixed question types for further practice.

Tips

- Have students complete the comprehension tasks independently in this section.
- Have students check their own answers and compare them with the answer explanations.

Section 4 Answers

This section explains why answers are correct or incorrect. A suitable written answer is supplied for each short-answer question. The multiple-choice and short-answer questions enable the students to self-assess.

Tips

- Assess students' results. Analyse the patterns of correct and incorrect answers in students' results to identify areas of strength and weakness to assist with further development. Use this information to target and revise areas that need further attention.
- Identify the kinds of comprehension questions students are having difficulty with. ESL students often have most difficulty with inferring types of questions and questions which require background knowledge, or which use idioms that native speakers of English grow up using or knowing. English idioms can cause problems for many students, but especially students for whom English is an additional language or dialect (EAL/D). Comprehension questions that depend on these concepts and ideas are specifically taught in the language questions section of this book.

Text overview grid

The Text overview grid on pages 128–131 provides a summary of the types of texts covered in the reading comprehension section of this book. It also offers additional teaching points and suggested ideas for student writing. Writing practice in different forms and genres will consolidate students' understanding of how texts are constructed and help them develop critical literacy.

Types of texts

The texts included in this book are defined according to their purposes: informative, imaginative and persuasive. Extracts from classic texts have been chosen to support the Australian Curriculum English Literature strand. Texts have also been chosen to support General Capabilities (Ethical Behaviour, Intercultural Understanding) and Cross-curricular Priorities (Aboriginal and Torres Strait Islander Histories and Cultures, Sustainability, Asia and Australia's engagement with Asia) of the Australian Curriculum.

READING STRATEGIES

Step-by-step guide

This section provides a summary of the way the **Step-by-step guide** works for each type of comprehension question. On page 5 you will find definitions of the eight useful reading strategies frequently referred to in this book. Once students have worked through Sections 1 and 2 they can use the guide below to help them answer the mixed questions in Section 3.

Reading the text

Step		
STEP 1	**Skim** the text to see what it is about and how it is organised.	**Read** the title. Look at the illustrations and other visual elements. Make **predictions** about the subject and purpose of the text.
STEP 2	**Read** the text. **Monitor** your reading to make sure you understand it.	**Visualise** and **connect** with the ideas in the text. **Think** about what you already know about the subject and the type of text. Make **predictions.** Make **inferences**. Reflect on meanings and make **judgements**.

Answering specific types of comprehension questions

Step			
STEP 3	**Read** the question. **Think** about what type of question it is. Work out what you need to do to answer it.	For a **fact-finding** question you need to find the part(s) of the text where the answer is stated directly.	pp. 26–29
		For a **synthesis** question you need to think about how ideas and information relate to each other in the text.	pp. 34–37
		For an **inferring** question you need to read between the lines to work out an answer that is not stated directly in the text.	pp. 42–45
		For a **language** question you need to work out the meaning and effects of the language used in the text.	pp. 54–57
		For a **judgement** question you need to make judgements about the information and ideas in the text, the writer's purpose and the values and attitudes embedded in the text.	pp. 66–69
STEP 4	**Think about** the text. Remember what you have read and **visualised**. **Scan** the text to find the relevant parts. Look for key words or phrases. **Re-read** part or all of the text if necessary. Find answers directly stated in the text. **Infer** meanings or work out the answer using clues and evidence in the text and from your own knowledge. Think critically. Draw conclusions. Make **judgements**.	For a **fact-finding** question, scan the text to find the relevant parts. Look for words or phrases used in the question. Re-read parts of the text or the whole text if necessary, to find the answer.	
		For a **synthesis** question, scan the text to find the relevant parts. Look for words or phrases used in the question. Re-read parts of the text or the whole text if necessary. Pull together the threads of meaning and draw your own conclusions.	
		For an **inferring** question, scan the text for the relevant parts. Re-read parts of the text or the whole text if necessary. Use clues in the text to help you work out what is implied to answer the question.	
		For a **language** question, scan the text for the relevant parts. Re-read parts of the text or the whole text if necessary. Examine how language is used in context. Use your knowledge of language conventions, persuasive devices and figurative language to answer the question.	
		For a **judgement** question, scan the text for the relevant parts. Re-read parts of the text or the whole text if necessary. Think critically. Make judgements based on evidence in the text and your own knowledge and understanding to answer the question.	

Terms used in the Step-by-step guide

Skimming

- Skimming over the text before you start reading tells you a lot about the text and how it is organised.
- Look at the text's structure and features. Skim headings and subheadings. Look at visual elements. Predict the purpose and audience for the text.

Good readers notice all of these things as they skim a text.

pp. 6–7

Visualising

- Visualising (forming mental pictures) as you read helps you maintain focus during reading, connect to the meaning of the text and remember what you are reading about.

Good readers visualise what they are reading about and store these images in their short-term memory.

pp. 8–9

Connecting

- Connecting your own life and experiences with what you are reading helps you make sense of the text. Think: How is this story like my life? What does this remind me of? What do I already know about this subject? Have I seen this kind of text before? Where? What do I recognise about the language of the text and its structures and features?

Good readers connect to ideas in a text as they read. They relate new knowledge to existing knowledge and understanding about texts, themselves and the world.

pp. 10–13

Predicting

- Making predictions about a text before you start reading, as well as while you read, helps you engage with the text. Predict what the text will be about. Predict the purpose and audience for the text. If you come across a word you are unfamiliar with use the context to predict what the word could be and its likely meaning. Predict what will come next in the text.

Good readers continually make predictions about a text and revise their predictions as they read.

pp. 14–15

Inferring

- Making inferences as you read means working out what the writer is suggesting when it is not stated directly in the text.
- Writers often leave it up to the reader to read between the lines of a text. They give enough clues and contextual support for readers to be able to infer the intended meanings. Sometimes writers leave meaning open to the reader's interpretation.

Good readers make inferences as they read, reading between the lines to work out intended meanings in the text.

pp. 16–18

Monitoring

- Monitoring your reading means thinking about the text as you read and making sure it makes sense. When you monitor your understanding of a text you realise very quickly when meaning breaks down. You re-read parts of the text to revise your understandings.

Good readers monitor their reading to maintain meaning as they read. They read on, to confirm or refute predictions and inferences, then re-read and revise understanding when inferences don't make sense. They self-correct.

pp. 18–19

Judging

- Judging means thinking critically as you read. You judge the information and ideas in the text and the ways these are expressed or implied. Making judgements about a text is an important part of being critically literate.

Good readers make judgements about a text, its context and its purpose as they read. Critically literate readers can judge whether a text is reliable, trustworthy, relevant, current, accurate, interesting, entertaining or useful based on their own purposes for reading. Critically literate readers can make judgements about the attitudes and values embedded in texts.

pp. 19–23

Scanning

- Scanning means looking quickly through sections of a text for specific words, phrases or images. Scanning is useful when checking for facts.

Good readers can quickly find what they need in a text without having to read whole texts or sections of text.

pp. 24–25

Reading with understanding

This section provides practice activities for the eight strategies referred to in the **Step-by-step guide** on page 4. These strategies support reading with understanding and answering comprehension questions.

They are:

1. Skimming
2. Visualising
3. Connecting
4. Predicting
5. Inferring
6. Monitoring
7. Judging (reading reflectively and critically)
8. Scanning.

Effective readers use these strategies simultaneously without even being aware that they are doing so. They make decisions about which strategies to use depending on the text and their purposes for reading.

1 Skimming

What is it? **Skimming** is a useful quick 'first glance' strategy to get a general idea of what a text is about and how it is organised, as well as its purpose and audience. Skimming a text's structure and features helps you make predictions and judgements about the text before you even read any of the text.

When you skim a text you can often tell whether it is an informative, imaginative or persuasive text. You notice features such as lists, paragraphs, columns, diagrams and maps. You skim a text to judge whether you want to read it.

How do you do it? When you skim a text your eyes move quickly across and down, or zigzag over the text, stopping briefly at the parts that get your attention such as headings, words in bold or illustrations. You notice how the text is organised. You might read the headings and subheadings or you might just look at the illustrations.

For example, you might:

- skim a novel to get a general idea of the author's style, the chapter titles and what the illustrations tell you, then use this information to make a judgement about whether or not to read the novel
- skim a recipe book for a photo of something that you'd like to eat then read that recipe
- skim a reference book to judge whether it will be useful for a class project.

Have a go!

Skim the texts below. You don't need to read the texts. Just skim over each text's structures and features and identify what kind of text it is. Be as quick as you can. Choose a label from the box for each text.

poem   explanation   playscript   newspaper article

MELBOURNE CHRONICLE

26TH JANUARY 2012

Robogal a winner!

The Young Australian of the Year Award for 2012 has been awarded to Marita Cheng. Prime Minister, Julia Gillard, presented the trophy on the steps of Parliament House in Canberra for Australia Day.

Ms Cheng is founder of Robogals, an organisation that encourages females to take an interest in engineering. As an engineering student at the University of Melbourne Ms Cheng realised that males outnumbered females in engineering courses and careers by 10 to 1, right across Australia, so she decided to do something about that.

Engineers design, invent and build everything from buildings and bridges to aeroplanes and bicycles, appliances and the millions of devices that improve lives but Ms Cheng is especially interested in robotics. As a child, helping her mother do the household chores, Marita dreamed of a day when robots could do all the chores for her. That idea has been a major inspiration for her choice of engineering and computer science courses at university. She believes that, in the future, robots will improve the lives of people all around the world.

Ms Cheng founded 'Robogals' in 2008 working as a volunteer, with her university peers, to visit schools and talk to girls about careers in engineering and technology. Robogals makes sure that girls know that engineering is not just for boys, running workshops in robotics to demonstrate that engineering is a great career choice. Ms Cheng hopes more girls become engineers. She has been described as a visionary leader: Robogals was internationally recognised in 2011 as an outstanding youth social initiative.

The Young Australian of the Year Award is presented each year to Australians aged between 16 and 30 who have made outstanding contributions to the community or who have achieved excellence in their chosen fields.

Extremes

Wind: fluttery breezes brush my cheek
but bullying gusts tear at my shirt; rip off my hat.
And raging storms snatch branches off trees
and roofs off the houses along city streets.

Rain: gentle drips feed the earth
but driving rain fills up the drain pipes;
rushes in torrents.
And flooding rain blocks off the roads
and isolates people in small country towns.

Heat: sunshiny mornings hasten new growth
but blistering heatwaves send us indoors,
seeking cool places.
And scorching drought cracks open the earth
and dries up all life on parched open plains.

by Tanya Dalgleish

A ....

B ....

Why sea levels are rising

Climate change is causing sea levels to rise at a faster rate than previously predicted by scientists.

Sea levels rise in two ways

1 Land-based ice melts into the sea.

a In Greenland warmer weather is causing the ice sheet to melt at the surface and the melted water is running off the top of the ice sheet and into the sea.

b In Antarctica warmer seas are undermining the ice shelf from below, causing large masses of ice to break off. As soon as these chunks of ice hit the sea they cause the sea level to rise in the same way that a chunk of ice added to a glass of water will make the water level in the glass rise. These icebergs float in the sea until they melt. If the West Antarctic ice sheet fully breaks up, the sea is predicted to rise by 6 m.

c The world's glaciers are melting and contributing to sea-level rise. Diminishing glaciers will also result in water shortages for millions of people because glaciers are fresh water storehouses.

2 Warm water expands.

Water expands as it heats so sea levels are rising because oceans are taking up more space.

Major consequences

A rise in sea levels has two major consequences.

Inundation of low-lying coastal areas. Seawater floods agricultural land contaminating it with salt. It is estimated that for every 2.5 cm of sea-level rise there is a corresponding 2.4 m horizontal shoreline loss due to erosion.

Some Pacific Islands will be completely submerged during this century.

Teacher trouble

Scene: Two boys are seated on a bench.

George: I don't like him.

Nikolas: Mmmm.

George: He made me redo that whole page of work because he didn't like it.

Nikolas: (nodding) Yeah.

George: I hate him. He's so unfair and mean. He picks on me all the time. I wish he'd go to another school.

Nikolas: Yeah.

George: Why do you think he picks on me? Maybe he just doesn't like me. Why would that be? I didn't do anything to him ... I muck around a little bit and have a joke but so does Lila and she doesn't get into trouble like me. I think she's funny, too.

Nikolas: Hmmm (sighs).

George: I get a little loud sometimes ...

Nikolas: (emphatic nodding) Yeah.

George: (pause) ... but that couldn't be why he picks on me (pause) ... He just hates me, don't you think?

Nikolas: (silence)

George: (pause) ... So maybe I don't ALWAYS do my homework (pause) ... and (pause) ... maybe

Nikolas: Yeah?

George: and ... well... maybe ... I rarely do my homework ...

Nikolas: Mmmmm.

George: but that's no excuse for him to pick on me. Telling me I can do better, telling me he's disappointed in me, saying he expects more from me. Who does he think he is?

Nikolas: (eyebrows lift)

George: (whining) He's just too bossy! He's just unfair. He's a bully; telling me I have "unfulfilled potential". Huh! ... and "a poor attitude". What a joke! He drives me nuts.

C ....

D ....

Answers **A** newspaper article **B** poem **C** explanation **D** playscript

② Visualising

What is it? **Visualising** means making mental pictures or picturing information in your mind as you read. Visualising helps you engage with a text so you understand it more readily and remember what you've read.

How do you do it? You picture in your mind what is described in the text.

For example, you could visualise:

- what an animal looks like based on a factual description
- what the finished dish will look like from reading a recipe
- a setting described in a narrative
- a character in a novel based on a description given by the author or another character as narrator.

Have a go!

Extract from *Black Beauty* by Anna Sewell

The Hunt

I and the other colts were feeding at the lower part of the field when we heard, quite in the distance, what sounded like the cry of dogs. And soon the dogs were all tearing down the field. After them came a number of men on horseback, all galloping as fast as they could.

Read one line of the text at a time. Close your eyes after each line and visualise what you have read. Engage all your senses. Think about the sounds, smells, feelings and sensations, as well as the images described in the text. Compare what you visualised with the answers provided.

A I and the other colts were feeding at the lower part of the field ...

What do you see? What's happening? Imagine it in motion like a film strip.

Answer You should have visualised a field (paddock or meadow) with a number of colts (young male horses). The *colts* are *feeding* so there must be grasses. The *field* slopes down to where the colts are *at the lower part.*

B

> … when we heard, quite in the distance, what sounded like the cry of dogs.

What do you see?

Answer You should see the colts stop feeding to listen. As they listen they might lift their heads. Their ears might twitch. You should hear the *cry of dogs* (barking, yapping, yelping).

C

> And soon the dogs were all tearing down the field.

What do you see?

Answer You should see the dogs running *down the field. Tearing down the field* means they were racing fast, pushing to get ahead of each other. Hear their cries.

D

> After them came a number of men on horseback, all galloping as fast as they could.

What do you see?

Answer You should see *men* galloping *on horseback* chasing after the dogs that are barking and howling. You might hear the galloping hooves of the horses. Maybe you can see their hooves kick up clods of earth. Visualise the colts looking on from where they were feeding at the lower part of the field.

E As you visualise the text, think about what it means. Connect the ideas in the text with your existing knowledge. Have you seen a scene like this on television, or in a movie? Do you think you know what's happening? Can you infer what the men and dogs are up to?

Write your ideas.

....

....

....

....

Answer You might be able to infer that the dogs are tracking an animal such as a rabbit in an activity called hunting. The dogs are following the scent trail and the men on horseback are following the dogs. The dogs are very excited. That's why they make a lot of noise. You should recognise that the text was either written many years ago or is set in the past (in fact, it was written in 1877). The type of hunting activity described in the book *Black Beauty* is rare now because of people's awareness of animal cruelty. Modern laws specify that any hunted animal be killed humanely.

③ Connecting

What is it? **Connecting** with a text means engaging with it and relating the ideas in it to yourself and your life. It means making connections between things you already know or know about and the new information in the text. Connecting helps you understand and remember what you are reading. Readers connect to texts in different ways based on their own life experiences.

How do you do it? Read the text and think about the ways you connect with it. You connect with a text when you think:

'This reminds me of …'

'I've been to a place like that.'

'I've done that.'

'I saw something like that …'

'I already know some things about this subject.'

'I've read this kind of text before …'

'I recognise the kind of language used in this text.'

For example, you might:

- connect with characters in a novel when you empathise with them and relate to their experiences
- connect with the ideas in a newspaper article if you are interested in the topic (a topic of interest will capture your attention and engage your feelings in a way that makes you connect to what is written)
- connect your experiences of cooking and your understanding of recipes to your reading of a new recipe.

Have a go!

You connect with characters in a text when you empathise with them and their situation.

Read *Bruno*, connect with the ideas in the text and answer the questions.

To *empathise* means to put yourself in someone's position and understand how they feel.

Bruno

Scott was really worried about his dog. Bruno hadn't been himself for days. He hadn't been eating and that was NOT normal. And now Bruno was just lying on his beanbag, not moving; also not normal. Scott had phoned his mother in a panic after school. She said they'd take Bruno to the vet when she got home from work. Scott knew what the vet would say. She'd say, "Bruno is 16 years old. That's a good long life. You don't want Bruno to suffer do you, Scott?"

The same thing had happened with his cat. She got cancer and stopped eating and the vet said she was in pain. Mum and Dad decided it was better to have her put down than let her suffer. Scott agreed but that didn't make it any easier to say goodbye. And he didn't want to say goodbye to Bruno. Bruno was really his Dad's dog. His Dad got Bruno from the Animal Shelter when Bruno was just a sad unwanted puppy. Oh no, Dad was going to be really upset. Scott felt sick.

A Have you ever lost a pet or a loved one, or felt like Scott feels? Explain an experience of your own that connects somehow to the text.

....

....

....

B Explain how Scott feels about telling his father.

....

....

....

C What would the author want readers to do about Bruno in Scott's place?

....

....

....

D Describe Bruno as you visualised him.

....

....

....

Compare your answers with these suggestions:

Answers

A Your response to the text will depend on your personal experience of loss or grief and how it is similar to or different from Scott's situation. If you have not experienced loss for yourself you might connect the text to a novel your have read or a film you have seen.

B If you connect with Scott's character and situation you will easily recognise that Scott feels concerned and worried about his father because his father and Bruno have been together for 16 years, since Bruno was just a puppy. You read *Oh no. Dad was going to be really upset.* Scott knows his father is going to be extremely sad when Bruno dies.

C You can judge that the author wants readers to accept that the kindest thing is to put Bruno to sleep so he doesn't suffer any more pain.

D The way you visualised Bruno will depend on dogs you have owned or known, or read about, or seen on television or in film. The Bruno you visualised will vary from the way other readers would have visualised him. The writer hasn't described Bruno so you can visualise him how you like. This is how you connect to the text and make it personally relevant.

Elaborating

What is it? Another way to help you connect with a text is to elaborate on it. **Elaborating** means adding extra details not stated directly or implied in the text. A reader's elaborations don't alter the meaning of the text but add fine details that make the text more relevant personally.

How do you do it? As you read think about the meaning of the text and fill in details for yourself.

For example:

The main character in a novel has a pet cat. The cat is not described by the author/narrator because its appearance does not affect meaning in the story. You elaborate on the text by visualising a grey cat because you have a grey cat. This is a way you connect your personal life to the ideas in a text. You can continue to visualise a grey cat for the rest of the narrative, unless the writer eventually describes the cat and you find out that the cat is not grey. Usually a writer will only do that for a reason—to shock or surprise the reader or to make the reader question what has happened earlier in the text.

Have a go!

Read this extract from *Black Beauty*, visualise the scene as the author has described it and then fill in details for yourself by elaborating on the ideas in the text.

> I and the other colts were feeding at the lower part of the field when we heard, quite in the distance, what sounded like the cry of dogs. And soon the dogs were all tearing down the field.

Write three elaborations about the text. Make sure you add fine details without altering the meaning.

A ....

B ....

C ....

Compare your answers with these suggestions:

Your elaborations on the text will be personally related to your experiences of the ideas in the text.

Answers

A If you've seen horses you might visualise these colts lifting their heads and twitching their ears when they hear the dogs, as they become alert and stop eating.

B You might fill in details such as the colours of the colts based on horses that you have seen somewhere.

C You might also elaborate on the breed of dog and how many there were.

The author doesn't need to specify these things as they don't alter meaning. You can elaborate in your own way to connect with the text.

Have a go!

Read *Gone fishing* and visualise the scene. Then answer the questions below to elaborate on the text, filling in the details that the writer hasn't stated directly or inferred in the text.

Gone fishing

Jordan woke with a start. It was the first day of the school holidays. He jumped out of bed and shook his brother's shoulder. "Ben, wake up. We need to get moving."

Ben opened his eyes and was out of bed in a flash reaching for his shorts and pulling on a T-shirt. They'd organised their backpacks with provisions the night before; all their favourite snacks. Now they just needed to collect their drink bottles from the fridge and their fishing gear from beside the front door and they were on their way. It was a kilometre walk to the creek from Grandma's house and they wanted to be there by sunrise.

A How old is each boy? What do the boys look like?

....

....

B What snacks did the boys take?

....

....

C Describe the walk to the creek from Grandma's.

....

....

D Compare your answers with someone else's. How were your elaborations similar?

....

....

How were they different? ....

....

Answer Your elaborations help you connect to the text. They can't be wrong as long as you haven't changed the meaning of the text. Your elaborations will be different from other people's based on your own experiences and background.

For example: you might have visualised the boys' snacks as muesli bars and cookies. Another person might have visualised apples and sandwiches. It would depend on each person's understanding of the word *snacks* and their experience of heading outdoors on an adventure.

④ Predicting

What is it? **Predicting** means thinking ahead as you read a text and guessing what might come next based on what you understand so far. Predicting makes you an active reader. It helps you connect to the text and remember what it is about.

How do you do it? As you read you use evidence in the text to make predictions. You can change your predictions as you read on and get new evidence.

This one might be useful.

For example, you can predict:

- the contents of a book by skimming its cover
- the meaning of a word from its context or from reading on and finding out more
- the next word in a text using your knowledge of language patterns
- what an article in a newspaper will be about from the photograph that accompanies it
- what might happen next in a narrative.

Have a go!

You can predict or anticipate what might happen next in a narrative, confirming your predictions or rejecting them and changing your mind as you read on.

You read *Sammy loved mice …*

You are likely to predict and visualise a boy or girl with a pet mouse.

Read on. *She loved them a lot.*

You now know Sammy is a girl's name and you visualise a girl handling a pet mouse.

Read on. *Yes, Sammy the python loved mice very much. They were delicious.*

You now know Sammy is a python so you correct your predictions and adjust your mental picture.

Have a go!

You can predict the meaning of an unfamiliar word in a text by thinking about how it's used in context. You do not need to read or decode every word. You can usually predict and then work out meanings when you read on and consider word use in the context of the sentence, paragraph or whole text.

You read *Marine turtles have a large carapace.*

You might not be familiar with the word *carapace* but you needn't stop reading at *carapace* and grab a dictionary. You can predict that a *carapace* is something on the turtle's body because it's described as *large* and something that turtles *have*. But read on and find out.

This shell varies in colour from greenish with dark mottling in Green Turtles, to black with light mottling in Leatherback Turtles …

So now you realise a *carapace* is a *shell*.

Have a go!

Read *Who goes there?* and predict what will happen in the end.

Who goes there?

Suzi peeked out into the dark from behind the curtain. She was sure she'd seen a shadow cross the front of the house. She was home alone while her mum drove to the train station to collect her sister. She hoped they'd be back soon. Her mum had locked every door and window before she'd left but Suzi ran quickly around the house and quietly checked them all again. The lights were out due to the storm otherwise she'd have turned on the verandah light.

She should have gone with her mum but it was cold out and she didn't want to get dragged out because of her sister, yet again. She kept her torch switched off so whoever was outside wouldn't know she was here. What was taking Mum so long?

She crept back to the window. There was the shadow again. She ducked down to the floor below the window ledge. She held the phone in her hand ready to dial 000 if she had to. She tried to steel her nerve to raise her head and peek though the gap in the curtain again. But she was too scared.

Write your predictions here.

....

....

....

Answer Your predictions will depend on your own experiences (including your experiences of scary stories, family relationships or older siblings) and the ways you connect these to the text. You might predict that the writer continues to build the suspense but you could predict that Suzi's mum will arrive home, check the front porch and discover the neighbour's cat or a tree blowing in the wind, the power will be reconnected, the lights will come back on and all will be well. You might infer that Suzi's imagination has created suspense and danger where there is none.

Compare your predictions with a friend's. How were they similar?

....

....

How were they different? ....

....

Have a go!

Use your knowledge of language (grammar and vocabulary) to predict the words that are missing in the following sentences.

A The children quickly .... across to the fence.

B The children smiled. The ice-cream was ....

C Dad was .... annoyed. The car wouldn't start, again.

Compare your answers with these suggestions:

Answers

A When you read the sentence you can readily predict that the missing word will be an action verb and you can infer the missing word's meaning. The answer can be any verb that gets children quickly to the fence. Suitable verbs include 'ran', 'raced', 'sprinted' and 'rushed'.

B You can predict that the missing word is an adjective. You can infer that it is a positive evaluation because the children *smiled.* The answer is 'delicious' or any positive adjective that means 'delicious' and can be used to describe the taste of ice-cream.

C You can predict that the missing word is an adverb such as 'really' or 'very'. The adverb increases the intensity of *annoyed*. The use of an intensifying adverb also increases the modality of the sentence.

⑤ Inferring

What is it? **Inferring** meaning is when you use all the information in the text to work out what the writer means when information is not stated directly in the text.

How do you do it? You think as you read, reading between the lines to work out what is implied by the writer.

Have a go!

Read the following, infer meaning and then answer the questions.

It was Monday. Sophie did not want to get out of bed. She had a maths test today and she was still tired after a big weekend at her dad's place. She heard Mum in the kitchen. She pulled the covers over her head and willed it to be Sunday again.

A Why didn't Sophie want to get out of bed?

....

Answer You read that *It was Monday* and *She had a maths test today.* You can infer that Monday is a school day and Sophie didn't want to go to school and do her maths test. You also read that *She was still tired after a big weekend at her dad's place.*

B Did Sophie enjoy going to her dad's place?

....

Answer You can infer that Sophie enjoyed going to her dad's place. She'd had a *big weekend,* which implies a good weekend, and the fact that she *willed it to be Sunday again* implies that Sunday at her dad's place was enjoyable.

Have a go!

Read the following text and then make inferences to answer the question.

Oscar jumped out of bed before his alarm went off. Today was the swimming carnival. He was very excited. He'd registered for four races and had been training hard.

Why did Oscar jump *out of bed before his alarm went off*?

....

Answer You can infer that Oscar got up early because he was keen to get to the swimming carnival. You can infer that he thinks he will do well at the swimming carnival because the text says he's *very excited* about it and he's been *training hard.*

Have a go!

You can often infer how writers feel about a subject from their use of emotive or evaluative language.

Read *The circus* and make inferences about the writer's attitude towards the subject. Write your answer on the lines below.

The circus

An animal circus is currently performing for audiences in my town. An animal circus is a circus that uses animals to amuse and entertain people. Exotic animals such as elephants and tigers are confined to small cages and hauled from town to town on the backs of trucks. I won't be attending the circus!

What is the writer's attitude towards circuses?

....

....

Answer The writer does not directly state an opinion about circuses but you can infer that the writer does not agree with animal circuses. *Confined* and *hauled* are emotive terms. *Uses animals to amuse* and *I won't be attending* imply that the writer has a negative attitude towards animal circuses.

Have a go!

You can infer the way characters in narratives feel about each other through their interactions, what the narrator tells you, and through what they say about each other.

How does Suzi feel about her sister in the text *Who goes there?* (See page 15.)

Answer The narrator tells you what Suzi is thinking. You can infer that Suzi feels resentful and annoyed. You could probably infer that she blames her sister somewhat for the situation she's in: home alone, in the dark and scared. You could also infer that there are other unresolved issues between the sisters. You could wonder: Why does Suzi feel that way about her sister? What has gone on before the events in the text?

⑥ Monitoring

What is it? **Monitoring** meaning means noticing as you read when a text doesn't make sense. Monitoring meaning means thinking as you read so that you immediately recognise when meaning breaks down or you lose the thread of the text. Maintaining the thread of the text is part of remembering what you have read. It is important for understanding the text and for connecting meaning across the text.

How do you do it? Think as you read.

Question the text: Does that make sense?

Self-correct when meaning breaks down, by re-reading previous sentences, sections of the text or the whole text to clarify things you might have misunderstood, misinterpreted or forgotten.

Adjust your predictions and rethink your inferences if necessary.

Have a go!

You read *A green turtle has a sharp, finely serrated beak-like mouth to share or crush food.*

If you are monitoring meaning as you read, you think about what you have read—*share food*.

You decide 'that doesn't make sense'.

You question the text: Why would turtles have beak-like mouths to *share food*? and How could turtles *share food* with their beak-like mouths?

You try to visualise turtles 'sharing' food in this way but it doesn't seem correct.

So you re-read the text.

This time you read *A green turtle has a sharp, finely serrated beak-like mouth to shear or crush food*.

You understand that you have misread *shear* for 'share'. You are not sure what *shear* means so you read on.

Their beaks are perfectly adapted for grazing on seagrass where they act like lawn mowers, cutting the tops off the grass but leaving the roots so that the grass grows back healthily.

You work out that the meaning of *shear* is 'cut' or 'trim'. This is vastly different in meaning to 'share'.

If you didn't monitor meaning you would have missed this important piece of information.

Monitoring meaning, in this way, happens instantaneously as you read if you THINK!

⑦ Judging

What is it? **Judging** a text means reading critically and evaluating as you read.

How do you do it? Think beyond the words in the text as you read and make judgements about ideas, the writer's purpose and values, and the intended audience for the text.

For example, you can judge:

- an informative text's usefulness or trustworthiness
- a character's behaviour in a narrative
- the context in which a text was created
- the values and attitudes embedded in a text about gender, race, religion, culture, society, sexuality, appearance, age and ability
- the effectiveness of a text in achieving what you judge to be the writer's purpose
- the importance or relevance of ideas in a text
- the effectiveness of the way language is used in a text (emotive and evaluative language, persuasive devices, figurative language)
- whether there are alternative perspectives on the ideas in the text
- whether a text represents a dominant or minority viewpoint.

Have a go!

Read *Huntsman spiders* and make judgements about the text's usefulness for the purposes listed below.

Huntsman spiders

A huntsman is a large hairy spider with eight long legs and eight eyes. They can grow to 15 cm across their leg span. There are approximately 1000 species of huntsman spider in the world and around 90 different kinds of huntsman live in Australia. Most huntsman spiders are a grey-brown colour but some can be mottled, banded or even a yellow colour, like the rare tiger huntsman found in North Queensland.

Circle the correct answer. Is the text relevant to your needs if your purpose is to:

A do a project on the tiger huntsman? yes no maybe

B find out what to do if a red-back spider bites you? yes no maybe

C write a horror story about giant huntsman spiders attacking humans? yes no maybe

Answers

A No. The text does not have enough detailed information about the tiger huntsman to be useful for a project.

B No. The text does not instruct on first aid for a red-back spider bite.

C Maybe. The text gives information about the huntsman spider species. Authors often research factual information and use it in narratives to give their texts credibility.

Have a go!

Make a judgement about the usefulness of websites.

Your purpose is to research koalas. Which website would you choose?

A maryjoe'skoalablog@hotmail.com.au

B http://www.environment.nsw.gov.au/animals/thekoala.htm

C http://www.abc.net.au/news/2014-01-10/new-koalas-introduced-to-tidbinbilla-nature-reserve/5193526

....

Answer **B** is correct because it is a NSW Government website. You would expect an Australian government website to have more accurate and unbiased information than a personal blog such as in website **A**. You would judge **C**, the ABC News, to be more reliable than a personal blog but because it is news coverage you would judge it unlikely to be useful for this particular research purpose. Also the title is about koalas introduced to Tidbinbilla reserve so you would judge the text as not useful for your specific research purposes.

Have a go!

Read *Tennis* and make judgements about the character's behaviour.

Tennis

It was too hot. She purposely hit the ball over the fence and into the park. There. That'll show him. He could just go fetch. She sat down and ignored the looks he was giving her. It was just too hot to practise today. She'd told him that. And she had a blister on her toe. She'd told him that, too. He should have listened. It's his fault she was hot. Who cares about stupid tennis anyway?

Write your judgements on the lines.

....

....

Answer You can judge that the character is not behaving nicely. She doesn't want to practise. She's whinging about the heat. She hits the ball over the fence on purpose to inconvenience her coach/brother/father/playing partner. You can judge that her behaviour seems sulky and uncooperative.

Have a go!

Read the extract from *The Adventures of Huckleberry Finn* by Mark Twain. Use evidence in the text to make judgements, including about the time and place in which the text was created.

The Adventures of Huckleberry Finn

At first I hated the school, but by and by I got so I could stand it. Whenever I got uncommon tired I played hookey, and the hiding I got next day done me good and cheered me up. So the longer I went to school the easier it got to be. I was getting sort of used to the widow's ways, too, and they warn't so raspy on me. Living in a house and sleeping in a bed pulled on me pretty tight mostly, but before the cold weather I used to slide out and sleep in the woods sometimes, and so that was a rest to me. I liked the old ways best, but I was getting so I liked the new ones, too, a little bit.

Write your judgements on the lines.

....

....

Compare your answers with these suggestions:

Answers

You might judge that:

- the story was written long ago or was set long ago. You can tell this because of the old-fashioned English used: *by and by, uncommon tired, hookey, the hiding I got, warn't so raspy* and that the narrator often chose to *slide out of bed* and *sleep in the woods*. In fact the story was published in 1884. It was set a few decades earlier than that in the Mississippi area of America.

- the story is set in America long ago because you connect the language used in the text with how you've heard characters speak in movies set in America in the past. You might recognise that *playing hookey* is an American term. It means skipping school or work.
- the narrator (Huckleberry Finn) is a school boy who isn't used to going to school and plays *hookey* when he gets tired of school. For this he gets a *hiding.*
- the narrator has missed a lot of school because he uses expressions such as *done me good.*
- the narrator is used to sleeping outdoors and fending for himself because he says *Living in a house and sleeping in a bed pulled on me pretty tight mostly.* You can judge that the expression *pretty tight* is not a good feeling because the narrator escapes to the woods *for a rest* and likes *the old ways best.*

Have a go!

1 A writer's choice of words can reinforce negative stereotyping. You can judge the values and attitudes embedded in a text by examining the language choices of the writer. From each pair of expressions below, choose the one that is the more inclusive and unbiased.

A a handicapped person/a person with a disability ....

B given name/Christian name ....

C the Koori lawyer/the lawyer ....

D Ms Jenkins/Miss or Mrs Jenkins ....

Answers

A *A person with a disability* is the appropriate term. The term *handicapped person* defines the person in a negative way instead of recognising that he or she is a person foremost who also happens to have a disability.

B *Given name* is the appropriate term. It is a non-religious term. Many Australians do not identify themselves as Christians. The term *Christian name* is inappropriate for people from non-Christian religious backgrounds or for people of no religion. The term *given name* is less confusing than a term such as *first name* for people from cultures in which the first name is the family name.

C *The lawyer* is the correct term. Labelling the lawyer according to cultural background is irrelevant. It implies that this aspect of the lawyer is unusual and so has to be pointed out.

D *Ms* is the appropriate term for all females regardless of marital status in the same way that *Mr* is the appropriate term for all males, regardless of marital status. Whether a person is married or not is irrelevant when you address them by a formal title such as Ms Jenkins. Some women choose to be called Mrs or Miss but that is a personal choice that they can make known to others.

2 Write a judgement about the way language reinforces negative attitudes and stereotyping in each of the following sentences.

A A school principal has an important job. He needs to be a good educator as well as communicator.

....

B Throughout the centuries man has shown he is an amazing inventor.

....

C Two police officers escorted the Aboriginal prisoner to the courthouse for the hearing.

....

D A blind guitarist came to school today to talk to us about music.

....

E The old man next door is stuck in a wheelchair.

....

F He's a big girl on the football field.

....

Answers

A By referring to a school principal as *he*, the writer implies that people in positions of authority are automatically male or more likely to be male. The writer should have said 'School principals have … They need to be …' or 'A school principal … She/He …'

B The writer's attitude discounts women's place in history. The writer should have used the more inclusive terms 'humankind' or 'people' instead of *man*.

C The fact that the prisoner is identified as Aboriginal is evidence of the writer's attitudes. It is an aspect of racial stereotyping to identify a prisoner by his or her ethnicity. It connects the crime to cultural background.

D The writer focuses on a disability instead of the ability of the guitarist. The fact that the guitarist was visually impaired is irrelevant because the guitarist was talking to students about music. The writer should have said a guitarist came to school today to talk to us about music. Later in the text, if relevant, the writer could have said the guitarist was visually impaired.

E The writing displays negative attitudes towards the elderly as well as towards people with disabilities. A wheelchair is a mobility device. It should be viewed positively as it helps the person maintain independence and remain active. The use of *stuck* is negative. The use of *old man* is also negative. It implies frailty, incompetence and uselessness.

F The writing displays a sexist attitude. The phrase *big girl* is a put-down. Describing a male as a girl in this way is implying that girls are inferior.

8 Scanning

What is it? **Scanning** is a strategy that helps you find specific information in a text. When you scan a text you look quickly through it for particular words, phrases or images you want to locate. You scan a text when it is not necessary to read or re-read the whole text to find the specific information you need. Scanning is useful for fact checking.

Note that when answering reading comprehension questions it is important to read the whole text before attempting to answer any questions. If you read the question first and try to simply scan the text for answers you are unlikely to answer inferring, synthesis, language and judgement questions accurately, and you might not find the exact answer required for a fact-finding question.

How do you do it? Look quickly through the text to find the part you need and then examine that area more closely. You can scan a page, a paragraph, a list, an index, a menu bar in digital texts, a glossary or a Table of Contents. You can scan headings and subheadings.

For example, you can scan:

- a text that you have already read to check your memory for the facts
- for your name in an alphabetical list
- a list of ingredients in a recipe to look for particular ingredients
- a product catalogue to see if the item you want is available or on special
- an invitation to a function to find out what time it starts
- a group photo for your image
- a map for a place name or icon
- a graph for a particular item.

Have a go!

1 You plan to cook ANZAC Biscuits. You're not sure that you have enough golden syrup. Don't read through every ingredient in the list. Just scan the list to find out how much golden syrup is required. Write your answer.

> **ANZAC biscuits**
> **Ingredients**
> 1 cup oats
> 1 cup flour
> 1 cup desiccated coconut
> ½ cup sugar
> ¼ cup golden syrup
> 1 tablespoon water
> 1 teaspoon bicarb soda

....

Answer You should have scanned the list to find golden syrup. You read *¼ cup golden syrup.*

2 Scan the text *Huntsman spiders.* You do not need to read the whole text. Find answers to these questions:

A How big can a huntsman grow?

....

B What is a baby huntsman called?

....

Huntsman spiders

Appearance

A huntsman is a large hairy spider with eight long legs and eight eyes. They can grow to 15 cm across their leg span. There are approximately 1000 species of huntsman spider in the world and around 90 different kinds of huntsman live in Australia. Most huntsman spiders are a grey-brown colour but some can be mottled, banded or even a yellow colour, like the rare tiger huntsman found in North Queensland. All spiders moult as they grow, shedding their old skin.

Caring for the young

The female huntsman makes a silken egg sac and then lays about 200 eggs inside it. She guards her egg sac for three weeks. She does not eat at all during this time. She will defend the eggs, rearing up on her back legs. When the spiderlings hatch they are tiny and quite pale. In some huntsman species the young stay with their mothers while they moult several times and grow larger.

Compare your answers with these suggestions:

Answers

A Scan the subheadings to narrow your search. You would expect to find information about how big a huntsman can grow under the subheading *Appearance*. You might already have an idea about the answer in your head so you know the sort of number you are looking for. Scan the paragraph for words related to size or measurement. You read a fact in the text: *They can grow to 15 cm across their leg span.*

B Scan the text for the subheading that is most likely to give you information about baby spiders. You know that baby spiders are the spiders' young so you would expect the information to be found under the subheading *Caring for the young.* You might already know what a baby spider is called but you need to confirm what baby huntsman spiders are called. Scan the paragraph for words that might tell you the answer. You read *the female … lays about 200 eggs*. Further on you read *When the spiderlings hatch.* Connect this information with existing knowledge and understanding that some baby creatures hatch from eggs, and you can work out that baby huntsman spiders are called *spiderlings.*

TYPES OF QUESTIONS

Step-by-step guide to **fact-finding** questions

Fact-finding questions involve finding information that is stated directly in the text.

Use this **Step-by-step guide** to help you read the text and **find facts** to answer the questions below. Circle the correct answers or write your answer on the lines.

STEP		
STEP 1	**Skim** the text to see what it is about and how it is organised.	**Read** the title of the text *An emergency*. Look at the illustration and other visual elements. Notice that the text is written in paragraphs. Make **predictions** about the subject and purpose of the text.
STEP 2	**Read** the text. **Monitor** your reading to make sure you understand the text.	**Visualise** and **connect** with the ideas in the text**. Think** about what you already know about the subject and the type of text, a recount. Make **predictions** Make **inferences**. Reflect on meanings and make **judgements**.

An emergency

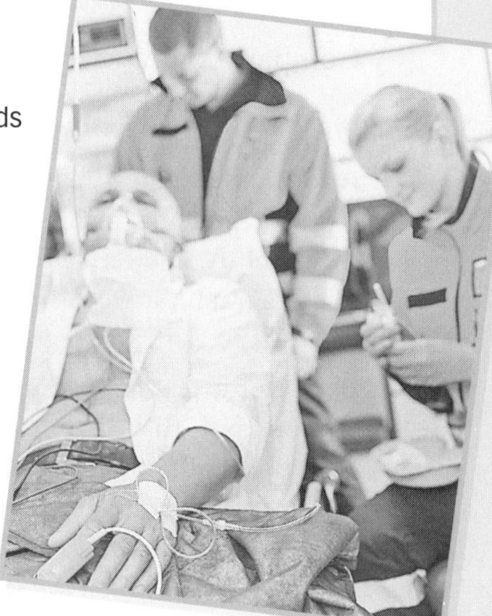

A week ago, when my mum and I were visiting Grandad he suddenly said he felt giddy, then his knees started to crumple and he leant towards my mum and she sort of held him as he collapsed onto the ground. Mum told me to call an ambulance and tell the operator that Grandad was having a heart attack.

I dialled 000 and asked for an ambulance. I had to recite the address, the nearest cross street and the phone number. For a minute I couldn't remember Grandad's phone number so the lady said she'd come back to that. Her name was Joanne. She asked me to tell her exactly what had happened. She said she had contacted the paramedics and they were on their way and that she would relay information to them about my grandad. She told me to open the front door and look out for them. Mum said Grandad was looking worse and having trouble breathing. I could tell she was really scared. Then I heard the sirens and the ambulance pulled up out the front, so Joanne said goodbye.

The paramedic in charge was Shawnie. She used needles to give Grandad some medicine in both his arms. She used scissors to cut off his shirt in order to attach him to a machine that would monitor his heart rate. The paramedics rolled Grandad onto a stretcher, carried him to the ambulance and drove away, sirens blaring.

Mum and I drove to the hospital in our car. We were really worried about Grandad but when we got to the hospital he looked much better. We thanked those paramedics for saving Grandad's life but Shawnie said everyone had played their part and contributed. Grandad is going to be fitted with a defibrillator, a tiny device that will be wired up to his heart all the time to give it an electric shock if it ever needs it.

Question 1 What was wrong with Grandad?

A He leant towards the narrator's mother.
B He needed an ambulance.
C He was having a heart attack.
D He collapsed and fell on the ground.

STEP 3 **Read** the question. **Think** about what type of question it is. Work out what you need to do to answer it.
✪ This is a **fact-finding** question. You need to find the part of the text that tells what was wrong with Grandad.

STEP 4 **Think** about the text. Remember what you have read and **visualised**.
✪ **Scan** the text. Paragraph 1 is the part of the text that tells what was wrong with Grandad.

C is correct. The answer is stated directly in the text. You read *Grandad was having a heart attack* (see lines 5–6).

Check to confirm that the other options are incorrect. **A** and **D** are incorrect because they tell you what Grandad did but not what was wrong with him. **B** is incorrect because it tells you what Grandad needed but not what was wrong with him.

Question 2 Why is Grandad getting a defibrillator?

A to give his heart an electric shock
B to help cure him
C to give him some medicine for his heart condition
D to call the ambulance

STEP 3 **Read** the question. **Think** about what type of question it is. Work out what you need to do to answer it.
✪ This is a **fact-finding** question. You need to find the part of the text that tells why Grandad is getting a defibrillator.

STEP 4 **Think** about the text. Remember what you have read and **visualised**.
✪ **Scan** the text. Look for the key word *defibrillator*.

A is correct. The answer is stated directly in the text. You read *Grandad is going to be fitted with a defibrillator, a tiny device that will be wired up to his heart all the time to give it an electric shock if it ever needs it* (see line 23).

Check to confirm that the other options are incorrect. The defibrillator will not cure Grandad (**B**), give him medicine (**C**) or call an ambulance (**D**).

Question 3 What were some of Grandad's symptoms?

A giddy, trouble breathing, unable to talk
B giddy, collapsing to the ground, difficulty breathing
C hungry and thirsty
D giddy, then looking worse and not breathing

STEP 3 **Read** the question. **Think** about what type of question it is and what you need to do to answer it.
✪ This is a **fact-finding** question. You need to find the part of the text that tells you Grandad's symptoms.

Symptoms are the signs of illness.

STEP 4 **Think** about the text. Remember what you have read and **visualised**.
✪ **Scan** the text. Look for the parts of the text that tell you Grandad's symptoms.

B is correct. The answer is stated directly in the text. In paragraph 1 you read, *Grandad … said he felt giddy, then … he collapsed* (see lines 2–5). In paragraph 2 you read *Mum said Grandad was looking worse and having trouble breathing* (see lines 14–15).

Check to confirm that the other options are incorrect. **A** is incorrect because Grandad was talking when he said *he felt giddy*—unable to talk is incorrect. **C** and **D** are incorrect, as the text doesn't tell you that Grandad was hungry and thirsty, or that he stopped breathing.

Fact-finding questions involve finding information that is stated directly in the text.

An emergency

A week ago, when my mum and I were visiting Grandad he suddenly said he felt giddy, then his knees started to crumple and he leant towards my mum and she sort of held him as he collapsed onto the ground. Mum told me to call an ambulance and tell the operator that Grandad was having a heart attack.

I dialled 000 and asked for an ambulance. I had to recite the address, the nearest cross street and the phone number. For a minute I couldn't remember Grandad's phone number so the lady said she'd come back to that. Her name was Joanne. She asked me to tell her exactly what had happened. She said she had contacted the paramedics and they were on their way and that she would relay information to them about my grandad. She told me to open the front door and look out for them. Mum said Grandad was looking worse and having trouble breathing. I could tell she was really scared. Then I heard the sirens and the ambulance pulled up out the front, so Joanne said goodbye.

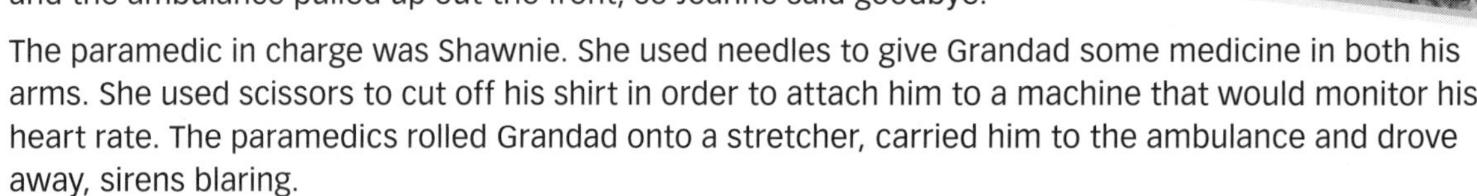

The paramedic in charge was Shawnie. She used needles to give Grandad some medicine in both his arms. She used scissors to cut off his shirt in order to attach him to a machine that would monitor his heart rate. The paramedics rolled Grandad onto a stretcher, carried him to the ambulance and drove away, sirens blaring.

Mum and I drove to the hospital in our car. We were really worried about Grandad but when we got to the hospital he looked much better. We thanked those paramedics for saving Grandad's life but Shawnie said everyone had played their part and contributed. Grandad is going to be fitted with a defibrillator, a tiny device that will be wired up to his heart all the time to give it an electric shock if it ever needs it.

Question 4 **When did Joanne say goodbye?**

A when she had all the information she needed
B after the ambulance had driven off with Grandad
C when the ambulance arrived
D when the narrator had given her grandad's address

STEP 3 **Read** the question. **Think** about what type of question it is. Work out what you need to do to answer it.

- This is a **fact-finding** question. You need to find the part of the text that tells when Joanne said goodbye.

STEP 4 **Think** about the text. Remember what you have read and **visualised**.

- **Scan** the text. Look for the key words *Joanne* and *goodbye*.

C is correct. The answer is stated directly in the text. You read *Then I heard the sirens and the ambulance pulled up out the front, so Joanne said goodbye (see lines 15–16)*. The conjunction *so* tells you that once the ambulance had arrived Joanne was no longer needed on the phone to relay information to the ambulance *SO* she said goodbye. *So* is a causal conjunction. It shows that events are connected through cause and effect.

Check to confirm that the other options are incorrect. **B** is incorrect because the conversation ended when the ambulance arrived. **A** and **D** are incorrect because Joanne continued to converse with the narrator after this information had been given.

Question 5 Who saved Grandad's life?

A the paramedics
B Shawnie, Joanne and Mum
C Mum, Joanne and the paramedics
D Mum, Joanne, the narrator and the paramedics

STEP 3 **Read** the question. **Think** about what type of question it is. Work out what you need to do to answer it.

- This is a **fact-finding** question. You need to find the part of the text that tells who saved Grandad's life.

STEP 4 **Think** about the text. Remember what you have read and **visualised**.

- **Scan** the text. Look for the key words *saved Grandad's life.*

D is correct. The answer is stated directly in the text. You read *We thanked those paramedics for saving Grandad's life but Shawnie said everyone had played their part and contributed* (see lines 22–23). *Everyone* means Mum, Joanne, the narrator and the paramedics. Note that the question uses *saved* and the text has *saving.* When you scan you need to look for all forms of the key words.

Check to confirm that the other options are incorrect. **A**, **B** and **C** list combinations of people involved in saving Grandad but only **D** lists everyone.

Question 6 What information did the narrator have to tell Joanne?

....

....

STEP 3 **Read** the question. **Think** about what type of question it is. Work out what you need to do to answer it.

- This is a **fact-finding** question. You need to find the parts of the text that tell what information Joanne was told.

STEP 4 **Think** about the text. Remember what you have read and **visualised**.

- **Scan** the text. Look for the part in paragraph 2 that tells of the phone call to the ambulance service.

The answer is stated directly in the text. You read *I had to recite the address, the nearest cross street … the phone number …* (and) *exactly what had happened* (see lines 7–11). Your answer must mention those four things.

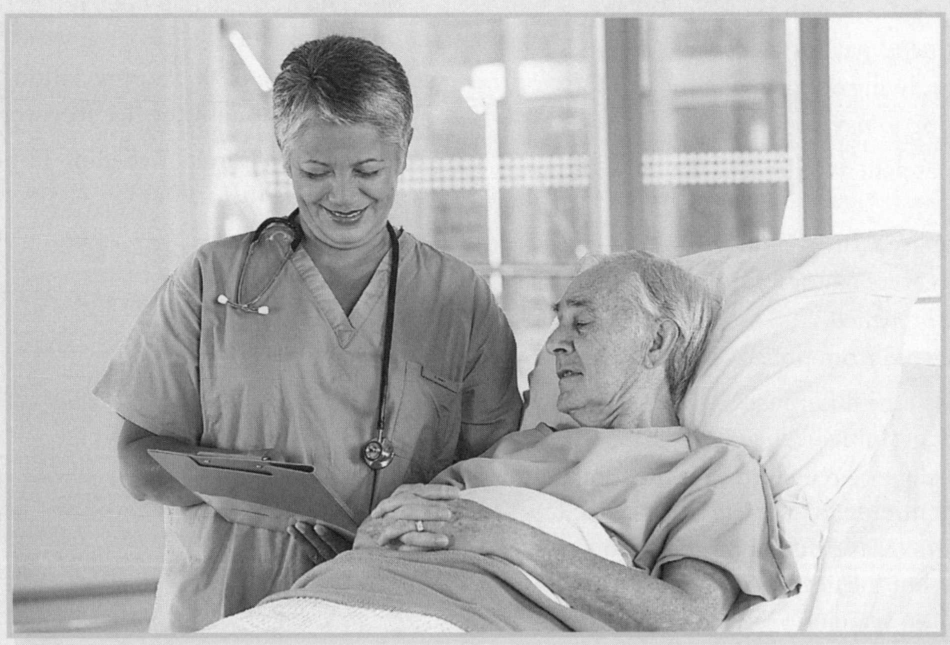

Fact-finding questions

Use the **Step-by-step guide** on pages 26–29 to help you read the text and **find facts** to answer the questions below. Circle the correct answers or write your answer on the lines.

The Eureka Stockade

Life for miners on the Victorian goldfields during the 1850s was extremely difficult. The name given to a miner at that time was 'digger'. Few diggers actually found any gold and even fewer struck it rich. Mostly diggers struggled in poor conditions. They struggled with the weather and living conditions in an often harsh environment and they were often ill-equipped.

The worst thing about being a digger was the requirement to pay for a mining licence. This licence entitled a miner to search for gold. Without a licence a digger could be fined and arrested. The police regularly raided mining camps to enforce this licensing law. Few miners could afford the licence fee and were resentful of a law they believed was unjust. In June 1854 Governor Hotham announced that police would conduct twice weekly mining licence checks. This outraged the miners further and set them towards armed rebellion against police.

The rebellion at the Eureka diggings in 1854 is often referred to as the Eureka Stockade. Led by Peter Lalor, the diggers constructed a barricade and burned their unfair licences as a form of protest. The miners pledged, 'We swear by the Southern Cross to stand truly by each other to defend our rights and liberties'. The Southern Cross referred to was a flag with a white cross joining five white stars on a dark blue background. It is now known as the Eureka Flag.

The diggers lost the battle of the Eureka Stockade but they won the legal battle that their rebellion instigated. In 1855 the Victorian Government implemented a mining tax, as a tax on gold found, to replace the unfair miner's licence which had to be paid regardless of whether the miner found gold or not. In Australia's history the Eureka Rebellion is the only time armed rebellion has been used to change unfair laws. The Eureka Stockade Rebellion is considered the birthplace of Australian democracy.

1. What is a digger in the text?
   - **A** a World War I soldier
   - **B** a goldminer
   - **C** a gravedigger
   - **D** someone who digs for treasure

2. What was the diggers' biggest complaint?
   - **A** the weather on the goldfields
   - **B** having to pay for a licence
   - **C** harsh living conditions
   - **D** having to pay a mining tax

3. What happened to diggers caught without a licence?
   - **A** They were fined or arrested.
   - **B** They were banned from the goldfields.
   - **C** They rebelled.
   - **D** They hid from police.

4. What was the difference between a mining tax and a mining licence?
   - **A** The digger's rebellion won the legal battle for a mining tax instead of a licence fee.
   - **B** The tax was paid if a miner discovered gold but the licence fee was paid for the right to search for gold.
   - **C** The tax was popular with the diggers.
   - **D** The police couldn't find and arrest miners anymore.

5. Why did the miners burn their licences? Choose all that apply.
   - **A** It was a protest.
   - **B** The licences had been replaced by a mining tax.
   - **C** It was a mark of appreciation.
   - **D** They thought the licences were unfair.

6. Why is the Eureka Rebellion important in Australia's history?

   ....

   ....

   ....

   ....

   ....

   ....

   ....

Answers and explanations on p. 96

Fact-finding questions

Use the **Step-by-step guide** on pages 26–29 to help you read the text and **find facts** to answer the questions below. Circle the correct answers or write your answer on the lines.

Huntsman spiders

There are more than 1000 different species of huntsman spider around the world. Most huntsman spiders are grey or brown but they can be varied in colour, including tones of orange or yellow. Some are mottled or have bands of brown or black. Females are larger than males. Their bodies can be 2 cm with a 15 cm leg span. A huntsman is a fast runner. The huntsman is often confused with a tarantula but the two species have differently jointed legs. A huntsman spider's legs are jointed so that their legs twist forwards and sideways, giving them a crab-like look and the ability to run sideways.

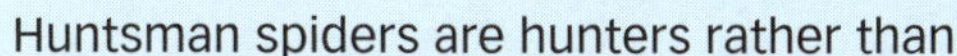

Huntsman spiders are hunters rather than web-building spiders. They hide in plants, under rocks or under loose tree bark, coming out at night to search for prey such as cockroaches which they run after to catch and eat. Spiders inject venom into their prey through their fangs. The venom paralyses the prey and begins the chemical breakdown of the prey's tissues. Spiders also regurgitate onto their food to help dissolve it. A spider sucks its liquid meal up through a tube-like mouth.

The female huntsman makes a silken egg sac and then lays approximately 200 eggs inside it. She guards her egg sac for three weeks, not eating at all during this time. She will defend the eggs, rearing up on her back legs in a threatening pose and will bite if provoked. These bites are relatively harmless to people but the huntsman prefers to run away from humans rather than chase or attack them. When the spiderlings hatch they are tiny and pale, usually undergoing several moults and darkening in colour, before leaving their mother. Birds, geckoes and wasps eat huntsman spiders.

1 What is special about the huntsman spider's legs?
- **A** They can run backwards and sideways.
- **B** They twist forwards and sideways.
- **C** They twist so a crab can run sideways.
- **D** They catch cockroaches.

2 Where might a huntsman spider hide?
- **A** under a rock
- **B** in a fridge
- **C** on tree bark
- **D** in a silken egg sac

3 How does a huntsman spider eat?
- **A** by sucking up liquid
- **B** by chewing
- **C** by swallowing prey whole
- **D** insects

4 What eats huntsman spiders?
- **A** people
- **B** other spiders
- **C** cockroaches
- **D** wasps

5 What is the role of a huntsman spider's venom?
- **A** It is injected through fangs.
- **B** It kills prey.
- **C** It begins the chemical breakdown of the prey's tissues.
- **D** It paralyses and helps dissolve prey.

6 How does a huntsman behave around humans?

Answers and explanations on pp. 96–97

Fact-finding questions

Use the **Step-by-step guide** on pages 26–29 to help you read the text and **find facts** to answer the questions below. Circle the correct answers or write your answer on the lines.

Australian bush tucker

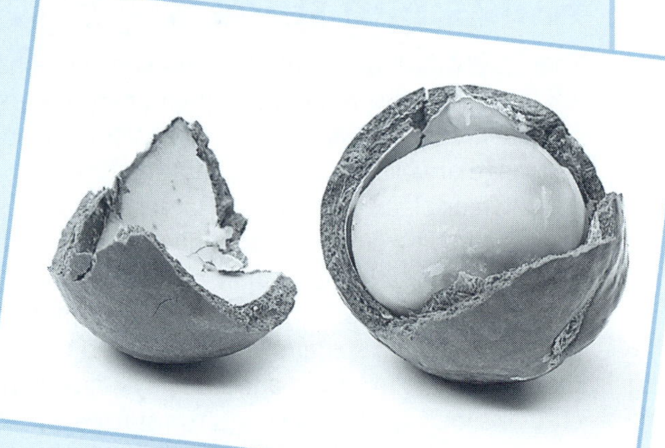

Bush tucker is food that is native to Australia. It includes fruit, vegetables, nuts, seeds, flowers, herbs, spices and animals.

Quondongs (also spelt quangdang or quangdong and called wild peaches or native peaches) are an example of bush tucker and a really useful Australian native plant. The highly nutritious fruit is bright red and can be eaten raw or dried while quandong leaves can be made into a medicinal ointment to treat skin sores. Quondong trees grow in arid and semi-arid areas of Australia.

The delicious and healthy macadamia nut is another example of Australian bush tucker. The macadamia tree is indigenous to Australia but is now grown commercially in other parts of the world. The nuts are actually toxic to dogs and can make them quite sick for a day or two. Names for this bush tucker in First Nations languages include gyndl, jindilli and boombera.

Witchetty grubs are another type of bush tucker. Witchetty grubs are the larvae stage of a few kinds of moth. The grubs can be eaten raw or cooked. Some people say the raw grubs taste like almonds. They are an excellent source of protein.

Honey ants are bush tucker. A honey ant's abdomen is used to store food for the ant colony. The food is in the form of a sweet liquid. The honey ant's abdomen can grow to the size of a grape as it fills with liquid. When food is needed by the colony the worker ants stroke the honey ant's antennae. This makes the honey ant regurgitate the liquid from its abdomen into the worker ant's mouth. People can eat honey ants whole.

1 What is bush tucker?
   - **A** any plant grown in the bush
   - **B** food native to Australia
   - **C** any plants and animals used for food
   - **D** all food from the bush

2 What part of the quondong tree do you eat?
   - **A** just the leaves
   - **B** any part of it
   - **C** bark
   - **D** fruit

3 Macadamia nuts are
   - **A** toxic to people.
   - **B** delicious but unhealthy.
   - **C** harmful to dogs.
   - **D** indigenous to various parts of the world.

4 Witchetty grubs
   - **A** shouldn't be eaten raw.
   - **B** turn into moths.
   - **C** look like almonds.
   - **D** can't be cooked.

5 Why is the honey ant's abdomen important?
   - **A** It grows to the size of a grape.
   - **B** It is bush tucker.
   - **C** It stores sweet liquid to feed the colony.
   - **D** The ant regurgitates it.

6 Write in your own words why quondong trees are useful.

....

....

....

....

....

....

Answers and explanations on p. 97

Use the **Step-by-step guide** on pages 26–29 to help you read the text and **find facts** to answer the questions below. Circle the correct answers or write your answer on the lines.

Bridport School News

October

Day for Children

The school has recently participated in UNICEF Australia's Day for Children, announcing at a school assembly that $1680 has been raised as a donation towards the education of children in Timor-Leste.

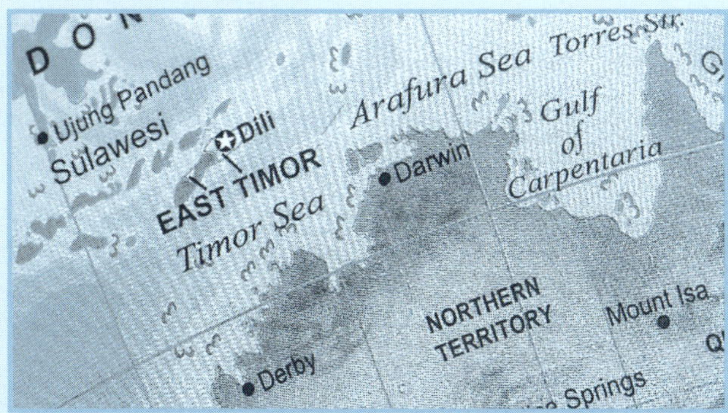

Timor-Leste

UNICEF Australia's Day for Children was established in 2006 as an annual fundraising event for Australian Schools. It supports the general work of UNICEF (United Nations International Children's Education Fund) to raise awareness of every child's right to an education, clean drinking water, sanitation, food and a safe home.

Bridport State School's Day for Children was launched by school captains Ahmed Khan and Melissa Jordan at an assembly of the whole school, parents and other community members. Principal Ms Julia Wong explained the Day for Children using a Powerpoint presentation of materials provided by UNICEF. Then students in Year 6 recited poems they had written in response to learning about Timor-Leste. Students were surprised to learn that Timor-Leste is only 450 km from Australia, off the coast of Western Australia and the Northern Territory.

Australian Aid (AusAID) is given to Timor-Leste to improve educational outcomes for children there. AusAID funding helps children attend school and stay at school for longer so that they have a better education and improved prospects for their future. Every year Bridport School has a fund-raising activity to help educate children in other countries.

1. Why did the school participate in the Day for Children?
   - **A** to raise awareness of the work of UNICEF
   - **B** to raise money for education
   - **C** to help feed children in other countries
   - **D** to participate in UNICEF's Day for Children

2. The school assembly included
   - **A** singing.
   - **B** a dramatic performance.
   - **C** poetry recitals.
   - **D** a debate.

3. Why did the Principal speak at the assembly?
   - **A** to tell the school where Timor-Leste is situated
   - **B** to welcome parents to the school
   - **C** to present information about the Day for Children
   - **D** to introduce Year 6 children

4. Why does AusAID want children to stay at school for longer?
   - **A** so that they can learn about Australia
   - **B** because a better education will give them a better future
   - **C** so that they stay at school longer
   - **D** so that they are happy

5. What facts did you learn about Timor-Leste in this article? Choose all answers that apply.
   - **A** It's 450 km from Australia.
   - **B** AusAID provides funding to Timor-Leste for education.
   - **C** It's in the Northern Territory.
   - **D** Timor-Leste children stay at school for longer than Australian children.

6. Who attended the launch of the school's Day for Children?

   ....

   ....

Answers and explanations on pp. 97–98

Step-by-step guide to **synthesis** questions

Synthesis questions involve connecting ideas and information from across the text.

Use this **Step-by-step guide** to help you read the text and **synthesise** information to answer the questions below. Circle the correct answers or write your answer on the lines.

STEP 1	**Skim** the text to see what it is about and how it is organised.	✪ **Read** the title *The Grey Cub*, an extract from *White Fang* by Jack London. Notice the visual elements. The extract consists of two paragraphs. Make **predictions** about the subject and purpose of the text.
STEP 2	**Read** the text. **Monitor** your reading to make sure you understand the text.	✪ **Visualise** and **connect** with the ideas in the text. **Think** about what you already know about the subject and the type of text, a narrative. Make **predictions. Infer** meanings. Reflect on and make **judgements**.

The Grey Cub

He was a fierce little cub. So were his brothers and sisters. It was to be expected. He was a carnivorous animal. He came of a breed of meat-killers and meat-eaters. His father and mother lived wholly upon meat. The milk he had sucked with his first flickering life was milk transformed directly from meat, and now, at a month old, when his eyes had been open for but a week, he was beginning himself to eat meat—meat half-digested by the she-wolf and disgorged for the five growing cubs that already made too great demand upon her breast.

But he was, further, the fiercest of the litter. He could make a louder rasping growl than any of them. His tiny rages were much more terrible than theirs. It was he that first learned the trick of rolling a fellow-cub over with a cunning paw-stroke. And it was he that first gripped another cub by the ear and pulled and tugged and growled through jaws tight-clenched. And certainly it was he that caused the mother the most trouble in keeping her litter from the mouth of the cave.

Extract from *White Fang* by Jack London, 1906, Part II Chapter III

Question 1 **What is the function of paragraph 1?**

A to establish the setting of the narrative
B to describe the carnivores
C to introduce the wolf family
D to introduce the fierce little cub

STEP 3	**Read** the question. **Think** about what type of question it is. Work out what you need to do to answer it.	✪ This is a **synthesis** question. You need to work out the function of paragraph 1 in the text as a whole.

Function means 'role' or 'job' so the question is asking *What job does paragraph 1 do?*

STEP 4 **Think** about the text. Remember what you have read and **visualised**.

✪ **Scan** the text. Find and re-read paragraph 1. **Think** about the information included in it. Ask yourself: What is the paragraph about? What does it tell the reader? To work out the answer you need to think about the whole of paragraph 1.

D is correct. The function of the paragraph is to 'introduce the fierce little cub'. Notice that most of the clauses start with, or include a reference to, the grey cub. You read *He was a fierce little cub* (see line 2). *He was a …* (see line 3) *He came …* (see line 4) *His father and mother …* (see line 5) *The milk he had …* (see line 6) *when his eyes …* (see line 8) *he was beginning himself …* (see line 9).

Check to confirm that **A**, **B** and **C** are incorrect. The paragraph does not describe the setting (**A**). It does not describe the carnivores (**B**). It mentions the wolf family members (**C**) but does not fully introduce them in the way that the grey cub is introduced.

Question 2 What is the function of paragraph 2?

A to describe the cub in more detail
B to set the scene for the complication
C to explain the cause of the mother wolf's problems
D to give the narrator's point of view about the wolves

STEP 3 **Read** the question. **Think** about what type of question it is. Work out what you need to do to answer it.

✪ This is a **synthesis** question. You need to **think** about the function of paragraph 2 in the text as a whole.

STEP 4 **Think** about the text. Remember what you have read and **visualised**.

✪ **Scan** to find paragraph 2. Re-read the paragraph. To work out the answer you need to **think** about the whole of paragraph 2.

A is correct. The function of paragraph 2 is to describe the cub in more detail. The information in the paragraph describes the cub's fierceness, its growl, its cunning and its habit of worrying its mother.

Check to confirm that the other options are incorrect. The paragraph does not set the scene for the complication (**B**), explain the cause of the mother wolf's problems (**C**) or give the narrator's point of view about the wolves (**D**).

Question 3 Which are the two topic sentences for the paragraphs?

A He was a carnivorous animal. His tiny rages were much more terrible than theirs.
B His father and mother lived wholly upon meat. He was a carnivorous animal.
C He was a fierce little cub. But he was, further, the fiercest of the litter.
D He was a fierce little cub. And certainly it was he that caused the mother the most trouble in keeping her litter from the mouth of the cave.

STEP 3 **Read** the question. **Think** about what type of question it is. Work out what you need to do to answer it.

✪ This is a **synthesis** question It is asking you to identify the topic sentence of each paragraph.

> The topic sentence is often (but not always) the first sentence in a paragraph. It summarises what a paragraph is about; it is the essence of the paragraph.

STEP 4 **Think** about the text. Remember what you have read and **visualised**.

✪ Re-read each paragraph if necessary. To work out which sentences are topic sentences you need to **think** about information included in each paragraph.

Answer **C** is correct. These sentences are the essence of their paragraphs about 'the fierce little cub'.

The other options do not include both topic sentences.

Step-by-step guide to **synthesis** questions *continued*

Synthesis questions involve connecting ideas and information from across the text.

The Grey Cub

He was a fierce little cub. So were his brothers and sisters. It was to be expected. He was a carnivorous animal. He came of a breed of meat-killers and meat-eaters. His father and mother lived wholly upon meat. The milk he had sucked with his first flickering life was milk transformed directly from meat, and now, at a month old, when his eyes had been open for but a week, he was beginning himself to eat meat—meat half-digested by the she-wolf and disgorged for the five growing cubs that already made too great demand upon her breast.

But he was, further, the fiercest of the litter. He could make a louder rasping growl than any of them. His tiny rages were much more terrible than theirs. It was he that first learned the trick of rolling a fellow-cub over with a cunning paw-stroke. And it was he that first gripped another cub by the ear and pulled and tugged and growled through jaws tight-clenched. And certainly it was he that caused the mother the most trouble in keeping her litter from the mouth of the cave.

Extract from *White Fang* by Jack London, 1906, Part II Chapter III

Question 4 **What do you understand of the story so far? Choose all that apply.**

A The cub belongs to a family of wolves.
B The cub is likely to be important to the story.
C The cub is insignificant in the story.
D The cub is likely to be a mischief-maker.

STEP 3	**Read** the question. **Think** about what type of question it is. Work out what you need to do to answer it.	This is a **synthesis** question. The question is asking you to summarise your understanding of the story so far. **Think** about the information included in the text by the narrator.
STEP 4	**Think** about the text. Remember what you have read and **visualised**.	**Scan** the text. To work out the answer you need to **think** about information across the text and what the narrator has told you.

A, **B** and **D** are correct. You have been told that the cub is part of a wolf family. You can recognise that the narrator is telling you that the cub is important in the story because your attention has been focused on it. You can predict that the cub will get into mischief when you read that he was the loudest and fiercest cub and he caused *the mother the most trouble (see lines 17–18)*.

C is incorrect. It contradicts the focus of the text.

Question 5 What is most likely to have occurred earlier in the story? Choose all that make sense.

A The mother wolf gave birth to the cubs.

B The wolf family moved into the cave.

C The mother wolf was killed.

D The adult wolves hunted for meat.

STEP 3 **Read** the question. **Think** about what type of question it is. Work out what you need to do to answer it.

✪ This is a **synthesis** question. It is asking you to **think** about events likely to have occurred before the events of the text.

STEP 4 **Think** about the text. Remember what you have read and **visualised**.

✪ To work out the answer you need to **think** about the facts given in the text.

A, **B** and **D** are correct. You know that the mother wolf gave birth to the cubs because you read *He was a fierce little cub … at a month old (see lines 2–8)*. You know that the wolves are living in a cave. You read *he was beginning himself to eat meat—meat half-digested by the she-wolf and disgorged for the five growing cubs (see lines 9–11)* so you know that the adult wolves have hunted for meat.

C is incorrect. You know that the mother wolf (or she-wolf) has not been killed as you read about her current activities in the text.

Question 6 What would you expect to happen next? Use your understanding of the story so far to make a prediction.

....

....

....

STEP 3 **Read** the question. **Think** about what type of question it is. Work out what you need to do to answer it.

✪ This is a **synthesis** question. It is asking you to **predict** what might happen next in the story. To answer this question correctly you need to **think** about the whole text so far and what it sets up for the future in the story.

STEP 4 **Think** about the text. Remember what you have read and **visualised**.

✪ **Scan** and re-read the text if necessary. **Think** about the story so far. Make **predictions** based on evidence in the text. At the end of paragraph 2 you read *And certainly it was he* [the cub] *that caused the mother the most trouble in keeping her litter from the mouth of the cave (see lines 17–18)*. The narrator says this to let readers know that something is going to happen. This is called foreshadowing. Writers use foreshadowing to alert readers to an upcoming issue or problem in a story. Foreshadowing can help build suspense.

Your predictions about what might happen next in the story need to involve the cub exploring beyond *the mouth of the cave (see line 18)*.

Synthesis questions

Use the **Step-by-step guide** on pages 34–37 to help you read the text and **synthesise** information to answer the questions below. Circle the correct answers or write your answers on the lines.

Book review: *Home and Away*

Home and Away is a picture book for mature readers. It gives a grim but realistic account of one family's desperate struggle for survival in Australia after a war breaks out and the family members become refugees. The book is confronting and sad. It challenges readers to put themselves in the shoes of people who become refugees or asylum seekers.

The story is narrated in the first person through a series of journal entries. There is a mum, a dad and the three children aged fifteen (the narrator), eleven and five. Both parents work. Grandma lives next door. The story begins with an introductory description of each family member and an account of a typical busy morning routine as parents and children have breakfast and leave the home for work and school. The family behaves just like every other average family but on the next page readers are shocked to learn that a war has started.

The narrator tells of the family's growing desperation. They pay people smugglers to take them to a place called Hollania where they hope to find sanctuary and begin new lives. They spend weeks at sea on a small, leaky, ill-equipped boat. Then when the children finally reach Hollania they are placed in a detention centre behind razor wire fences and labelled illegal immigrants by a country that does not want them.

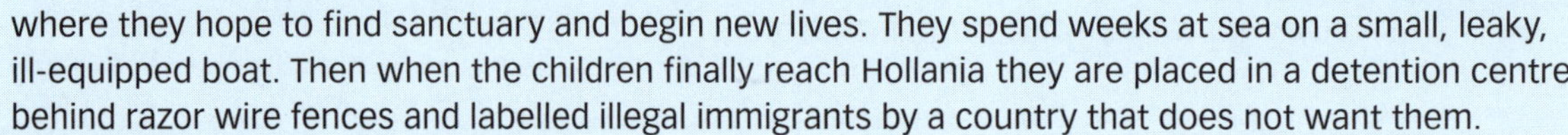

This thought-provoking picture book was a Children's Book Council of Australia Honour Book in 2009. It is definitely not for little children but it should be read and discussed in upper primary and secondary classrooms across Australia.

Home and Away by John Marsden and illustrated by Matt Ottley, 2008

1. What is the function of paragraph 2?
   - **A** to summarise the plot of a story
   - **B** to tell readers about journal writing
   - **C** to summarise the main events in a story
   - **D** to introduce the main characters in a picture book

2. What is the function of paragraph 4?
   - **A** to tell about the Children's Book Council Award
   - **B** to tell John Marsden's point of view
   - **C** to make a recommendation
   - **D** to summarise the story's conclusion

3. What is the purpose of the text?
   - **A** to tell readers about a picture book
   - **B** to help people empathise with refugees
   - **C** to retell a story about a family of asylum seekers
   - **D** to provide information about asylum seekers

4. What is the reviewer's attitude to refugees?

   ....

   ....

   ....

5. Does the reviewer's recommendation make YOU want to read the book. Explain your answer.

   ....

   ....

   ....

6. If John Marsden wrote a sequel for *Home and Away* what would you like it to be about?

   ....

   ....

   ....

Answers and explanations on p. 98

Synthesis questions

Use the **Step-by-step guide** on pages 34–37 to help you read the text and **synthesise** information to answer the questions below. Circle the correct answers or draw your answer in the box.

The woylie

Transcript: Radio interview

Radio host: Today on our program we welcome Nerida Kazumi who's going to talk to us about woylies. Good afternoon Nerida.

Nerida: Good afternoon and thank you for having me.

Radio host: Nerida tell us about the woylie.

Nerida: Yes, certainly. The woylie is a critically endangered Australian marsupial. It's sometimes called a brush-tailed bettong. There used to be two kinds of woylie but one kind is now extinct and so there's only one subspecies of woylie left and it is very, very rare.

Radio host: What does a woylie look like?

Nerida: It looks a bit like a miniature kangaroo but with a pointier nose and smaller ears. It's cute, furry, nocturnal, about 30 cm tall and has a long tail. It uses its tail to carry nesting materials. It forages for food so it plays an important role in aerating the soil and spreading seeds and fungi for a healthy ecosystem.

Radio host: Why is the woylie critically endangered?

Nerida: It once lived across half of Australia but now it only survives in a couple of small isolated pockets of Western Australia. Woylies have suffered a 90% population decline in recent years. Predators such as foxes, as well as loss of habitat and disease, have played a part but scientists aren't sure exactly why numbers of woylies have dropped so drastically so quickly. We've instigated a captive breeding program to ensure their survival.

Radio host: Are you confident the woylies will breed in captivity?

Nerida: Yes, we currently have three females with joeys in their pouches. We've used the generous donations from the public to recreate the woylies' natural environment as much as possible at our centre.

Radio host: Thank you for sharing your knowledge and insights into the plight of the woylie. It's been a pleasure.

Nerida: Thank you for having me.

1. What is the purpose of the text?
   - **A** to raise money for woylies in the wild
   - **B** to convince people to help prevent woylie extinction
   - **C** to present a point of view about endangered animals
   - **D** to inform people about woylies
2. What information about woylies is covered in the interview?
   - **A** the problems faced by woylies including loss of habitat
   - **B** what type of creature it is and the problems it faces
   - **C** what it is; what it looks like; why it's endangered; what's being done to help it
   - **D** a description of woylies and their habitat; what's being done to ensure the species survives
3. What information could a follow-up interview include? Choose all that apply.
   - **A** an update about the state of the captive breeding program
   - **B** what the woylie looks like
   - **C** how listeners can donate to help the woylies
   - **D** why foxes are killing woylies
4. Draw a conclusion about the future of woylies based on Nerida's attitude.
   - **A** They will become extinct in the near future.
   - **B** Three females have joeys.
   - **C** Captive breeding will ensure their survival.
   - **D** They are killed by foxes.
5. Draw your impression of a woylie. Draw it next to another object to show scale.

Answers and explanations on pp. 98–99

Synthesis questions

Use the **Step-by-step guide** on pages 34–37 to help you read the text and **synthesise** information to answer the questions below. Circle the correct answers or write your answer on the lines.

John Macarthur

John Macarthur holds an honoured place in Australia's history for his part in co-founding the Australian wool industry. There is, however, another side to his story—the story of a man who used his positions in the public service aggressively to further his own interests and build his personal fortune.

Macarthur arrived in the colony of NSW in 1790 as lieutenant in the New South Wales Corp. He gained favour with his Commanding Officer, Major Francis Grose, who promoted him to Paymaster for the Corps in 1792. In 1793 Grose, now acting governor, granted Macarthur 200 acres of land near Parramatta where Macarthur and wife, Elizabeth, established Elizabeth Farm. In 1805 under the patronage of Lord Camden in England, Macarthur was granted 10 000 acres (40 square kilometres) in the Cowpastures, which he renamed Camden Park. It was arguably the best farming land in all of NSW at that time and the Macarthurs farmed it using free convict labour.

Macarthur was known to be argumentative, ambitious and determined. He courted favour with powerful people and plotted to undermine anyone who stood in the way of his ambitions, including Governors Hunter, King, Bligh and Macquarie.

Macarthur was often accused of profiteering and was twice recalled to London to face court martial. On one occasion it was for his role against Governor Bligh during the Rum Rebellion, when Macarthur supported the commander of the NSW Corps in an armed takeover of the government. This rebellion is the only time in Australia's history that the government has been overthrown by armed action.

Macarthur is a man held in high regard in Australian history for his work with merino sheep, but at the same time it must be acknowledged that, in his day, he was regarded by many as corrupt and self-serving.

1 What is the purpose of the text?
- **A** to provide an autobiography
- **B** to report factual events in history
- **C** to present a point of view
- **D** to describe the history of the wool industry

2 What is the function of paragraph 1?
- **A** to provide an orientation to the wool industry
- **B** to describe John Macarthur
- **C** to describe the setting for Macarthur's life
- **D** to provide a thesis statement

3 What key point does the writer make about Macarthur's success in paragraph 2?
- **A** Macarthur was given a lot of land for free.
- **B** Macarthur served in the New South Wales Corps.
- **C** Macarthur was a public servant.
- **D** His properties were called Elizabeth Farm and Campden Park.

4 The writer thinks Macarthur got rich because
- **A** he was a lieutenant in the New South Wales Corps.
- **B** he plotted against governors.
- **C** he used Governors Hunter, King, Bligh and Macquarie.
- **D** he had powerful friends and allies.

5 Which statement is the main point of paragraph 4?
- **A** Macarthur faced court martial.
- **B** Macarthur was involved in illegal activities.
- **C** Macarthur started the rum rebellion.
- **D** Macarthur conspired to overthrow Governor Bligh.

6 Write a positive statement about John Macarthur.

....

....

Answers and explanations on pp. 99–100

Synthesis questions

Use the **Step-by-step guide** on pages 34–37 to help you read the text and **synthesise** information to answer the questions below. Circle the correct answers or write your answer on the lines.

The Chinese on the goldfields

The transportation of convicts to NSW ceased in 1840 causing a labour shortage in the colony. In order to overcome the labour shortage, the government organised for Chinese workers to be brought to Australia as indentured labourers. They were used for jobs such as clearing areas of bush, felling trees and digging wells.

When gold was discovered in the colony, Chinese workers, along with gold seekers from nations across the world, were drawn to the goldfields. By 1860 there was a large number of Chinese miners working on the goldfields. The Chinese miners were generally peaceful and industrious.

Many European miners were distrustful of the Chinese because of their different clothing, habits, customs and traditions. The harsh conditions on the goldfields fuelled these resentments. There were six anti-Chinese riots on the Lambing Flat goldfields of NSW in a period of 10 months during 1860–1861. The miners accused the Chinese of wasting water, which was costly to purchase when the creeks ran dry. The most serious riot saw 250 Chinese miners injured, and their property burnt or stolen. Not all residents of NSW held racist attitudes and some helped the Chinese in whatever ways they could, providing food and shelter, and risking the ire of angry mobs themselves.

The Governor of NSW sent troops to quell the rioting and insist that European miners obey the law and not harm the Chinese or their property. Public pressure mounted and the government was forced to do something about the civil unrest on the gold fields. The *Chinese Immigration Restriction and Regulation Act* was passed into law in 1861. This Act was designed specifically to restrict the numbers of Chinese immigrants to the colony. It is considered a precursor to the Federal Government's *Immigration Restriction Act* of 1901.

1 Which headline might have been found in a Chinese newspaper in 1861?

- **A** Chinese anger miners
- **B** Miners angry about water wastage
- **C** Miners injured in riots
- **D** Miner's call for government support

2 The anti-Chinese miners

- **A** accepted that the Chinese had rights under the law.
- **B** appreciated that the Chinese were industrious.
- **C** distrusted the Chinese because they were different.
- **D** disliked the Chinese for using all the water.

3 For the majority of miners, life on the goldfields was

- **A** exciting.
- **B** boring.
- **C** difficult.
- **D** profitable.

4 What is the purpose of the text?

- **A** to complain about racism on the goldfields
- **B** to give information about racism on the goldfields
- **C** to justify racism on the goldfields
- **D** to deny racism on the goldfields

5 What extra information belongs in the report? Choose all that apply.

- **A** information about the search for gold in China
- **B** how water is used in mining
- **C** what happened during the riots
- **D** how the troops quelled the riots

6 Draw some conclusions about being Chinese in NSW at that time.

....

....

....

Answers and explanations on p. 100

Step-by-step guide to **inferring** questions

Inferring questions involve reading between the lines to work out an answer that is not stated directly in the text.

Use this **Step-by-step guide** to help you read the text and make **inferences** to answer the questions below. Circle the correct answers or write your answer on the lines.

STEP 1	**Skim** the text to see what it is about and how it is organised.	**Read** the title, *Someone's been eating my porridge*. Notice that the text is written in paragraphs. Make **predictions** about the subject and purpose of the text.
STEP 2	**Read** the text. **Monitor** your reading to make sure you understand the text.	**Visualise** and **connect** with the ideas in the text**. Think** about what you already know about the subject and the type of text, a narrative. Make **predictions. Infer** meanings. Reflect on and make **judgements**.

Someone's been eating my porridge

Goldie watched from behind a tree across the street as the family left the house, the three of them, Mother, Father and Junior. They did this every day at the same time. They set the breakfast out on the table and then went for their morning walk. They'd be gone for an hour. It was a nice family routine and for a moment Goldie was envious but she shook any longings out of her head and hurried across the road, moving quietly down the side of the house and around to the back. The window above the kitchen sink was wide open, as usual, so she climbed through and lowered herself onto the kitchen bench and then to the floor.

She went straight to the breakfast table. The porridge smelled great. Usually she ate a small amount from each bowl, enough to satisfy her hunger but not so much that the family would notice. Today she was really starving and couldn't stop herself from eating all the porridge in Junior's bowl.

A rare full tummy made Goldie feel sleepy. She needed to rest for a moment. There were three chairs in the lounge room, the largest chair obviously belonging to the Father. It looked quite upright and uncomfortable. The mother's chair looked way too lumpy and squishy. Junior's chair was the right size so she sat on it.

Crack! One of the chair legs collapsed under her. She propped the chair back up on its broken leg and moved into the bedroom.

Goldie eyed the three beds in a row. Father's was large and had a brown checked cover. It was neatly made. Mother's bed was also neatly made. Junior's bed, on the other hand, was rumpled and unmade. Goldie put her hand on the mattress. It was still warm. There was a huge pile of deliciously soft quilts. She decided to stretch out in the bed, just for five minutes. She still had time before the family returned. She snuggled in under the covers and quickly fell asleep.

Question 1 **How does Goldie know the family's routine?**

A She asked them.
B She lives across the street.
C She spies on them.
D They are her friends.

STEP 3	**Read** the question. **Think** about what type of question it is. Work out what you need to do to answer it.	This is an **inferring** question. The answer is not stated directly in the text. You need to read between the lines and work out how Goldie knows the family's routine.

STEP ④ **Think** about the text. Remember what you have read and **visualised**.

✪ You can work out the answer using the clues in the text. **Scan** the text. Look for key words related to the *family's routine*. Re-read paragraph 1 to work out how Goldie knows the *routine*.

C is correct. You can infer that Goldie spies on the family. You read *Goldie watched from behind a tree across the street as the family left the house … They did this every day at the same time … They'd be gone for an hour* (see lines 2–4).

There is no evidence in the text to support an inference that Goldie talks to the family (**A**) or that they are her friends (**D**). If Goldie lived across the street (**B**) she wouldn't need to watch the family *from behind a tree* (see line 2).

Question 2 What *longings* does Goldie shake *out of her head*?

A longings for breakfast

B longings to belong to a happy family

C longings for a morning walk

D longings to be rid of her headache

STEP ③ **Read** the question. **Think** about what type of question it is. Work out what you need to do to answer it.

✪ This is an **inferring** question. The answer is not stated directly in the text. You need to read between the lines and work out what *longings* Goldie shook *out of her head*.

STEP ④ **Think** about the text. Remember what you have read and **visualised**.

✪ **Scan** the text. Look for the key words *longings* and *out of her head*. Re-read that part of the text if necessary. You can work out the answer using the clues in the text.

B is correct. You read *the family left the house, the three of them, Mother, Father and Junior … It was a nice family routine and for a moment Goldie was envious but she shook any longings out of her head and hurried across the road …* (see lines 2–6) You can infer that Goldie is envious of a happy family with their *nice family routine*.

Check the other options to confirm they are incorrect. **A** and **C** are incorrect because the longings relate to what Goldie thinks as she sees the family together. **D** is incorrect because there is no evidence in the text to suggest that Goldie has a headache she wants to get rid of.

Question 3 How does Goldie feel about breaking the chair?

A She is annoyed.

B She doesn't seem to care.

C She props the chair back up on its broken leg and moves into the bedroom.

D She is upset and worried.

STEP ③ **Read** the question. **Think** about what type of question it is. Work out what you need to do to answer it.

✪ This is an **inferring** question. The answer is not stated directly in the text. The question is asking you to work out how Goldie feels about breaking the chair.

STEP ④ **Think** about the text. Remember what you have read and **visualised**.

✪ **Scan** the text to find the part that deals with the broken chair. **Think** about any clues in the text and **infer** how Goldie feels.

B is correct. You read *Junior's chair was the right size so she sat on it. Crack! One of the chair legs collapsed under her. She propped the chair back up on its broken leg and moved into the bedroom* (see lines 14–17). You can infer that Goldie doesn't seem to care that she has broken the chair.

Check the other options to confirm they are incorrect. There is no evidence to support **A** or **D**, that she feels annoyed or upset and worried. **C** is what Goldie does after breaking the chair. It is evidence that she doesn't seem to care but the statement does not describe her feelings about breaking the chair.

Inferring questions involve reading between the lines to work out an answer that is not stated directly in the text.

Someone's been eating my porridge

Goldie watched from behind a tree across the street as the family left the house, the three of them, Mother, Father and Junior. They did this every day at the same time. They set the breakfast out on the table and then went for their morning walk. They'd be gone for an hour. It was a nice family routine and for a moment Goldie was envious but she shook any longings out of her head and hurried across the road, moving quietly down the side of the house and around to the back. The window above the kitchen sink was wide open, as usual, so she climbed through and lowered herself onto the kitchen bench and then to the floor.

She went straight to the breakfast table. The porridge smelled great. Usually she ate a small amount from each bowl, enough to satisfy her hunger but not so much that the family would notice. Today she was really starving and couldn't stop herself from eating all the porridge in Junior's bowl.

A rare full tummy made Goldie feel sleepy. She needed to rest for a moment. There were three chairs in the lounge room, the largest chair obviously belonging to the Father. It looked quite upright and uncomfortable. The mother's chair looked way too lumpy and squishy. Junior's chair was the right size so she sat on it.

Crack! One of the chair legs collapsed under her. She propped the chair back up on its broken leg and moved into the bedroom.

Goldie eyed the three beds in a row. Father's was large and had a brown checked cover. It was neatly made. Mother's bed was also neatly made. Junior's bed, on the other hand, was rumpled and unmade. Goldie put her hand on the mattress. It was still warm. There was a huge pile of deliciously soft quilts. She decided to stretch out in the bed, just for five minutes. She still had time before the family returned. She snuggled in under the covers and quickly fell asleep.

Question 4 **What clues in the text help you infer that Goldie doesn't want the family to know she's been in their home. Choose all that apply.**

A She usually eats a small amount from each bowl so that the family won't notice.

B She's thinking about how much time she has.

C She eats all the porridge in Junior's bowl.

D She props the chair back up on its broken leg.

STEP 3 **Read** the question. **Think** about what type of question it is. Work out what you need to do to answer it.

- This is an **inferring** question. The answer is not stated directly in the text. The question is asking what clues help you **infer** that Goldie doesn't want the family to know she's been in their home.

STEP 4 **Think** about the text. Remember what you have read and **visualised**.

- **Scan** the text to find the relevant parts. You can work out the answer from clues in the text.

A, **B** and **D** are correct. Goldie's behaviour helps you infer that she doesn't want the family to know she's been there. Goldie waited for the family to leave and then *moving quietly down the side of the house and around to the back … she climbed through* (the window) *(see lines 6–7)* and *They'd be gone for an hour … (see line 4)* and *Usually she ate a small amount from each bowl, enough to satisfy her hunger but not so much that the family would notice … (see lines 9–10)* and *She propped the chair back up on its broken leg … (see line 16)* and *She decided to stretch out in the bed, just for five minutes. She still had time before the family returned (see line 21).*

C is incorrect because that behaviour would alert the family to the fact that someone had been in their home.

Question 5 **Why does Goldie sneak into the house every day?**

A to play

B to upset Junior

C to eat

D to feel like part of the family

STEP 3	**Read** the question. **Think** about what type of question it is. Work out what you need to do to answer it.	This is an **inferring** question. The answer is not stated directly in the text. The question is asking you to read between the lines and work out why Goldie would sneak into the house every day.
STEP 4	**Think** about the text. Remember what you have read and **visualised**.	**Scan** the text to re-read what Goldie does in the house. **Think** about the clues in the text.

C is correct. You read *Usually she ate a small amount from each bowl, enough to satisfy her hunger (see lines 9–10)*. You know that Goldie eats some porridge every day. It's the first thing she does when she enters the house.

Check the other options to confirm that they are incorrect. **A** is incorrect. Goldie does not play with anything in the house. **B** is incorrect because Goldie does not break Junior's chair on purpose and she usually doesn't eat all his porridge. **D** is incorrect. You can infer that Goldie is envious of the happy family but there's nothing in the text to make you infer that she wants to be a member of this family.

Question 6 **What do you predict will happen next?**

....

....

....

STEP 3	**Read** the question. **Think** about what type of question it is. Work out what you need to do to answer it.	This is an **inferring** question. The answer is not stated directly in the text. The question is asking you to read between the lines to **infer** what will happen next in the story.
STEP 4	**Think** about the text. Remember what you have read and **visualised**.	**Scan** the final paragraph to re-read how the text ends with Goldie asleep and the family due home. You should **infer** that the family will return in an hour as per their regular routine and find Goldie asleep. The extract is a narrative so you should **infer** that there would be a complication to create drama or conflict in the story. You should recognise that the best means of creating conflict is to have the family arrive home while Goldie is still sleeping. If you recognise the fairy tale, *Goldilocks and the Three Bears*, you can **infer** that the family returns to find Goldie in Junior's bed and she runs away.

Inferring questions

Use the **Step-by-step guide** on pages 42–45 to help you read the text and make **inferences** to answer the questions below. Circle the correct answers or write your answers on the lines.

The finals

"Will you be home for dinner?" asked Dad from the kitchen. "I'm defrosting some chicken."

Sam called out "No thanks, Dad, I have soccer practice. Ling's mum is driving Olivia and me and we're having noodles afterwards. Mum's picking me up from Ling's at 7 o'clock."

Sam loved having something to eat with her teammates after practice. They did it every Friday night. Sometimes they had sushi. It was a time when the team could relax and have fun before their competition game on the Saturday morning. The team had trained hard three afternoons this week. They had a semi-final game the next day. The competition was tough but they expected to win. Sam played soccer for the local team called Runaway Bay Rascals. They were keen to do well, working hard but having fun too. Sam had some good friends on the team and the girls were well matched in terms of their skills.

Sam entered the kitchen. She kissed her dad goodbye. "OK. Have fun," said Dad. "I'll see you tomorrow." Sam's dad was currently on night shift as a nurse at the hospital. He was pleased that he had Saturday off work and would be able to watch Sam's semi-final. He attended all the games he could, depending on his shifts. Sam said she liked it when he watched her play.

1. What is Dad cooking for dinner?
   - **A** sushi
   - **B** chicken
   - **C** noodles
   - **D** pizzas

2. On what day of the week does the conversation in the text take place?
   - **A** Saturday
   - **B** Monday
   - **C** at dinner time
   - **D** Friday

3. Which sentence is unlikely to be true?
   - **A** Sam likes to do well at soccer.
   - **B** Sam's team has fun together.
   - **C** Sam plays in a good soccer team.
   - **D** Sam trains harder than the rest of the team.

4. Why didn't Sam's dad attend all Sam's soccer games?
   - **A** because he was a nurse at the hospital
   - **B** because he didn't like soccer
   - **C** because he had to work
   - **D** because he had to cook dinner

5. How does Sam feel about soccer?

6. Does Sam's Dad always work night shift? Explain your answer.

Answers and explanations on pp. 100–101

Use the **Step-by-step guide** on pages 42–45 to help you read the text and make **inferences** to answer the questions below. Circle the correct answers or write your answers on the lines.

MELBOURNE CHRONICLE

26TH JANUARY 2012

Robogal a winner!

The Young Australian of the Year Award for 2012 has been awarded to Marita Cheng. Prime Minister Julia Gillard presented the trophy on the steps of Parliament House in Canberra for Australia Day.

Ms Cheng is founder of Robogals, an organisation that encourages females to take an interest in engineering. As an engineering student at the University of Melbourne Ms Cheng realised that males outnumbered females in engineering courses and careers by 10 to 1, right across Australia, so she decided to do something about that.

Engineers design, invent and build everything from buildings and bridges to aeroplanes and bicycles, appliances and the millions of devices that improve lives but Ms Cheng is especially interested in robotics. As a child, helping her mother do the household chores, Marita dreamed of a day when robots could do all the chores for her. That idea has been a major inspiration for her choice of engineering and computer science courses at university. She believes that, in the future, robots will improve the lives of people all around the world.

Ms Cheng founded Robogals in 2008 working as a volunteer, with her university peers, to visit schools and talk to girls about careers in engineering and technology. Robogals makes sure that girls know that engineering is not just for boys, running workshops in robotics to demonstrate that engineering is a great career choice. Ms Cheng hopes more girls become engineers. She has been described as a visionary leader: Robogals was internationally recognised in 2011 as an outstanding youth social initiative.

The Young Australian of the Year Award is presented each year to Australians aged between 16 and 30 who have made outstanding contributions to the community or who have achieved excellence in their chosen fields.

1. What did Marita Cheng win an award for?
   - **A** studying engineering at university
   - **B** making engineering fun
   - **C** her encouragement of girls to study engineering
   - **D** being a Young Australian

2. What motivated Marita to start Robogals?
   - **A** an interest in robotics
   - **B** a realisation that there weren't many female engineers in Australia
   - **C** discussions with university colleagues
   - **D** her desire to improve the lives of people around the world

3. Which statement would Marita disagree with?
   - **A** Engineering improves people's lives.
   - **B** Boys make better engineers than girls.
   - **C** Engineering students study at university.
   - **D** Engineering is an exciting field.

4. Which idea can you infer from the text?
   - **A** Engineering will always be a boy's subject.
   - **B** Engineering is part of everyone's life.
   - **C** Very few people can experience an engineered product.
   - **D** The Young Australian of the Year Award is for engineering.

5. What is the aim of Robogals?
   - **A** to visit schools and have fun
   - **B** to visit schools and make robots
   - **C** to encourage students to go to university
   - **D** to encourage girls to study engineering

6. Make a prediction about some things Marita Cheng might achieve in her life.

....

....

....

Answers and explanations on pp. 101–102

Inferring questions

Use the **Step-by-step guide** on pages 42–45 to help you read the text and make **inferences** to answer the questions below. Circle the correct answers or write your answers on the lines.

My grandmother

My grandmother is my hero. My grandmother migrated from Romania in 1948, after World War II. She came to Australia as a little girl with her mother, both as refugees under the international Refugee Organisation Scheme. They settled in Victoria.

My grandmother's mother (that's my great grandmother who I never met) worked as a house cleaner and was always telling my grandmother to work hard at school. This is advice my grandmother took because she became a nurse and then went on to specialise in obstetrics so she got to help deliver a lot of babies. My grandmother no longer works as a nurse but is a palliative care volunteer. Palliative care is given to people who are dying. I think it sounds very depressing but when my grandmother talks about it her eyes sparkle. She says that it is very rewarding.

My grandmother is proud of her Romanian heritage. She speaks Romanian and has taught me how to speak a little of it. She jokingly says Romania is only famous for two things: Count Dracula and Nadia Comaneci. The story of Count Dracula the Vampire is based on a Romanian general and is set in the region of Transylvania in Romania. Nadia Comaneci, one of the world's most famous gymnasts, competed for Romania in the 1976 Montreal Olympic Games and earned a perfect score of 10. But grandmother also says proudly that Romania has some of the best-preserved forest areas in all of Europe, with brown bears, wolves and hundreds of animal species unique to Romania.

My grandmother is kind and patient. She is brave and smart. She is a role model. I call her Bunica. That's Romanian for grandmother.

1 Where was the writer's grandmother born?

- **A** 1948
- **B** Australia
- **C** Victoria
- **D** Romania

2 What advice was given to the writer's grandmother by her mother?

- **A** become a nurse
- **B** speak Romanian
- **C** be kind and patient
- **D** get a good education

3 What makes the writer's grandmother proud of Romania?

- **A** its forests and animals
- **B** Count Dracula and Nadia Comaneci
- **C** She has learned English.
- **D** brown bears, wolves and hundreds of unique animals

4 How does the writer's grandmother feel about palliative care?

- **A** It's a waste of time.
- **B** She feels she is doing something worthwhile.
- **C** She finds it depressing.
- **D** It's too hard.

5 What doesn't a palliative care volunteer do?

- **A** helps sick people
- **B** delivers lots of babies
- **C** assists families and people who are dying
- **D** a good job

6 Why does the writer refer to Bunica as *my hero*?

....

....

....

....

Answers and explanations on p. 102

Inferring questions

Use the **Step-by-step guide** on pages 42–45 to help you read the text and make **inferences** to answer the questions below. Circle the correct answers or write your answers on the lines.

Halloween

New | Reply | Delete | Archive | Junk | Sweep | Move to

Halloween

31st October

Hi Billy

Spoilt, greedy children will soon be roaming my street expecting every adult to give them sweets and treats. It annoys me intensely. Does it annoy you? They know nothing about the history of All Hallows' Eve or the fact that the ancient Gaels believed that on the 31st of October the dead could come back to walk the earth. They have no idea that the reason for wearing scary masks and skeleton costumes at Halloween is to mimic the dead or appease them. I think Halloween's just so commercial now and greedy children revolt me. One vomited chocolates and lollies on my doormat last year. Let's start a petition to ban Halloween! I hope you don't get too many door-knockers at your place tonight. See you at work tomorrow.

Regards, Rhonda

Justin, Do not go out tonight unless Matt's dad goes too. I will email Doug to check his plans. And make sure you are home by 7 pm. I'll be home from work at 5 pm. Wait for me. Love Mum XXX

New | Reply | Delete | Archive | Junk | Sweep | Move to

Hi Matt, I'll meet you at 5 pm outside my gate. Mum says I can trick-or-treat as long as your dad comes with us and I'm home by 7 pm. I hope we score heaps of loot. My sister's helping me with my costume. It's a surprise. See you soon. Justin

New | Reply | Delete | Archive | Junk | Sweep | Move to

Hi Matt, My parents won't let me trick-or-treat. They say it's unhealthy—all those lollies and the potential for germs. My parents say they'll give money to UNICEF to help poor children in other countries rather than spend it on sweets for neighbourhood kids. I actually agree with them. My sister vomited on some poor lady's doormat last Halloween. It was ugly! See you at school tomorrow, Ava.

1. According to Rhonda, what is the worst thing about Halloween?
   - **A** too many door-knockers
   - **B** scary masks and costumes
   - **C** greedy children
   - **D** the idea that the dead come back to walk the earth

2. You can infer that Rhonda and Billy are
   - **A** boyfriend and girlfriend
   - **B** work associates
   - **C** neighbours
   - **D** friends from work

3. Who is Matt's dad?
   - **A** Justin
   - **B** Billy
   - **C** Doug
   - **D** Matt's dad's name is not mentioned.

4. How does Justin's mum feel about Halloween?
   - **A** excited that Justin might score lots of loot
   - **B** happy that it's a fun time for everyone
   - **C** concerned about safety
   - **D** annoyed that she has to come home early from work

5. How does Ava feel about Halloween?
   - **A** disappointed she can't trick-or-treat
   - **B** doesn't care about trick-or-treating
   - **C** angry that she can't trick-or-treat
   - **D** jealous because her parents are giving money to other children

6. Infer how Matt feels about Halloween.

   ....

   ....

Answers and explanations on pp. 102–103

Inferring questions

Use the **Step-by-step guide** on pages 42–45 to help you read the text and make **inferences** to answer the questions below. Circle the correct answers or write your answers on the lines.

Landcare

Hebe Wickham (age 11) spoke at her school assembly about the benefits of becoming a Landcare volunteer and member of Landcare Australia. A transcript of her speech is included here.

Landcare Australia is a not-for-profit organisation that aims to protect and restore the natural environment. I joined Landcare Australia two years ago. I have been involved in tree planting, wildlife monitoring and community clean-up days. Now I hope to inspire other students to join Landcare and get involved too.

One of the great things about Landcare is that the work starts at a local level—in your own backyard, park, neighbourhood and school, and the whole family can get involved. The projects are actually lots of fun. My parents joined Landcare five years ago and have been recently helping rid bush areas of weeds such as lantana.

You should sign up for the e-newsletter. That way you can find out about projects in the local area that you might be interested in, as well as what's going on across the country. You can read about schools that have created worm farms, bush tucker gardens and waterwise native gardens to attract native birds. Some schools have created vertical gardens to grow herbs and vegetables for their school canteens. You can get involved in bush regeneration and restoring wildlife habitats and corridors to their natural state. There's so much you can do.

I've met really great people while volunteering and I feel that I am doing something very important. And if everyone just did one little thing for the natural environment the world would be a better place for plants, animals and people. It's actually really easy to get involved and be part of something wonderful—helping nature. So, I recommend you get involved in Landcare!

1 Why did Hebe join Landcare?

- **A** to help the environment
- **B** to learn how to grow food
- **C** to make friends
- **D** to win an award

2 Hebe's attitude suggests she is trying to

- **A** annoy everyone.
- **B** show off.
- **C** be bossy.
- **D** share her enthusiasm.

3 How do you think Hebe became involved in Landcare?

- **A** through school
- **B** through her teachers
- **C** through her parents
- **D** through a friend

4 What can you infer Landcare volunteers do when they restore wildlife habitats?

- **A** plant native bushes and trees
- **B** create animal parks
- **C** build homes for wildlife
- **D** pull down old sheds

5 How do Hebe's parents feel about her involvement in Landcare? Explain your reasoning.

....

....

....

....

....

Answers and explanations on p. 103

Use the **Step-by-step guide** on pages 42–45 to help you read the text and make **inferences** to answer the questions below. Circle the correct answers or write your answers on the lines.

Missing person

Cindy Ella (surname unknown)

Personal Details

Last seen: Saturday, 12th July	Eyes: Brown
Year of birth: 2003	Hair: Brown
Height: 168 cm	Complexion: Fair
Build: Athletic	Gender: Female

Circumstances

Cindy was last seen at the Royal Palace Gala Ball. She had arrived at 8 pm in a chauffeur driven limousine. She was wearing a cream-coloured, floor-length, organza-and-silk gown with a sequined bodice. She was last seen dancing with a happy Prince Harry but raced off the dance floor when the clock struck midnight, leaving behind one of her shoes, size 9, on the grand staircase. The Prince picked up her shoe and ran after her as far as the palace gates, but was forced to stop by his security guards. The Prince watched until she was out of sight somewhere past Victoria Memorial. Witnesses report seeing a lone female in a ball gown running awkwardly in St James Park, sometime after midnight. Cindy has not been seen since. Local police are concerned.

Updated 15th July. The Palace has offered a reward.

If you have any information please contact the Missing Persons' hotline.

1 Why might the female running in St James Park after midnight be Cindy?
- **A** She was seen by witnesses.
- **B** She was in a ball gown and running awkwardly.
- **C** There was no-one else out that late.
- **D** The lone female was running swiftly.

2 Why do you think Prince Harry ran after her? Choose all that apply.
- **A** He had enjoyed dancing with her.
- **B** He wanted to give her back her shoe.
- **C** He liked her and wanted her to stay.
- **D** He didn't understand why she was running away.

3 Why do you think the guards forced Prince Harry to stop chasing Cindy?
- **A** They thought he might get lost in the dark.
- **B** Prince Harry was not allowed to run anywhere.
- **C** Prince Harry had other guests to dance with.
- **D** They were concerned for his safety.

4 Why might the witness statements be important to police?
- **A** The witnesses might be involved in a crime.
- **B** They confirm Cindy's last known whereabouts.
- **C** She has not been seen since the ball.
- **D** The witnesses know what happened to Cindy.

5 Why are local police concerned?
- **A** Prince Harry needs a girlfriend.
- **B** Cindy has been missing for 3 days.
- **C** Cindy was last seen in St James Park, which is a dangerous place.
- **D** Cindy's surname is unknown.

6 Make some predictions about the outcome of the Missing Persons' Hotline enquiry.

....

....

....

....

Answers and explanations on pp. 103–104

Use the **Step-by-step guide** on pages 42–45 to help you read the text and make **inferences** to answer the questions below. Circle the correct answers or write your answers on the lines.

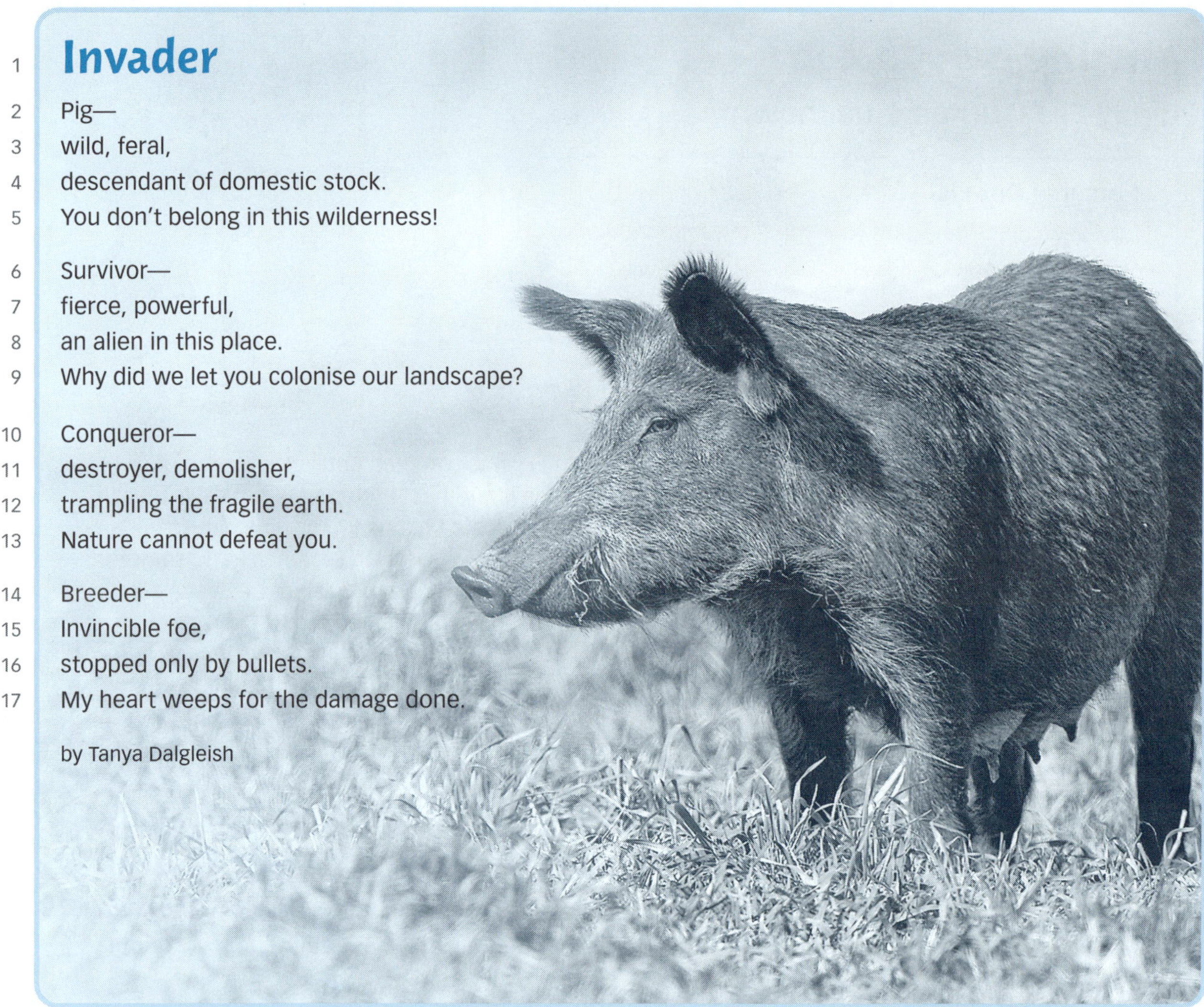

Invader

Pig—
wild, feral,
descendant of domestic stock.
You don't belong in this wilderness!

Survivor—
fierce, powerful,
an alien in this place.
Why did we let you colonise our landscape?

Conqueror—
destroyer, demolisher,
trampling the fragile earth.
Nature cannot defeat you.

Breeder—
Invincible foe,
stopped only by bullets.
My heart weeps for the damage done.

by Tanya Dalgleish

1 Why does the poet say *You don't belong in this wilderness*!

- **A** The poet doesn't like pigs.
- **B** The pig escaped from a farm.
- **C** The pig is not a native animal.
- **D** The pig is wild.

2 How did the pig *colonise our landscape*?

- **A** The pig killed all other creatures.
- **B** The pig is an alien from outer space.
- **C** The pig invaded and bred successfully.
- **D** The pig lives in colonies.

3 Why does the poet say *Nature cannot defeat you*?

- **A** The pig eats everything in its path.
- **B** The pig tramples the fragile earth.
- **C** The pig is too powerful.
- **D** The pig has no natural predator.

4 Why does the poet's heart weep?

- **A** for damage done by bullets to pigs
- **B** for damage to the environment
- **C** with sadness because the pigs can't survive
- **D** with sympathy for the pigs

5 How does the poet want readers to feel?

- **A** shocked
- **B** amazed
- **C** happy
- **D** concerned

6 Infer how the poet feels about feral foxes.

Answers and explanations on pp. 104–105

Inferring questions

Use the **Step-by-step guide** on pages 42–45 to help you read the text and make **inferences** to answer the questions below. Circle the correct answers or write your answers on the lines.

The jungle above

Ben and Min were playing in the yard of the derelict house at the end of their street when they noticed a rope ladder hanging from a huge old tree. Ben began to climb the ladder and Min followed. Up and up they went past branches and leaves. Min was just wondering if they'd ever reach the top when she looked up and saw a large hairy purple hand reach out and grab Ben's arm. She screamed as Ben was dragged up through the tree's canopy. Min climbed up as fast as she could after him.

At the top of the canopy they found a dense tropical jungle, filled with giant purple leaves and vines, and fluorescent flowers. They looked around in amazement but then the creature was off again dragging Ben through the trees. It looked something like a gorilla, but purple, and it pulled Ben to the edge of a deep pit in the ground. There it dropped Ben's arm and sat looking down into the pit and then back at the children, from one to the other, its face and shoulders sagging. Min followed its gaze and knew instantly why it was sad. She saw a larger creature sitting forlornly in the bottom of the pit. It was trapped. Ben spotted a fallen tree trunk and the children manoeuvred the log towards the pit and carefully lowered one end of the log down into it. The creature climbed along the log and up to the top of the pit where it hugged the now jubilant smaller one.

By then it was nightfall and there were strange noises the children couldn't identify. The children looked at each other. It was time to go home. The creatures seemed to understand. They led the children back to the tree where the rope ladder was waiting for them. The children waved goodbye, vowing to return. They climbed through the canopy, and back into the yard of their very own neighbourhood.

1 How did Min know that the smaller creature was sad?

- **A** It was trapped.
- **B** She worked it out by observing the situation.
- **C** The smaller creature told her.
- **D** It wanted the children to help.

2 How did the children and creatures communicate?

- **A** through body language
- **B** in writing
- **C** by talking in English
- **D** through mental telepathy

3 The writer implies that

- **A** Min is the leader and Ben is a follower.
- **B** Min is the main character as the story is more about her.
- **C** Ben is the character in charge.
- **D** Min and Ben are equals in the story.

4 Why did the children decide that it was time to go home?

- **A** They didn't want to get into trouble.
- **B** They were hungry and tired.
- **C** It was dark and it sounded scary.
- **D** They heard wild noises.

5 What is implied in the text by the line *The creatures seemed to understand*?

- **A** that the creatures understood they'd never see the children again
- **B** that it was nightfall
- **C** that the children wanted to leave
- **D** that the children were tired

6 Will the children revisit the jungle? Explain.

....

....

....

....

Answers and explanations on p. 105

Step-by-step guide to **language** questions

Language questions involve examining how language is used in a text.

Use this **Step-by-step guide** to help you read the text and examine the way **language** is used to answer the questions below. Circle the correct answers or write your answer on the lines.

STEP 1	**Skim** the text to see what it is about and how it is organised.	✪ **Read** the title, *Royal Kidnapping Thwarted.* Look at the illustration and other visual elements. Notice the layout, newspaper banner and columns. Make **predictions** about the subject and purpose of the text.
STEP 2	**Read** the text. **Monitor** your reading to make sure you understand the text.	✪ **Visualise** and **connect** with the ideas in the text**. Think** about what you already know about the subject and the type of text, a newspaper article. Make **predictions** Make **inferences**. Reflect on meanings and make **judgements**.

THE DAILY CHRONICLE

LONDON, 14TH JULY

Royal kidnapping thwarted

Palace security is on high alert after a mysterious woman who attended the Royal Gala Ball on Saturday night has now vanished. The unidentified woman, who introduced herself only as Cindy Ella, danced all night with a smiling Prince Harry and then vanished into St James Park and has not been seen since midnight.

Palace Security Chief Poly Minions believes the woman may be associated with an international kidnapping gang known as 'The Step-sisters'. Ms Minions said, 'The woman attempted to lure the Prince into the Park. We believe he was in grave danger. We have advised the Prince to remain inside Palace grounds until the woman is apprehended.'

Official spokesperson for Palace Events and Event Organiser Eva Rafter believes the woman gained access to the Ball using a forged invitation. A horrified Ms Rafter said, 'Invitations were only sent to the best and richest families. That woman clearly didn't belong here. Heads will roll over this breach of security.'

Ms Minions denies accusations of any fault with her security team. She claims her people saved the Prince from the kidnappers. 'My staff responded quickly and followed all protocols appropriately. We saved the Prince's life. The fault lies with the invitation process.'

Lady Camellia attended the ball and commented, 'She seemed like a lovely girl. I don't think I can believe she's a kidnapper. She had a truly lovely smile. The Prince seemed quite smitten by her. I watched them dance all night.'

Lord Montybaton said, 'She definitely looked shifty. I'm not surprised she is a kidnapper.'

The Queen has offered a reward of £5000 to any person who assists the police in apprehending the woman.

Scotland Yard has not confirmed allegations of any attempted kidnapping or the existence of a Step-sisters gang.

Question 1 Which statement is an opinion?

An *opinion* is a point of view. It does not have to be based on fact.

A Ms Minions denied accusations of fault.
B The Prince was nearly kidnapped.
C Poly Minions is head of Palace Security.
D Lady Camellia attended the ball.

STEP 3 **Read** the question. **Think** about what type of question it is. Work out what you need to do to answer it.

- This is a **language** question. You need to examine the way language is used in the text to work out which of the statements is an opinion.

STEP 4 **Think** about the text. Remember what you have read and **visualised**.

- **Scan** the text. Look for evidence in the text to work out which statement is an opinion.

B is correct. There is no proof in the text that the prince was nearly kidnapped. It is only an accusation and an opinion about events expressed by characters in the text.

Check the other options to confirm that they are incorrect. Notice that **A**, **C** and **D** are facts that are stated directly in the text.

Question 2 Which statement expresses a fact?

A *fact* in the text is something stated as true in the text.

A The Prince was nearly kidnapped.
B Poly Minions is head of Palace Security.
C Cindy Ella looked shifty.
D Palace security saved the Prince's life.

STEP 3 **Read** the question. **Think** about what type of question it is. Work out what you need to do to answer it.

- This is a **language** question. You need to work out which statement is factual in the text.

STEP 4 **Think** about the text. Remember what you have read and **visualised**.

- **Scan** the text to find statements made by each character or about each character in the question.

B is correct. You read that the *Palace Security Chief,* (is) *Poly Minions* **(see lines 15–16)** so you know that **B** is a fact in the text.

Check the other options to confirm that they are incorrect. **A**, **C** and **D** are all opinions expressed in the text by characters who have particular points of view about the events.

Question 3 What does *heads will roll* mean in the text?

Heads will roll is a figure of speech. It doesn't actually mean that heads will roll.

A The Queen will have heads chopped off for breaches of security.
B Ms Rafter will roll her eyes at staff behind the Queen's back.
C Staff found to be responsible will lose their jobs
D The heads of departments will have to answer to the Queen.

STEP 3 **Read** the question. **Think** about what type of question it is. Work out what you need to do to answer it.

- This is a **language** question. You need to work out the meaning of the idiomatic expression *heads will roll.*

STEP 4 **Think** about the text. Remember what you have read and **visualised**.

- **Scan** the text to find the key words *heads will roll.* Re-read that part of the text. To work out the answer you need to examine how the expression is used in context.

C is correct. You read *A horrified Ms Rafter said, 'Invitations were only sent to the best and richest families. That woman clearly didn't belong here. Heads will roll over this breach of security.'* **(see lines 28–32)** Ms Rafter means that she will find out who was responsible for an uninvited guest at the ball and they will be dealt with by losing their jobs. Ms Rafter uses the expression *heads will roll* figuratively and not literally.

Check the other options to confirm they are incorrect. **A** is a literal interpretation of the expression and is incorrect. **B** is incorrect as it refers to eyes rolling and not heads. **D** is incorrect because it refers to heads of departments, meaning the managers of government departments, and is not the figurative meaning of *heads will roll.*

Language questions involve examining how language is used in a text.

THE DAILY CHRONICLE

LONDON, 14TH JULY

Royal kidnapping thwarted

Palace security is on high alert after a mysterious woman who attended the Royal Gala Ball on Saturday night has now vanished. The unidentified woman, who introduced herself only as Cindy Ella, danced all night with a smiling Prince Harry and then vanished into St James Park and has not been seen since midnight.

Palace Security Chief Poly Minions believes the woman may be associated with an international kidnapping gang known as 'The Step-sisters'. Ms Minions said, 'The woman attempted to lure the Prince into the Park. We believe he was in grave danger. We have advised the Prince to remain inside Palace grounds until the woman is apprehended.'

Official spokesperson for Palace Events and Event Organiser Eva Rafter believes the woman gained access to the Ball using a forged invitation. A horrified Ms Rafter said, 'Invitations were only sent to the best and richest families. That woman clearly didn't belong here. Heads will roll over this breach of security.'

Ms Minions denies accusations of any fault with her security team. She claims her people saved the Prince from the kidnappers. 'My staff responded quickly and followed all protocols appropriately. We saved the Prince's life. The fault lies with the invitation process.'

Lady Camellia attended the ball and commented, 'She seemed like a lovely girl. I don't think I can believe she's a kidnapper. She had a truly lovely smile. The Prince seemed quite smitten by her. I watched them dance all night.'

Lord Montybaton said, 'She definitely looked shifty. I'm not surprised she is a kidnapper.'

The Queen has offered a reward of £5000 to any person who assists the police in apprehending the woman.

Scotland Yard has not confirmed allegations of any attempted kidnapping or the existence of a Step-sisters gang.

Question 4 **What does *seemed quite smitten* mean?**

A He argued with her.

B He appeared to like her a lot.

C He wanted to marry her.

D He seemed quite annoyed by her.

STEP 3 **Read** the question. **Think** about what type of question it is. Work out what you need to do to answer it.	This is a **language** question. The question is asking you to work out the meaning of an expression *seemed quite smitten*.
STEP 4 **Think** about the text. Remember what you have read and **visualised**.	**Scan** the text for the key words from the question *seemed quite smitten*. Re-read that part of the text. To work out the answer you need to examine how the expression is used in context.

B is correct. You read *Lady Camellia … commented, 'She [Cindy Ella] seemed like a lovely girl … She had a truly lovely smile. The Prince seemed quite smitten by her. I watched them dance all night.'* (see lines 42–49) Lady Camellia speaks positively about Cindy Ella. The expression *seemed quite smitten* means that the Prince appeared to like her a lot.

Check the other options to confirm they are incorrect. **A** and **D** are incorrect because they are negative evaluations. There is nothing in the text to support **C**.

Question 5 Which statement is expressed with the greatest degree of certainty (highest modality)?

A She seemed like a lovely girl.

B We probably saved the Prince's life.

C I don't think I can believe she's a kidnapper.

D She definitely looked shifty.

STEP 3 **Read** the question. **Think** about what type of question it is. Work out what you need to do to answer it.

- This is a **language** question. The question is asking you to work out which statement has the highest modality.

STEP 4 **Think** about the text. Remember what you have read and **visualised**.

- Re-read parts of the text if necessary. Examine the way language is used to express modality.

Modality means how certain or likely something is judged to be. It is expressed in verbs (*must*, *should*, *might*), adverbs (*definitely*, *probably*) and nouns (*probability*, *certainty*).

D is correct. *Definitely* is an adverb that expresses a high degree of certainty.

Check to confirm that the other options are incorrect. The use of *seemed* in **A** makes the statement less certain; it implies that there might be some doubt. The use of *probably* in **B** means that it is more likely than not the Prince's life was saved by the guards but not absolutely so. **C** is a low modality statement. The use of *don't think I can believe* is less certain. It implies that with a little more evidence you might believe it.

Question 6 Write a quote from Prince Harry to include in the newspaper article.

Prince Harry made the following statement:

....

....

....

STEP 3 **Read** the question. **Think** about what type of question it is. Work out what you need to do to answer it.

- This is a **language** question. You need to use language to represent the point of view of a character in the story.

STEP 4 **Think** about the text. Remember what you have read and **visualised**.

- **Scan** the text to find the parts that specifically relate to the Prince. You read *Cindy Ella danced all night with a* <u>*smiling*</u> *Prince Harry and then vanished into St James Park and has not been seen since midnight* (see lines 10–14). To write the answer you need to **think** about Harry's involvement in the events, what he witnessed, what he did and how he might feel about events. You would expect the Prince to be worried about Cindy Ella and concerned about her whereabouts. You need to use thinking and feeling verbs to express his point of view.

For example:

'I am deeply concerned about the whereabouts of Cindy Ella. I am hoping that further witnesses will come forward with information to assist the police in finding her. I sincerely hope that she is safe and is able to respond to this public appeal. I would truly like to see her again.'

Language questions

Use the **Step-by-step guide** on pages 54–57 to help you read the text and examine the way **language** is used to answer the questions below. Circle the correct answers or write your answer on the lines.

A dog

My labradoodle is as cute as a button. She loves attention and likes nothing better than to sit on my lap and watch TV or to lean on my feet if I'm sitting at the table. She loves to go for walks and to swim. If I take her to the park she gets so excited. I have to keep her on a leash as she just loves to chase and terrify any birds she spies. She loves people and rolls over onto her back in a submissive position so that people can tell her how cute she is and rub her on the tummy. She likes to bark but she's all bark and no bite. She is as smart as a whip.

My neighbour's labradoodle is a loose cannon. It runs around madly and creates chaos. It does not know how to come when it is called. Once in a blue moon it will obey a command. It can't be trusted at the park to leave the poor birds alone and has to be kept on a leash even in the off-leash areas. It barks all day when the owners are out and annoys me intensely. I've told the owners about it but they haven't done anything. It is a stupid-looking dog with zero brains and no common sense. I'm afraid it is a waste of space.

1 What opinion do both writers share?

- **A** Both texts describe a pet dog.
- **B** Neither writer likes the birds to be disturbed.
- **C** They both recognise the dog loves attention and to be patted.
- **D** They both think the labradoodle is cute.

2 A *loose cannon* in the text means

- **A** not coming when it's called.
- **B** a weapon used in wars.
- **C** out of control and likely to cause problems.
- **D** it has to be kept on a leash.

3 The expression *all bark and no bite* means

- **A** it barks all day at home but wears a muzzle in public.
- **B** it sounds and acts like a guard dog.
- **C** it barks all day long when it's home alone and has no-one to bite.
- **D** it sounds fierce but it won't hurt you.

4 *Once in a blue moon* means

- **A** when the moon turns red.
- **B** very rarely.
- **C** once a week.
- **D** when it is a full moon.

5 The expression *a waste of space* means

- **A** an animal that destroys things.
- **B** its head is empty as it has zero brains.
- **C** something of no value.
- **D** something that takes up too much space.

6 Imagine you are the writer of Text 2. Write your main problem with the dog in one non-emotive sentence.

....

....

....

....

....

Answers and explanations on pp. 105–106

Language questions

Use the **Step-by-step guide** on pages 54–57 to help you read the text and examine the way **language** is used to answer the questions below. Circle the correct answers or write your answer on the lines.

Bella's party

Liam continued arguing. "But Mum, everybody's going."

"Not you," replied Leanne.

"But it's not fair! I'm the only one not allowed."

"I'm sure there will be others not going and I really don't want to hear any more about it."

"All my friends are going."

"I said no," she sighed wearily.

Liam had been trying to persuade his mum to allow him to go to a party at Bella's on Friday night. He had started nagging while she was sorting out school lunches and breakfasts and continued as they ate. He'd tried asking nicely. He'd tried all his best arguments. He'd tried making her feel guilty for spoiling his life. Now he sat brooding, mulling over ideas. He absently pushed his cereal around in the bowl, while his mind desperately tried to come up with extra strategies or arguments to convince his mother to let him go to the party. The trouble was that his mum knew Bella's parents were away for the week and Bella's brother, Sean, would be in charge. Sean was seventeen and Liam thought he was super cool. His mum liked Sean but didn't think he was responsible enough to supervise a party of twelve year olds.

Liam thought about asking his stepdad for permission to go to the party. Sure as eggs his stepdad would say yes but he decided against it as his mum would go ballistic and he'd just get his stepdad into trouble. He'd have to come up with a different strategy.

"I'll do the dishes and tidy the kitchen, Mum. You go get ready for work."

His mum looked at him sideways.

1. *"I said no," she sighed wearily.* What does this tell you about Liam's mum at this moment?
   - **A** She's tired of arguing.
   - **B** She's annoyed with Liam.
   - **C** She's had too little sleep.
   - **D** She's very busy in the kitchen.

2. *Now he sat brooding.* What does *brooding* mean?
   - **A** crying
   - **B** not hungry
   - **C** sulky and deep in thought
   - **D** angry

3. *He absently pushed his cereal around in the bowl.* What does *absently* mean here?
   - **A** The cereal was absent—he'd eaten it all and didn't realise.
   - **B** His mind was focused on other things and he stirred his food without thinking about it.
   - **C** He didn't like the cereal so just pushed it around the bowl, not eating it.
   - **D** His attention was focused on the cereal.

4. What does the expression *sure as eggs* mean?
   - **A** hopefully
   - **B** certainly
   - **C** probably
   - **D** possibly

5. What does the expression *his mum would go ballistic* mean?
   - **A** have hurt feelings
   - **B** get very angry
   - **C** scream and cry
   - **D** punish him in some way

6. *His mum looked at him sideways.* Explain what this means.

   ....

   ....

   ....

   ....

   ....

   ....

Answers and explanations on p. 106

Language questions

Use the **Step-by-step guide** on pages 54–57 to help you read the text and examine the way **language** is used to answer the questions below. Circle the correct answers or write your answer on the lines.

The neighbours

I live in a unit. Living in a block of units means you have to be considerate of all your neighbours all the time with regard to noise, cooking smells, clutter left in foyers and stairwells, parking in front of people's garages, the behaviour of your guests, and a whole list of other things included in the Body Corporate Rules. Sometimes problems with neighbours escalate but mostly issues with neighbours can be resolved amicably when people just consider the needs of others.

My dad recently gave me a lesson on how to resolve issues with neighbours. The man who lives in the unit below us often has a visitor who smokes cigarettes on the balcony. The neighbour shuts his balcony doors to keep the smoke out of his unit but the smoke drifts up into our unit. We hate that so Dad told our neighbour that we were worried about breathing in the toxic smoke. Our neighbour apologised. He said he hadn't realised the smoke was coming into our unit. He said he doesn't like cigarette smoke in his unit either. He banned his friend from smoking anywhere near our block of units. Dad was so happy.

My best friend, Amira, lives in a house. When she goes to school and her parents go to work her dog, Foxy, barks all day. Her neighbour complained about the noise. She sleeps in the day because she works at night. Amira's barking dog didn't give her any peace. Amira felt really bad for being so thoughtless. She now puts a bark control collar on Foxy before she goes to school. Foxy is learning not to bark and Amira learned a lesson about considering others.

Being considerate of others is important wherever you live.

1 What does *escalate* mean in the text?
- **A** going up an escalator
- **B** get worse
- **C** dry up
- **D** resolve by themselves

2 What does *amicably* mean in the text?
- **A** in a friendly way
- **B** forcefully
- **C** in a disagreeable way
- **D** silently

3 Who does *She* refer to in the sentence *She sleeps in the day …*?
- **A** Amira
- **B** Foxy
- **C** Amira's neighbour
- **D** Amira's mother

4 The writer's neighbour is depicted as
- **A** a forceful person.
- **B** a reasonable person.
- **C** a person with strong opinions.
- **D** a disagreeable person.

5 Amira is depicted as
- **A** a lonely girl.
- **B** a hard worker at school but noisy at home.
- **C** inconsiderate of others.
- **D** kind but unthinking.

6 What did the writer's dad say to the neighbour at the end of their conversation?

....

....

....

....

....

....

Answers and explanations on pp. 106–107

Use the **Step-by-step guide** on pages 54–57 to help you read the text and examine the way **language** is used to answer the questions below. Circle the correct answers or write your answer on the lines.

Pets

Animal Lover Too

As an owner of a pet shop I was insulted to read 'Puppy Factories and Kitten Farms' (Animal Lover, April 9th). The letter was biased and emotive, totally lacking in factual detail. Pet shops have regulations, enforced by law and all the managers and staff I deal with have the utmost integrity in caring for their animals. Animal Lover needs to find another cause as he/she is barking up the wrong tree with this one.

Shop Owner

Babies for sale

I agree with Animal Lover ('Puppy Factories and Kitten Farms', April 9th). Pet shops should not be allowed to display and sell puppies and kittens to walk-by shoppers. Buying a pet is something that should be thoroughly researched and planned for. Walk-by shoppers buy pets on impulse when they get their groceries. This is why we have so many unwanted cats and dogs needing to be rehomed by the RSPCA and other animal welfare groups. Pet shops should just sell pet accessories and pet foods.

Animal Righter

1 What does *barking up the wrong tree* mean in the text?

A barking like a dog

B making a mistake

C barking unnecessarily

D talking to the wrong people

2 *This is why we have so many unwanted cats and dogs needing to be rehomed ...* What does *This* refer to?

A people buying pets on impulse

B people taking time to research their choice of pet

C how easy it is to buy a pet at the grocery store

D research is needed before buying a pet

3 Which statement best represents *Shop Owner*'s point of view?

A that pet shops owners don't like to be insulted

B that pet shops have regulations

C that Animal Lover needs to find another cause

D that pet shops operate responsibly

4 Which command would *Animal Righter* want readers to obey?

A Buy a pet with your groceries.

B Take the decision to buy a pet seriously.

C Take unwanted pets to an animal welfare group.

D Advise walk-by shoppers to buy puppies and kittens.

5 Both of the letters were written in response to

A the RSPCA.

B Animal Lover Too.

C Puppy Factories and Kitten Farms.

D Animal Righter.

6 Choose one letter to agree or disagree with. Write your opinions about the topic.

Answers and explanations on p. 107

Language questions

Use the **Step-by-step guide** on pages 54–57 to help you read the text and examine the way **language** is used to answer the questions below. Circle the correct answers or write your answer on the lines.

1 How does the comic strip show the passage of time?

- **A** The frames are linked through cause and effect.
- **B** The images show time passing.
- **C** The narrative is sequenced in time.
- **D** The labels tell how time has passed.

2 The text is an example of political satire because it

- **A** makes fun of people by calling them names.
- **B** makes fun of politicians.
- **C** shows what happens at Parliament House.
- **D** shows a news event.

3 *I'm glad he's opposed to sledging.*

This is

- **A** irony because the main character is actually sledging.
- **B** an honest opinion: the speaker doesn't like sledging either.
- **C** a lie because the speaker agrees that the government should oppose sledging.
- **D** a truthful comment about sledging.

4 A *sandwich short of a picnic* means the same as

- **A** never has enough to eat.
- **B** a true blue Aussie.
- **C** as happy as a pig in mud.
- **D** not that smart.

5 Which term could the creator use to add an extra frame to the comic strip between frames 5 and 6? Draw the new frame.

- **A** terrific talent
- **B** tireless workaholic
- **C** despicable worm
- **D** esteemed and educated colleague

6 Explain what *sledging* is and the point the cartoonist makes in the comic strip.

....

....

Answers and explanations on p. 108

Language questions

Use the **Step-by-step guide** on pages 54–57 to help you read the text and examine the way **language** is used to answer the questions below. Circle the correct answers or write your answer on the lines.

The life of Herman

Storyboard for film: Scene 1: Another Busy Day

1. Why does the storyboard start with a close-up?
   - **A** to set the scene
   - **B** to establish the point of view of the main character
   - **C** to show what the ants are doing
   - **D** to build suspense

2. What impact is the view in frame 4 meant to have on readers?
   - **A** to show readers a human foot
   - **B** to introduce the human character
   - **C** to help readers empathise with the ant
   - **D** to make readers worried that the ant will bite the person

3. Why does the creator show this view of the human in frame 6?
   - **A** to show how the ants feel
   - **B** to show the human's point of view
   - **C** to put the size of the ant into perspective
   - **D** to show the background

4. Which sequence of emotions is displayed by the ant?
   - **A** happiness, fear, courage
   - **B** pride, concern, fear, anger
   - **C** worry, fear, anger
   - **D** adventurousness, fear, bravery

5. What is the reader shown of the human's emotions?
   - **A** The human is oblivious to the ants.
   - **B** The human has a fear of ants.
   - **C** The human is angry about the ants.
   - **D** The human's point of view is not shown.

6. Write the dialogue for frame 5.

   ....

   ....

   ....

   ....

   ....

Answers and explanations on pp. 108–109

Language questions

Use the **Step-by-step guide** on pages 54–57 to help you read the text and examine the way **language** is used to answer the questions below. Circle the correct answers or write your answer on the lines.

A foiled plan

Mel's face was inscrutable. She wasn't giving anything away.

"We could go after school," I suggest hopefully.

Still no reaction.

"Well don't just stand there, say something."

She looked at me.

I waited … and waited …

I raised my eyebrows … looking at her … waiting …

"You scratch my back and I'll scratch yours," I entreated, quoting my mum and using one of her favourite sayings; one she used whenever she wanted me to do something.

Mel ignored that; steely eyed; impervious to my mum's sayings. She'd heard them all before.

I shrugged sheepishly. Worth a try, I thought.

FINALLY, Mel looked me in the eye.

"No."

"Huh?"

Her eyes round like her mouth. "No."

I was stunned. This can't be. She always agrees. She's like putty—very malleable. I didn't understand. What was happening here? She always, always does what I say. Mel and Abigail, peas in a pod. I hesitated … I gave her my sucked-lemon face.

I waited … and waited …

"You're driving me up the wall!" I stormed off.

1. *You scratch my back and I'll scratch yours.* What does this mean in the text?
   - **A** The writer is itchy.
   - **B** The writer is offering to scratch Mel's back for a back scratch in return.
   - **C** Do something for me and I'll do something for you.
   - **D** You need to scratch someone's back to make them happy.

2. What does *impervious* mean in the text?
   - **A** not influenced
   - **B** not listening
   - **C** she'd heard it before
   - **D** impressed

3. What does it mean to shrug *sheepishly*?
   - **A** angrily
   - **B** stupidly
   - **C** in an embarrassed way
   - **D** with a bold attitude

4. The narrator's character
   - **A** tries to bully Mel into doing what she wants.
   - **B** expects Mel to do what she wants.
   - **C** cries and whines to get her way.
   - **D** is argumentative and very persuasive.

5. Readers learn about Mel's character through
   - **A** her facial expressions and gestures.
   - **B** what the narrator tells you.
   - **C** what she says about herself.
   - **D** what other people say about her.

6. *"You're driving me up the wall!" I stormed off.*

   How does Abigail feel at this point in the narrative?

   ....

   ....

   ....

Answers and explanations on pp. 109–110

Use the **Step-by-step guide** on pages 54–57 to help you read the text and examine the way **language** is used to answer the questions below. Circle the correct answers or write your answer on the lines.

Feral animals in Australia

Australia has a large number of feral animals including cane toads, cats, dogs, rabbits, foxes, pigs, goats, deer, buffalo, horses and camels. Feral animals are an environmental disaster. They kill native animals and they compete with them for food and shelter. They contribute to soil erosion, water degradation and habitat destruction. They can spread diseases to livestock and domestic animals. They have no natural predators and they reproduce quickly and successfully. They are very difficult to manage and eradicate from natural areas.

It is impossible to rid Australia of all the feral animals. Government agencies endeavour to clear feral animals from specific limited areas through baiting, trapping, shooting, erecting fences or using biological controls but no method is perfect.

Fences work in small areas but they are costly to erect and need to be regularly checked and maintained. Trapping is also labour intensive because the traps have to be set and then checked daily. Rabbits can be baited with a naturally occurring poison such as one derived from the West Australian native pea. (Western Australian native animals seem to have developed a tolerance for this poison so are not harmed and the bait is coloured black or green so that it is not attractive to native birds.) Biological controls include the introduction of natural predators or diseases such as the myxomatosis virus, which was released in 1950 to kill feral rabbits. The federal government department responsible for the environment believes that shooting, by professional licenced shooters, is the most humane method of dealing with larger feral animals like horses, pigs and buffalo. Shooters use helicopters in rugged mountainous areas.

Any methods used must be cost effective and also comply with government guidelines on the humane treatment of feral animals.

1 Find an emotive term in the text that sums up the writer's opinion of feral animals.

....

2 What does *endeavour* mean in the text?

A try **B** forget

C disregard **D** hate

3 What rights do feral animals have?

A the right to live peacefully

B no rights as they are an environmental disaster

C the right to live in remote areas of Australia

D the right under law to be treated humanely

4 What does *developed a tolerance* mean?

A have learned to avoid it

B have developed a distaste for something

C can eat it without being harmed

D have developed a taste for it

5 What is the writer's attitude to shooting feral animals?

A The writer doesn't give an opinion for or against.

B The writer doesn't like shooting as a means of controlling feral animals.

C The writer prefers shooting larger animals.

D The writer thinks baiting is more cost effective than shooting.

6 What does *humane* mean? Write in your own words.

....

....

....

....

....

....

Answers and explanations on p. 110

Step-by-step guide to **judgement** questions

Judgement questions involve making judgements.

Use this **Step-by-step** guide to help you read the text and make **judgements** to answer the questions below. Circle the correct answers or write your answers on the lines.

STEP 1	**Skim** the text to see what it is about and how it is organised.	**Read** the title, *Joose*. Look at the illustrations and other visual elements. Notice the types of images, the font style and size, and layout. Make **predictions** about the subject and purpose of the text.
STEP 2	**Read** the text. **Monitor** your reading to make sure you understand the text.	**Visualise** and **connect** with the ideas in the text**. Think** about what you already know about the subject and the type of text, an advertisement. Make **predictions** Make **inferences**. Reflect on meanings and make **judgements**.

Joose

GOODNESS YOU CAN **FEEL**
FLAVOUR YOU CAN **SEE**
HEALTH YOU CAN **TOUCH**

yellow orange red purple green blue
the colours of the garden packed into great-tasting drinks

healthy, delicious fruit juices, shakes and smoothies

Options: low fat, gluten free, dairy free, cruelty free, coconut and soy based alternatives to dairy

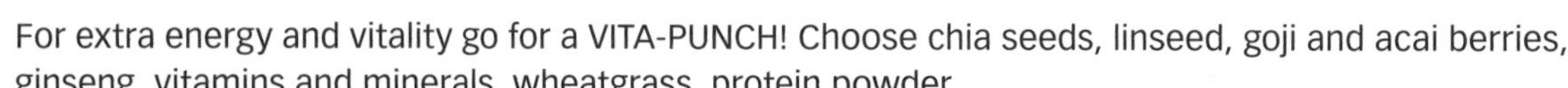

For extra energy and vitality go for a VITA-PUNCH! Choose chia seeds, linseed, goji and acai berries, ginseng, vitamins and minerals, wheatgrass, protein powder.

LIKE US ON FACEBOOK **JOIN US ON TWITTER** **and win a 'Go Green' Joose**

BUY JOOSE TODAY!

Question 1 **What judgements can you make about *Joose* drinks based on the claims in this advertisement? Choose all that apply.**

A They seem healthy.
B They are definitely tasty.
C They use some healthy ingredients.
D They must give you energy and vitality

STEP 3	**Read** the question. **Think** about what type of question it is. Work out what you need to do to answer it.	This is a **judgement** question. You need to use evidence in the text and your understanding about the language of advertisements to make **judgements** about the claims made in the advertisement.

STEP 4 **Think** about the text. Remember what you have read and **visualised**.

✪ You can work out the answer by looking for evidence to support each claim and judging how language is used to persuade. **Scan** the text to find and re-read the relevant parts.

A and **C** are correct. You read that *Joose* is made from ingredients that you should recognise as healthy (**A**) so you can judge that they seem healthy (**C**). Notice the low modality word *seem*. You cannot judge that they really are healthy but you can judge that they are likely to be healthy.

B and **D** are incorrect. You cannot make a judgement that *Joose* drinks are definitely tasty or that they must give you energy and vitality. Notice the high modality used in the language of options **B** and **D**.

Question 2 Who is the most likely target audience for the advertisement?

A children under five years of age

B children aged 5–12

C teenagers

D parents

STEP 3 **Read** the question. **Think** about what type of question it is. Work out what you need to do to answer it.

✪ This is a **judgement** question. You need to find evidence in the text to judge the *most likely* target audience for the advertisement.

STEP 4 **Think** about the text. Remember what you have read and **visualised**.

✪ **Scan** the text or re-read it if necessary. Look for evidence to help you make a judgement.

You can judge that the most likely target audience for the ad is **D**, parents. Notice the low modality phrase *most likely* used in the question. Members of other age groups might choose health drinks but you can judge that the ad targets older people, adults or parents because of the health claims.

Check to confirm that the other options are incorrect. **A**, **B** and **C** are incorrect because you should judge that children and teenagers are less likely to be persuaded to buy a drink because of ingredients such as *chia seeds, linseed, goji and acai berries, ginseng, vitamins and minerals, wheatgrass, protein powder* (see lines 11–12).

Question 3 Which statements best describe the methods used in the advertisement? Choose all answers that apply.

A uses scientific evidence to prove its claims

B lists ingredients available to the customer

C uses emotive words, phrases and imagery that appeal to the senses

D uses high modality to persuade customers to choose *Joose*

STEP 3 **Read** the question. **Think** about what type of question it is. Work out what you need to do to answer it.

✪ This is a **judgement** question. You need to judge the methods used by the advertiser of *Joose*.

STEP 4 **Think** about the text. Remember what you have read and **visualised**.

✪ **Scan** the text or re-read it if necessary. Make **judgements** based on evidence in the text.

B, **C** and **D** are correct. **B** is correct because the advertisement lists ingredients available to the customer: *chia seeds, linseed, goji and acai berries, ginseng, vitamins and minerals, wheatgrass, protein powder* (see lines 11–12). **C** is correct because the advertisement uses emotive words, phrases and imagery that appeal to the senses. You read *GOODNESS YOU CAN FEEL / FLAVOUR YOU CAN SEE / HEALTH YOU CAN TOUCH / the colours of the garden* (see lines 2–6). Examples of evaluative language are *great-tasting, healthy, delicious* (see lines 6–7). **D** is correct. The ad uses high modality persuasive commands. You read *go for a VITA-PUNCH! Choose chia seeds … LIKE US ON FACEBOOK. JOIN US ON TWITTER / win …* (see lines 11–13) You should also notice how images, layout and use of upper-case lettering persuade through emphasis.

A is incorrect. The advertiser does not use science or reasoning to promote the product.

Judgement questions involve making judgements.

Joose

GOODNESS YOU CAN **FEEL**
FLAVOUR YOU CAN **SEE**
HEALTH YOU CAN **TOUCH**

yellow orange red purple green blue

the colours of the garden packed into great-tasting drinks

healthy, delicious fruit juices, shakes and smoothies

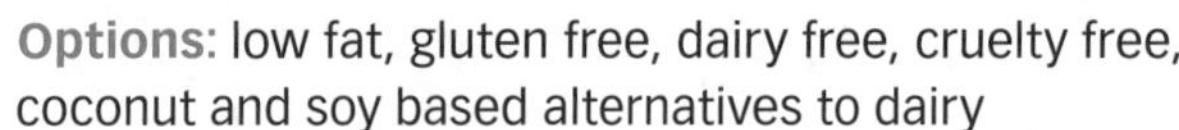

Options: low fat, gluten free, dairy free, cruelty free, coconut and soy based alternatives to dairy

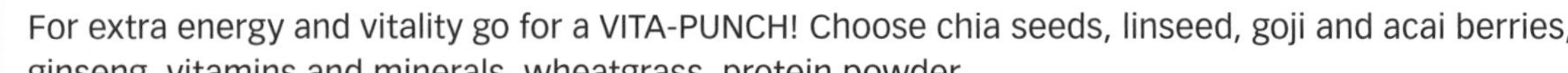

For extra energy and vitality go for a VITA-PUNCH! Choose chia seeds, linseed, goji and acai berries, ginseng, vitamins and minerals, wheatgrass, protein powder.

LIKE US ON FACEBOOK **JOIN US ON TWITTER** **and win a 'Go Green' Joose**

BUY JOOSE TODAY!

Question 4 **Judge which information in the advertisement would be least important to a potential customer.**

A Options: low fat, gluten free, dairy free, cruelty free, coconut and soy based alternatives to dairy
B delicious fruit juices, shakes and smoothies
C For extra energy and vitality go for a VITA-PUNCH!
D LIKE US ON FACEBOOK and win a 'Go Green' Joose

STEP 3 **Read** the question. **Think** about what type of question it is. Work out what you need to do to answer it.

- This is a **judgement** question. You need to **judge** the relevance of information in an advertisement to a potential purchaser.

STEP 4 **Think** about the text. Remember what you have read and **visualised**.

- **Think** about the question. Re-read it if necessary.

D is correct. You can judge that the information in **D** would be the least important to a purchaser in deciding whether to choose to buy a product.

Check to confirm that the other options are incorrect. **A**, **B** and **C** are incorrect because you can judge that ingredients, taste and health benefits would be more important to a purchaser than **D**. **A** would be important to people with allergies to dairy or gluten, or to people who are vegans. **B** would be relevant because taste is important in choosing a drink. **C** would be relevant to some people who might choose a drink based on claims that it has energy and vitality benefits.

Question 5 Does the advertisement place a greater emphasis on taste or health benefits? Explain how you reached your decision.

....

....

....

STEP 3	**Read** the question. **Think** about what type of question it is. Work out what you need to do to answer it.	✪ This is a **judgement** question. You need to examine the advertisement and judge whether it places greater emphasis on promoting the taste of *Joose* or the health aspects of *Joose.*
STEP 4	**Think** about the text. Remember what you have read and **visualised**.	✪ **Scan** the text to identify the taste claims and the health claims. A useful strategy would be to use a highlighter pen to colour or underline the parts of the text that appeal to taste and use a different colour to highlight the parts that promote health benefits.

The answer can be summarised as follows:

Taste: FLAVOUR, great-tasting, delicious

Health: the images of fruit, GOODNESS, HEALTH, healthy, low fat, gluten free, dairy free, coconut and soy based alternatives to dairy, extra energy and vitality, chia seeds, linseed, goji and acai berries, ginseng, vitamins and minerals, wheatgrass, protein powder.

Some people would argue that the colours of the garden and cruelty free are also for health benefits.

Your judgement should conclude that the advertisement focuses greater attention on the health benefits of the product than the taste and justify or explain how you reached this decision.

Question 6 Would an adult in your family buy a *Joose* drink? If so, who and why? If not, why not? Explain your judgements.

....

....

....

STEP 3	**Read** the question. **Think** about what type of question it is. Work out what you need to do to answer it.	✪ This is a **judgement** question. You need to **judge** the effectiveness of the advertisement and its likely impact on the buying decisions of an adult family member.
STEP 4	**Think** about the text. Remember what you have read and **visualised**.	✪ Re-read the text if necessary. Choose an adult in your family and make a **judgement** about the influence you think the advertisement would have on that person. **Judge** the impact of the visual elements (illustrations, layout, font, design) and the emotive and persuasive language.

You could judge the advertisement to be effective and cite the call to action (*BUY JOOSE TODAY!*), and its use of persuasive and emotive language to influence its target market. You could judge that the adult enjoys buying other similar products or that the adult is health-conscious. You could judge that the adult would like the fruit in the illustration.

Alternatively you could judge the advertisement to be ineffective. You might suggest that the adult you have chosen does not like so-called health foods or might not like to spend money on juice and smoothies. The adult might want to know the cost of the juice before making a purchase decision.

You need to have used evidence in the text and your knowledge of the preferences of your family member to justify your judgements.

Judgement questions

Use the **Step-by-step guide** on pages 66–69 to help you read the text and make **judgements** to answer the questions below. Circle the correct answers or write your answers on the lines.

Targeting Maths Year 5 app

By Blake Publishing

Open iTunes to buy and download apps.

Description

The Targeting Maths Year 5 app is an amazing new way to learn mathematics. Within this app students can access a huge range of activities that make learning maths facts fun, motivating and very rewarding!

This app includes:

- Training—81 question sets that cover the 9 big topics of Year 5 Mathematics. This section includes a scratch board for working out problems, along with a Dictionary of terms.
- Multiplayer—up to 4 players can play against each other in this game of speed and fun.
- Timed—increase speed in essential addition, subtraction, word and mixed mathematic facts.
- Badges—players earn more than 220 badges.
- Games—players earn tokens to spend on fun games in the circus area.

With the ability to make multiple accounts, each student's individual progress is tracked and recorded.

In creating the Targeting Maths apps we have brought together all we know about how children learn maths with the powerful interactivity and motivation provided by the iPad. The irresistible combination of engagement and learning will switch on all students, even those who don't think that they are good at maths!

1. Who is the most likely target audience for the advertisement?
   - **A** primary school children
   - **B** parents
   - **C** teachers
   - **D** Year 5 students

2. What judgements can you make about the Targeting Maths Year 5 App based on the claims in this advertisement? Choose all that apply.
   - **A** It seems fun.
   - **B** It must make students happy to do maths.
   - **C** It definitely helps children learn maths.
   - **D** It covers the important areas of maths for Year 5.

3. Which methods are used in the advertisement? Choose all that apply.
   - **A** uses scientific evidence to prove its claims
   - **B** claims expertise
   - **C** uses evaluative and emotive words
   - **D** uses high modality to persuade

4. Judge which information in the advertisement would be least important to Year 5 students.
   - **A** It's an amazing way to learn maths.
   - **B** It includes a Dictionary of terms.
   - **C** It has powerful interactivity.
   - **D** There's a huge range of activities.

5. Does the advertisement place a greater emphasis on fun or learning? Explain how you reached your decision.

   ....

   ....

   ....

6. Based on what you read in the advertisement, would you choose to try this App? If so, why? If not, why not? Explain your judgements.

   ....

   ....

   ....

Answers and explanations on pp. 110–111

Judgement questions

Use the **Step-by-step guide** on pages 66–69 to help you read the text and make **judgements** to answer the questions below. Circle the correct answers or write your answers on the lines.

The shark debate

Speaker 1: Shark nets kill turtles, dolphins, whales, stingrays and harmless sharks such as the grey nurse and hammerhead. Nets catch more harmless animals than dangerous ones. People: Don't swim or surf in shark territory or at shark-feeding times. Simple. The by-catch makes netting not worth it.

Speaker 2: Swimmers must be saved from horrific injuries or death inflicted by shark attacks on our beaches. Nets are one strategy amidst a range of useful strategies. Our tourist industry needs to be able to tell tourists the beaches are safe. People need protection.

Speaker 3: People need to put things in perspective here. Whenever a person is injured or killed by a shark in Australian waters, renewed calls are made to cull all sharks that roam near our coastline. Would we cull all dogs because some have attacked people?

Speaker 4: The ocean belongs to fish and marine mammals and when people trespass in the marine environment they should do so at their own risk. People are aware that sharks are out there. Sharks belong—we don't. We can't net the whole Australian coastline for the sake of a few shark attacks or a few deaths each year. As unfortunate and tragic as those fatal attacks are, there's no guarantee that if we did net off the whole coastline sharks wouldn't get through anyway and we'd be killing all those harmless creatures for nothing.

1. What is the most common point of view?
   - **A** in favour of shark nets to protect people
   - **B** against shark nets to protect harmless animals
   - **C** for shark nets to protect harmless animals
   - **D** against shark nets to protect people

2. Speaker 2 could be a member of the
   - **A** Grey Nurse Shark Study Group
   - **B** World Wildlife Fund
   - **C** Sydney City Tourism Board
   - **D** Save the Shark Alliance

3. Speaker 3 could be a representative from
   - **A** the Cull Feral Animals Action Group
   - **B** the Save the Shark Alliance
   - **C** Peoplefirst.org
   - **D** unitefordogs.com.au

4. How are the opinions of Speakers 1 and 4 similar?
   - **A** Speaker 1 is concerned about by-catch and Speaker 4 is not.
   - **B** Both speakers are in favour of netting.
   - **C** Speaker 1 is against netting and Speaker 4 is against people swimming in the ocean.
   - **D** Both speakers advise common sense and are against netting.

5. Which statement is the most emotive?
   - **A** Netting is not worth the by-catch.
   - **B** Swimmers must be saved from horrific injuries or death.
   - **C** People need protection.
   - **D** Sharks belong in the ocean.

6. Which speaker do you most agree with? Explain your reasons.

   ....

   ....

   ....

   ....

   ....

Answers and explanations on pp. 111–112

Judgement questions

Use the **Step-by-step guide** on pages 66–69 to help you read the text and make **judgements** to answer the questions below. Circle the correct answers or write your answers on the lines.

Teacher trouble

Scene: Two boys are seated on a bench.

George: I don't like him.

Nikolas: Mmmm.

George: He made me redo that whole page of work because he didn't like it.

Nikolas: (nodding) Yeah.

George: I hate him. He's so unfair and mean. He picks on me all the time. I wish he'd go to another school.

Nikolas: Yeah.

George: Why do you think he picks on me? Maybe he just doesn't like me. Why would that be? I didn't do anything to him … I muck around a little bit and have a joke but so does Lila and she doesn't get into trouble like me. I think she's funny, too.

Nikolas: Hmmm (sighs).

George: I get a little loud sometimes …

Nikolas: (emphatic nodding) Yeah.

George: (pause) … but that couldn't be why he picks on me (pause) … He just hates me, don't you think?

Nikolas: (silence)

George: (pause) … So maybe I don't ALWAYS do my homework (pause) … and (pause) … maybe

Nikolas: Yeah?

George: and … well… maybe … I rarely do my homework …

Nikolas: Mmmmm.

George: but that's no excuse for him to pick on me. Telling me I can do better, telling me he's disappointed in me, saying he expects more from me. Who does he think he is?

Nikolas: (eyebrows lift)

George: (whining) He's just too bossy! He's just unfair. He's a bully; telling me I have "unfulfilled potential". Huh! … and "a poor attitude". What a joke! He drives me nuts.

1 Why does George have a problem with his teacher?

- **A** The teacher is a bully and picks on George.
- **B** George gets into trouble in class.
- **C** George laughs at Lila's jokes.
- **D** George complains about everything.

2 Which sentence best describes Nikolas's character?

- **A** He is the teacher's favourite.
- **B** He likes the teacher.
- **C** He does his homework and works hard.
- **D** He is a good listener and George's friend.

3 What does the teacher think of George?

- **A** George is incapable of learning anything.
- **B** George is a nuisance and should move to another school.
- **C** George could do so much better.
- **D** George is lucky to be Nikolas's friend.

4 Which of the following would be appropriate for the end of the text?

- **A** Nikolas: Tell the teacher why you're upset.
- **B** Nikolas: Tell him he's a bully.
- **C** Nikolas: You are whinging too much. I'm tired of listening to it.
- **D** Nikolas: (sigh)

5 What do you think of George?

....

....

....

6 Is George a true-to-life, realistic character? Explain.

....

....

....

Answers and explanations on p. 112

Judgement questions

Use the **Step-by-step guide** on pages 66–69 to help you read the text and make **judgements** to answer the questions below. Circle the correct answers or write your answers on the lines.

THE CITY TIMES

17TH MARCH 2023

Endangered languages

An open letter to the Australian business community

We need your help.

When Great Britain colonised Australia there were hundreds of First Nations languages but now many of those languages are extinct and many are critically endangered. What a great shame!

The United Nations classifies a language as critically endangered if the language has less than ten speakers. Mostly these critically endangered languages are only spoken by older people and once these people die their languages become extinct.

Governments around the world NOW recognise the importance of working to save endangered languages from extinction. Language carries cultural identity, ancestral knowledge and tradition. Our world is richer for the variety of languages that are maintained and used.

Australian Indigenous languages are the oldest surviving languages in the world. Isn't that amazing! The Australian government is funding initiatives to help First Nations communities revive or maintain their languages. Early childhood programs, bilingual classrooms, local community Indigenous Language Centres and Indigenous language courses, in secondary schools, are just some of the ways that younger generations can learn the languages of their ancestors and preserve these languages for generations of the future.

You can help by sponsoring an Indigenous language program. Make a commitment today to support Aboriginal and Torres Strait Islander communities in preserving languages for the benefit of all Australians.

Thank you
V Curtis
savinglanguagefund.org.au

1 What is the purpose of the text?

- **A** to alert people to a language problem
- **B** to report an issue in the newspaper
- **C** to persuade people to learn to speak endangered languages
- **D** to persuade business leaders to support Indigenous language programs

2 Would this text be useful in compiling a government report about the status of endangered languages?

- **A** Yes, because it has information about saving languages.
- **B** No, because it isn't from a reliable source.
- **C** Yes, because it tells that many languages are endangered.
- **D** No, because it is an advertisement.

3 Why does the writer say *Isn't that amazing*?

- **A** to ask the reader a question
- **B** to express surprise
- **C** to engage the reader
- **D** to state a fact

4 Make a judgement about the writer based on what is said in the text. The writer

- **A** is a First Australian.
- **B** is a non-Indigenous person.
- **C** works for the government.
- **D** values culture.

5 Judge why the writer thinks it is so important to save Indigenous languages.

....

....

....

....

6 How have attitudes about preserving language changed over the years?

....

....

....

....

Answers and explanations on pp. 112–113

Use the **Step-by-step guide** on pages 66–69 to help you read the text and make **judgements** to answer the questions below. Circle the correct answers or write your answers on extra paper.

Longline fishing

Text 1

Longline fishing is a method of fishing that is often used to catch tuna. The fishing ship trails a fishing line up to 100 kilometres long that can have thousands of baited hooks. The longline is designed to catch as many fish as possible. The problem is that the hooks catch other sea creatures such as turtles and sea birds, dragging them through the ocean and drowning them. These animals are referred to as by-catch.

The Humane Society International says that longline fishing kills 400 albatrosses every week around the world. Nineteen of the world's 22 albatross species are classified as threatened or endangered. It is also estimated that 450 turtles and 50 000 sharks are wrongly caught each year on longlines in Australian waters alone. It is a tragedy that these animals die needlessly when there are other methods of fishing that don't cause a by-catch.

Text 2

Longline fishing is a highly productive, cost-effective, commercial fishing method used to catch the maximum number of fish from one vessel. The fishing ship trails a fishing line up to 100 kilometres long that can have thousands of baited hooks designed to catch as many fish as possible. Fish are an important food source for millions of people worldwide. As well as being cost effective, another benefit of longline fishing is that baited fish are alive when hauled aboard the fishing vessel so longline caught fish have a reputation for freshness.

1 What is the key point of view in Text 1?

- **A** Longline fishing catches tuna.
- **B** Longline fishing is inhumane and wasteful.
- **C** Longlines are designed to catch as many fish as possible.
- **D** There are methods of fishing that don't create by-catch.

2 What is the writer's purpose in Text 1?

- **A** to persuade people to think about problems with a fishing method
- **B** to describe the usefulness of longline fishing in catching turtles
- **C** to encourage people to find out about the Humane Society International
- **D** to describe methods of fishing

3 Reading Text 1 could be helpful before

- **A** learning how to fish for tuna.
- **B** compiling a report on marine turtles.
- **C** working with injured wildlife such as albatrosses.
- **D** creating a petition to ban longline fishing.

4 What is the writer's overall point of view in Text 2?

- **A** Countries need longline fishing to feed populations.
- **B** Longline fishing is a very successful fishing method.
- **C** Longline fishing has an excellent reputation.
- **D** There is no point of view evident.

5 Which text do you think would be the most effective at influencing opinions? Explain your reasons.

....

....

6 What do you think about longline fishing based on the evidence and opinions given in both texts? Make a judgement.

....

....

Answers and explanations on pp. 113–114

Judgement questions

Use the **Step-by-step guide** on pages 66–69 to help you read the text and make **judgements** to answer the questions below. Circle the correct answers or write your answers on the lines.

Book review*: *The One and Only Ivan*

The One and Only Ivan, a 2013 Newbery Medal winner, is a first-person narrative. The narrator is Ivan, a captive gorilla. The author uses Ivan's voice to give readers a very credible insight into the life of a captive animal. Gorillas in the wild live in social groups but Ivan never learned how to be a gorilla. He says, *I used to be a wild gorilla and I still look the part*.

The novel is based on the true story of an infant gorilla captured in Africa and shipped to America to become someone's pet. When Ivan grew too large and likely to become a problem for his owner he was sent to live in a circus-themed shopping mall, where he lived in a cage for 27 years. When the Mall went out of business he was taken to a zoo in Atlanta.

This story highlights the underlying immorality of keeping exotic animals as pets and in cages for human entertainment.

The story is beautifully told using poetic language such as *Gorillas are as patient as stones.* This simile shows readers Ivan's attitude to captivity. Ivan's friends are an elephant in an adjacent cage and a stray dog. The reader is able to empathise with the characters because of the caring and insightful way Ivan describes them and interacts with them.

This is a moving story with a strong voice for animals. It encourages readers to see zoos and circuses from the animals' points of view.

*Review by Kristy Sullivan
The One and Only Ivan by Katherine Applegate, 2013

1. What is the reviewer's judgement about Ivan as a narrator?
   - **A** A gorilla is the narrator, so it's unrealistic.
   - **B** Ivan is a believable narrator.
   - **C** Ivan's point of view is too biased because it's a true story.
   - **D** The narration is entertaining.

2. What is the reviewer's judgement of the author's ability to tell a story?
   - **A** She is talented.
   - **B** She must be good because the book is a Newbery Medal winner.
   - **C** She only writes stories for animal lovers.
   - **D** She takes the subject matter too seriously.

3. What is the reviewer's opinion of circuses?
   - **A** it is sad when animals are captured in Africa
   - **B** immoral
   - **C** worthwhile and entertaining
   - **D** interesting

4. Why do you think the reviewer is so impressed with Katherine Applegate's use of poetic language?

   ....

   ....

   ....

5. *I used to be a wild gorilla and I still look the part.* Why do you think the reviewer uses this quote?

   ....

   ....

   ....

6. Judge the effectiveness of the review in helping you decide whether or not to read the book. Explain your reasoning.

   ....

   ....

   ....

   ....

   ....

Answers and explanations on p. 114

Judgement questions

Use the **Step-by-step guide** on pages 66–69 to help you read the text and make **judgements** to answer the questions below. Circle the correct answers or write your answers on the lines.

Slaves for sugar

A group of male and female South Sea Islander farm workers on a sugar plantation at Cairns in 1890. (State Library of Queensland; The Commons) http://trove.nla.gov.au/version/47949612

Approximately 60 000 Pacific Islanders worked as indentured labourers on Queensland's sugar cane fields between 1863 and 1903. They were mainly males, aged 9 to 30, transported to Australia by ship. Some came freely, wanting the new life promised to them, some were lured with sweets and gifts, some were tricked, some were abducted.

The practice of kidnapping people for labour was called 'blackbirding'. 'Blackbird' was a term used instead of slave, because slavery was actually illegal. Britain had passed the *Slavery Abolition Act* of 1833 and as a British colony, Queensland was subject to the Act. Also, the government of the colony of Queensland at that time, before Federation, had passed a law to try to prevent people trafficking. It is estimated that a third of Pacific Islanders who worked as indentured labourers were either kidnapped or tricked into coming to Australia. Indentured labour was really just another name for slavery.

Indentured labourers had to work for a required period of time, usually three years, to pay back their passage to Australia and then they could earn wages as free labourers. It was hard, dirty work in the heat and dust in rural areas of Queensland. Most indentured labourers were badly treated, many returning to their homelands as soon as their indentured period was finished. A small number married into local communities and stayed. Free labourers were also badly exploited on the cane fields, working for meagre wages and living in extremely poor conditions.

After Federation, the Australian Government's White Australia Policy forced Pacific Islanders to leave Australia. Even people who were born in Australia to Pacific Islander parents were deported. If they didn't leave freely they were rounded up and deported forcibly between 1906 and 1908. This practice was devastating for many families. Some of the people had lived in Australia most, if not all, of their lives. Only a few who had married Australians were allowed to stay. A few managed to hide and evade deportation.

1 What is the writer's point of view?

A The writer doesn't have one.
B The Pacific Islanders were treated very badly.
C This is a factual report so there are no opinions.
D Slavery took place even though it was illegal.

2 What does the writer want you to think? Choose all answers that apply.

A that blackbirding was a common practice on sugar plantations
B that Pacific Islanders had a better life in Australia than in their homelands
C that blackbirds were not actually slaves
D that many Australians held racist attitudes at the time of Federation

3 A major theme of the text is

A greed. **B** exploitation.
C jealousy. **D** breaking the law.

4 Imagine you own a sugar plantation in 1890. How would you justify blackbirding? Choose all that apply.

A I need cheap labour to make a profit.
B The Pacific Islanders are hard workers.
C I can't get labourers any other way.
D I give the Islanders a job so they're better off here in Australia.

5 What concerns might you have if you were a Pacific Islander living in Queensland in 1906?

....

....

6 What is your opinion of indentured labour based on the information in this text?

....

....

....

Answers and explanations on pp. 114–115

Judgement questions

Use the **Step-by-step guide** on pages 66–69 to help you read the text and make **judgements** to answer the questions below. Circle the correct answers or write your answers on the lines.

The Hunt

I and the other colts were feeding at the lower part of the field when we heard, quite in the distance, what sounded like the cry of dogs. And soon the dogs were all tearing down the field. After them came a number of men on horseback, all galloping as fast as they could.

Just then a hare wild with fright rushed by and made for the woods. On came the dogs; they burst over the bank, leaped the stream, and came dashing across the field followed by the huntsmen. Six or eight men leaped their horses clean over, close upon the dogs. The hare tried to get through the fence; it was too thick, and she turned sharp round to make for the road, but it was too late; the dogs were upon her with their wild cries; we heard one shriek, and that was the end of her.

As for me, I was so astonished that I did not at first see what was going on by the brook; but when I did look there was a sad sight; a fine horse lay groaning on the grass.

My mother said, "I never yet could make out why men are so fond of this sport."

When Mr. Bond, the farrier, came to look at the black horse that lay groaning on the grass, he felt him all over, and shook his head; one of his legs was broken. Then someone ran to our master's house and came back with a gun; presently there was a loud bang and a dreadful shriek, and then all was still; the black horse moved no more.

My mother seemed much troubled; she said she had known that horse for years. She never would go to that part of the field afterward.

Extract from *Black Beauty* by Anna Sewell, 1877, Chapter 2, abridged

1. The narrator is the male horse of the title, *Black Beauty*. What is Black Beauty's attitude to the hunt?
   - **A** worried
   - **B** excited
   - **C** bewildered
   - **D** jealous

2. Which statement best describes the mother's opinion of the *sport?*
   - **A** She is sad but totally accepts that accidents happen during the hunt.
   - **B** She is powerless to change things.
   - **C** She is puzzled about the popularity of the hunt and sad for her friend.
   - **D** She is worried about the colts getting hurt.

3. Does the text make readers feel sorry for the hare? Explain.

4. *Black Beauty* became an important animal rights novel. Why do you think this might be?

5. Make a judgement about gender bias in this story.

6. *The Oxford English Dictionary* defines sport as 'an activity involving physical exertion and skill in which an individual or team competes against another or others for entertainment'. Is the hunt, in the text, sport? Explain.

Answers and explanations on pp. 115–116

BRINGING IT ALL TOGETHER

Mixed questions

Use the **Step-by-step guide** on page 4 to help you read the text and answer the questions below. Circle the correct answers or write your answer on the lines.

Extremes

Wind: fluttery breezes brush my cheek
but bullying gusts tear at my shirt; rip off my hat.
And raging storms snatch branches off trees
and roofs off the houses along city streets.

Rain: gentle drips feed the earth
but driving rain fills up the drain pipes; rushes
in torrents.
And flooding rain blocks off the roads
and isolates people in small country towns.

Heat: sunshiny mornings hasten new growth
but blistering heatwaves send us indoors, seeking
cool places.
And scorching drought cracks open the earth
and dries up all life on parched open plains.

by Tanya Dalgleish

1 The poem is about
- **A** predicting the weather.
- **B** what you should do in extreme weather conditions.
- **C** weather being gentle or destructive.
- **D** being unable to control the weather.

2 When is the wind a bully?
- **A** when it brushes your cheek
- **B** when it drives rain into drainpipes
- **C** when it rips at your clothes
- **D** when it blows dust storms

3 The poet infers that
- **A** climate change is affecting the weather.
- **B** extreme weather is fun.
- **C** heavy rain fills dams.
- **D** extreme weather can be dangerous.

4 What is the poet's attitude to the weather?
- **A** inspired by it
- **B** concerned that it causes harm
- **C** thrilled about its unpredictability
- **D** bored because weather happens every day

5 Judge which kind of weather the poet thinks is the worst.
- **A** rain
- **B** wind
- **C** flood
- **D** drought

6 Which kind of weather or weather event do you think is the worst? Explain your answer and your reasons.

....

....

....

Answers and explanations on pp. 116–117

Mixed questions

Use the **Step-by-step-guide** on page 4 to help you read the text and answer the questions below. Circle the correct answers or write your answer on the lines.

Waltzing Matilda

Oh there once was a swag-man[1] camped in the billabongs,
Under the shade of a Coolibah tree,
And he sang as he looked at the old billy boiling
Who'll come a Waltzing[2] Matilda[3] with me.
Who'll come a waltzing Matilda my darling
Who'll come a Waltzing Matilda with me,
Waltzing Matilda and leading a water bag
Who'll come a Waltzing Matilda with me.
Down came a jumbuck[4] to drink at that billabong
Up jumped the swagman and grabbed him with glee,
And he said as he put him away in the tucker bag
You'll come a Waltzing Matilda with me!
Waltzing Matilda, Waltzing Matilda,
You'll come a Waltzing Matilda with me …
Down came the squatter[5] a riding his thorough-bred
Down came policemen one, two, three
Whose is the jumbuck you've got in the tucker bag?
You'll come a Waltzing Matilda with me!
But the swagman he up and he jumped in the water-hole
drowning himself by the Coolibah tree.
And his ghost may be heard as it sings by the billabong
Who'll come a Waltzing Matilda with me …
Waltzing Matilda, Waltzing Matilda
Who'll come a Waltzing Matilda with me.

by AB 'Banjo' Paterson, original words transcribed in 1895 by Christina McPherson

Footnotes:

1 swagman: a person of no fixed address, who walks from town to town looking for work, carrying his bedroll and pack on his back
2 auf der Walz: a German term from that time meaning to move from place to place practising your trade
3 Matilda: a term of endearment for a swag which held all the swagman's possessions and was very important to him on the road.
4 jumbuck: sheep
5 squatter: landowner/farmer

1 The song's structure is
- **A** stanzas with a sequence of events.
- **B** orientation, complication, resolution.
- **C** orientation, complication, series of events, resolution.
- **D** orientation, complication, consequence, resolution, coda.

2 The orientation
- **A** introduces the main character.
- **B** introduces the homeless man and the setting.
- **C** introduces Matilda and the swagman.
- **D** sets the scene in the billabongs and asks a question.

3 What is the complication in the narrative?
- **A** *… camped in the billabongs.*
- **B** *Down came a jumbuck to drink at that billabong*
- **C** *Up jumped the swagman and grabbed him with glee,*
- **D** *Down came the squatter a riding his thorough-bred*

4 Why did Paterson use the phrase *with glee*?
- **A** to tell how happy the swagman was to have food
- **B** to tell listeners the swagman was excited when stealing things
- **C** to express the jumbuck's excitement
- **D** to tell how the swagman danced with Matilda

5 What does *Waltzing Matilda* mean?
- **A** go to jail
- **B** dance the waltz with a jumbuck
- **C** dance with a swag
- **D** go on the road with your swag

6 'Waltzing Matilda' has remained important to Australians for more than a century. Make a judgement: Why do you think this is so?

....

....

....

....

....

Answers and explanations on p. 117

Mixed questions

Use the **Step-by-step-guide** on page 4 to help you read the text and answer the questions below. Circle the correct answers or write your answer on the lines.

Kaili Valley Wetlands

Summary of a Queensland Government Report commissioned to describe the 'environmental values of the Wetlands and the threats to these values', February 2012.

The Kaili (Caley) Valley Wetlands* are a nationally important wetland system, located 21 km north-west of Bowen in Queensland.

The Kaili Valley Wetlands area is inhabited by 22 species of migratory birds including the endangered Little Tern and two threatened species, the Australian Cotton Pygmy-goose and the Eastern Curlew.

Resident water birds found at Kaili include species such as the near threatened Black-necked Stork and Freckled Duck, the vulnerable Beach Stone-curlew, as well as the Pacific Black Duck, Magpie Goose and Wandering Whistling-Duck. The wetlands are one of Queensland's largest nesting areas for the Black Swan.

The wetlands are used as a movement corridor and foraging area for native animals, including three threatened species: the Northern Quoll, Coastal Sheathtail Bat and the Water Mouse.

Habitat degradation has had a significant impact on migratory bird populations in Asia, especially over the last 25 years where numbers have declined, in some species by as much as 80%. Development activities and resulting habitat degradation, including human interference with the area's natural water cycle pose similar potential risks to animal life in Kaili Valley Wetlands. Sea level rise is considered a long-term risk.

*A wetland is an ecosystem comprising an area of land that is usually saturated with freshwater, saltwater or brackish water (a mix of the two). Wetlands support aquatic plants such as mangroves. The Amazon River Basin is one of the world's largest wetland areas.

1 Judge the trustworthiness of the text.

- **A** It is biased and emotive.
- **B** It is trustworthy but has some emotive content.
- **C** It is untrustworthy.
- **D** It is trustworthy and factual.

2 What is the conclusion of the report?

- **A** Migratory birds from Asia are fewer in number.
- **B** Human activity threatens fauna that use the area.
- **C** Humans have interfered with the natural water cycle in the area.
- **D** Sea level rise is a major threat.

3 The purpose of the report is to

- **A** list bird species that reside in or migrate to the wetlands.
- **B** assess any threats and risks related to the wetlands.
- **C** summarise the importance of the area and potential threats.
- **D** describe all fauna evident in the wetlands.

4 Which is NOT a fact in the text?

- **A** The wetlands are used as a useful corridor for animals.
- **B** The area is usually saturated with water.
- **C** Humans pose potential risks to animal life at Kaili Valley.
- **D** Sea level rise has disturbed the natural water cycle.

5 Which is a fact in the text?

- **A** The Northern Quoll is now extinct.
- **B** Migratory birds live in the wetlands some of the time.
- **C** Resident birds live in the wetland some of the time.
- **D** Foraging native animals migrate to the wetlands.

6 Make a judgement about the value of the wetlands to Australians. Explain your reasons.

....

....

....

Answers and explanations on pp. 117–118

Mixed questions

Use the **Step-by-step-guide** on page 4 to help you read the text and answer the questions below. Circle the correct answers or write your answer on the lines.

Monarch butterflies

Monarch butterflies, called Wanderer butterflies in Australia, are amazing orange and black butterflies. They are amazing because of their size (a wingspan of up to 10 cm), because they can migrate vast distances, because of their life cycle (which varies from generation to generation), and because they gather in large clusters in cooler months (called over-wintering).

Monarch butterflies are migratory insects. The Australian Wanderer has more limited migration patterns but the Monarch butterfly can travel over 4000 km in a migration to warmer weather. They travel from North America to Mexico every year. This is further than from Melbourne to Darwin by road (3750 km) or from Sydney to Perth by road (3935 km).

The Monarch was first seen in Australia around 1870–71. It is not an indigenous species. Scientists speculate that cyclone winds carried adult Monarchs to Australia from Vanuatu or New Caledonia. Adult Monarchs can feed on the nectar from any flower but Monarch caterpillars rely specifically on the milkweed plant. A diet of milkweed acts as a defence mechanism against the Monarch's predators. The milkweed plant is actually poisonous to animals such as frogs, lizards and birds so a build-up of the milkweed chemical in the Monarch's body means the insect is distasteful to predators.

Monarchs have the usual butterfly life cycle of egg-larvae-pupae-adult; however, the length of time spent in the adult stage varies from one generation to the next over the course of a year. Because of its long migration patterns, the North American Monarch butterfly breeds four generations each year. The first three generations only live for about six weeks each but the fourth generation lives for 6 to 8 months so that it has time to undertake the migration and breed before dying.

Monarch numbers in North America and Mexico are under threat due to habitat loss and loss of milkweed due to land clearing and pesticides.

1 Judge the writer's feelings about the subject.
- **A** The writer wants people to feel sad that the butterflies are under threat.
- **B** The writer is fascinated by the butterflies.
- **C** The writer writes factually with no evaluative words or phrases.
- **D** Monarchs are orange and black.

2 Why does the writer include examples of Australian distances? Choose all that apply.
- **A** so the reader will know how long it takes the Monarch to fly those distances
- **B** to put migration distances in perspective
- **C** to use real-life places to illustrate a point
- **D** to make the text more relevant to an Australian audience

3 The purpose of the text is to
- **A** compare Australian and North American butterflies.
- **B** inform about a species of butterfly.
- **C** explain a butterfly's life cycle.
- **D** explain the relationship between milkweed and Monarch butterflies.

4 What is the main idea in the text?
- **A** Monarchs have a different life cycle.
- **B** Monarch numbers are declining.
- **C** Monarchs are different from other butterflies.
- **D** Monarchs gather in clusters.

5 What does *the insect is distasteful to predators* mean?
- **A** Milkweed is poisonous to adult Monarchs.
- **B** The Monarch only likes milkweed.
- **C** Insect predators enjoy the full taste of Monarchs.
- **D** Insect eaters do not like the taste of Monarchs.

6 What else might a reader want to know about these butterflies?

....

....

....

Answers and explanations on p. 118

Mixed questions

Use the **Step-by-step-guide** on page 4 to help you read the text and answer the questions below. Circle the correct answers or write your answers on the lines.

Film review: *The Lost Thing*

Students in Year 5 were placed in groups. Each group's task was to share opinions about a film by Shaun Tan and then present a group consensus about the film to the rest of the class.

Jonah: I thought the animation was clever.

Luca: I thought the character of the Thing was really good, considering it only communicated with body language and bells, and I liked the boy's narration.

Molly: Oh, I loved the Thing from the minute it started jiggling on the beach, excited to play with the ball, and then it jumped when the dog barked at it. So cute. I think it's the best film, just awesome and I think the themes are belonging and being different.

Jonah: Yeah I agree, and I think another theme is responsibility because the boy looks after the Thing until he finds a place where it belongs. I think the sound effects and music suited the film really well.

Stephanie: I think it's a good story—it has an orientation, a problem to be solved, a series of events, and a resolution then a coda.

Luca: Yes, it has a solid plot and characters. I liked the scene showing the place full of lost things—really colourful and happy.

Molly: Yes, me too—I loved when the Thing started to walk in with the other things, but then turned around to say goodbye with its bells. I felt really happy that it had a place to belong. I loved that scene. It was a great contrast to the scenes in the dark, scary office for odds and ends.

Stephanie: I didn't really like the bit at the end where the boy grows a few years older and gets too busy to notice lost things any more—seems a bit sad. I guess one of the themes of the story is growing up.

1 What is the purpose of the discussion?

- **A** to discuss a character in a film
- **B** to share opinions
- **C** to argue points of view
- **D** to summarise the plot of a film

2 Who liked the film the most?

- **A** Stephanie
- **B** Jonah
- **C** Molly
- **D** Luca

3 How does the Thing communicate?

- **A** It talks and rings its bells.
- **B** It jumps and jiggles to show excitement.
- **C** It makes cute noises and rings its bells.
- **D** It uses body language and bells.

4 According to the text, what themes does the film explore?

- **A** sadness, happiness, responsibility, growing up
- **B** orientation, complication, events, resolution, coda
- **C** belonging, being different, growing up, responsibility
- **D** a solid plot and characters

5 Write the group's consensus for presentation to the rest of the class.

....

....

....

....

....

....

....

6 Do you think children your age would enjoy this film? Justify your answer.

....

....

Answers and explanations on p. 119

Mixed questions

Use the **Step-by-step-guide** on page 4 to help you read the text and answer the questions below. Circle the correct answers or write your answer on the lines.

Geoffrey Gurrumul Yunupingu

Geoffrey Gurrumul Yunupingu (1971–2017) was an internationally respected First Nations Australian musician, born in 1970 on Elcho Island off the coast of Arnhem Land.

In his early career Gurrumul played in the rock band Yothu Yindi, the band established by Gurrumul's uncle Mandawuy Yunupingu, who was awarded Australian of the Year in 1992. (Mandawuy passed away in 2013.) Gurrumul played drums, guitar and keyboard for Yothu Yindi, all self-taught. After leaving Yothu Yindi, Gurrumul became a member of the Saltwater Band.

As a solo performer Gurrumul received numerous awards, including Best World Music Album at the 2011 ARIA Artisan Awards. (ARIA stands for Australian Recording Industry Association.) He performed for US President Barack Obama, Crown Prince Frederik and Princess Mary of Denmark and at the Queen's Diamond Jubilee Concert at Buckingham Palace in 2013.

Gurrumul sang in the First Nations languages Galpu, Gumatj or Djambarrpuyngu, with a few English words added to the mix. He also played the didgeridoo. His music is hauntingly beautiful and evocative. Audiences around the world were spellbound by his lyrical voice and musicianship. His music speaks of his heritage and his love of family and his culture. On his recordings he sings the music of his ancestry.

Gurrumul was born blind but didn't let that deter him in any way from becoming a musician. His family members and the people in his community say that nature compensated by giving him extraordinary musical abilities.

Gurrumul was an important role model for First Australian youth. He established the Gurrumul Yunupingu Foundation to help young First Nations people reach their personal potential.

1. Which of the following describes Gurrumul's music as a solo musician?
   - **A** powerfully important didgeridoo music
   - **B** soulful and lyrical
   - **C** powerful rock music with guitar and drums
   - **D** appeals to young people
2. The writer of the text
   - **A** respects Gurrumul's remarkable abilities.
   - **B** wishes more people could hear Gurrumul's music.
   - **C** hopes that people will buy Gurrumul's music.
   - **D** was also born on Elcho Island.
3. What evidence is there of Gurrumul's international fame? Choose all that apply.
   - **A** Audiences around the world were spellbound.
   - **B** His albums sell around the world.
   - **C** He sang for royalty and world leaders.
   - **D** He won ARIA awards.
4. How do you know that Gurrumul values his heritage? Choose all that apply.
   - **A** He sings in First Nations languages.
   - **B** His music is hauntingly beautiful.
   - **C** His music speaks of his heritage and his love of family and his culture.
   - **D** He sings the music of his ancestry.
5. Which of the following would Gurrumul have judged the most important?
   - **A** He was famous.
   - **B** His music speaks of his heritage and his love of family and his culture.
   - **C** His uncle Mandawuy Yunupingu was awarded Australian of the Year in 1992.
   - **D** He played for the Queen.
6. Which words from the text could be used to advertise Gurrumul's music and sell his albums?

   ....

   ....

   ....

Answers and explanations on pp. 119–120

Mixed questions

Use the **Step-by-step-guide** on page 4 to help you read the text and answer the questions below. Circle the correct answers and draw the storyboard in the boxes.

Pieces of Eight

All was dark within, so that I could distinguish nothing by the eye. As for sounds, there was the steady drone of the snorers and a small occasional noise, a flickering or pecking that I could in no way account for.

With my arms before me I walked steadily in. I should lie down in my own place (I thought with a silent chuckle) and enjoy their faces when they found me in the morning.

My foot struck something yielding—it was a sleeper's leg; and he turned and groaned, but without awaking.

And then, all of a sudden, a shrill voice broke forth out of the darkness:

"Pieces of eight! Pieces of eight! Pieces of eight! Pieces of eight! Pieces of eight!" and so forth, without pause or change, like the clacking of a tiny mill.

Silver's green parrot, Captain Flint! It was she whom I had heard pecking at a piece of bark; it was she, keeping better watch than any human being, who thus announced my arrival with her wearisome refrain.

I had no time left me to recover. At the sharp, clipping tone of the parrot, the sleepers awoke and sprang up; and with a mighty oath, the voice of Silver cried, "Who goes?"

I turned to run, struck violently against one person, recoiled, and ran full into the arms of a second, who for his part closed upon and held me tight.

"Bring a torch, Dick," said Silver when my capture was thus assured.

And one of the men left the log-house and presently returned with a lighted brand.

Extract from *Treasure Island* by Robert Louis Stevenson, 1883

1 What could the narrator see?

A men sleeping
B nothing
C bodies on the floor, snoring
D his arms before him

2 Who shouted *Pieces of eight!*?

A Silver **B** Dick
C Captain Flint **D** one of the men

3 What is a *wearisome refrain*?

A a loud announcement
B a shrill noise
C something that sounds like the clacking of a tiny mill
D something that is continually repeated without pause or change

4 Who was in charge?

A Silver **B** Dick
C Captain Flint **D** the narrator

5 What is another word in the text for *torch*?

A portable light **B** lighted brand
C flashlight **D** lantern

6 Draw a storyboard to depict events. Use extra paper if necessary.

Answers and explanations on p. 120

Mixed questions

Use the **Step-by-step-guide** on page 4 to help you read the text and answer the questions below. Circle the correct answers or write your answers on the lines.

Coral reefs

Coral reefs are complex ecosystems. They are built by tiny organisms called coral polyps. The calcium carbonate skeletons of coral-forming polyps are the structures left behind as polyps die.

Coral reefs around the world are under threat due to:

1 Ocean acidification

Oceans absorb carbon dioxide. This helps reduce the effects of carbon dioxide pollution in the air. However, too much carbon dioxide in the ocean dissolves coral skeletons making the reefs weaker and more easily damaged by storms and boats.

2 Rising ocean temperatures

Like all animals, coral polyps need oxygen to survive. This oxygen is produced by algae that live within the coral. The coral polyp and the algae have a symbiotic relationship. This means they are of mutual benefit to each other. The polyp produces carbon dioxide, which algae need for photosynthesis. Warmer water stresses coral polyps and they expel the algae. This is referred to as coral bleaching because the algae give coral its colour. The coral eventually dies without the algae's oxygen.

3 Pollution

Shipping, oil, gas, and pesticide and fertiliser contamination caused by agricultural run-off pollute the ocean. Garbage such as plastic bags and discarded fishing nets snag on reefs and physically damage coral.

4 Erosion

The roots of trees and plants hold soil in place. When areas of land are cleared for development as in construction and mining along coastlines, loose soil is washed into the ocean when it rains. This dirt and sediment makes the water cloudy and it eventually settles over coral, smothering reefs and blocking out the sunlight needed by algae for photosynthesis.

1. What is a symbiotic relationship?
   - **A** coral produces carbon dioxide for algae to use
   - **B** a relationship where different species are beneficial to each other
   - **C** a relationship where a species helps another species to survive
   - **D** one species kills another species

2. Coral is made of
   - **A** coral polyps.
   - **B** calcium carbonate.
   - **C** coral reefs
   - **D** a species of algae.

3. Coral bleaching occurs because
   - **A** the ocean absorbs too much carbon dioxide.
   - **B** the coral polyps eat all the algae.
   - **C** oceans become colder.
   - **D** oceans become warmer.

4. How does acidification harm coral?
   - **A** Oceans absorb carbon dioxide.
   - **B** Coral is damaged by storms and boats.
   - **C** Carbon dioxide in the ocean dissolves coral.
   - **D** Carbon dioxide pollutes the air.

5. How can a coastal building project damage a coral reef?

6. How can farming practices damage a coral reef?

Answers and explanations on p. 121

Mixed questions

Use the **Step-by-step-guide** on page 4 to help you read the text and answer the questions below. Circle the correct answers or write your answers on the lines.

Heroism

Heroes: A hero is a person who displays great courage in helping others, sometimes at their own risk. Heroes are evident in war and in peace, in the military as well as in public services—think of police, firefighters and other emergency-service workers. Heroes are evident in local communities in times of disaster or need—think of ordinary people who rush to help others. A hero is someone we can admire and respect. Heroes inspire our faith in humanity because they are the best that people can be.

My Heroes: My Nan and Pa are my heroes. Pa was only 18 when he joined the army during WWII. He was sent to Darwin and was stationed there during the bombing. After the war he worked at the Commonwealth Bank for thirty years until retirement. My Nan is my hero because she has always worked to help others. Pa says she's a brick. She used to be a teacher and has always cared for foster children, helping children who needed a temporary home if their mother or father were unable to care for them.

Maybe Hero: When I get old enough I would like to join the navy. I think I would enjoy working with others as a member of a team. I would like to be involved in peace-keeping missions and working in areas of disaster relief such as after typhoons, earthquakes or tsunamis. I hope I never have to fight in a war.

by Chloe, age 11

1 What does the writer mean by *ordinary people*?

A people who aren't soldiers
B people who could be your neighbours
C people who aren't trained to deal with emergencies
D all of the above

2 How would the writer define *hero*?

A a famous person you can admire
B someone brave in a war
C someone who helps others
D a soldier who fights for others

3 The writer wrote the text to

A persuade others that her opinions about heroism are correct.
B reflect on the topic.
C define the concept of a hero.
D present arguments on the importance of heroism.

4 What does Pa mean when he says Nan is a brick?

....

....

....

5 What does the text tell you about the writer?

....

....

....

....

6 Reflect in your own words about heroes.

A A hero

....

....

....

B My hero

....

....

....

C Maybe hero

....

....

....

Answers and explanations on pp. 121–122

Mixed questions

Use the **Step-by-step-guide** on page 4 to help you read the text and answer the questions below. Circle the correct answers or write your answer on the lines.

Text 1: The Terracotta Army

New | Reply | Delete | Archive | Junk | Sweep | Move to

Search email

Folders Inbox **1**

Archive Junk

Drafts

Sent

Deleted

Greetings from Beijing

Christo and Nina Alonzo

To: Joshua Alonzo

Hi Josh

We are now in Beijing. It's amazing. Saw the Terracotta Army at Xian. It's a replica of the army of an emperor from over two thousand years ago. You'd love it. There are 8000 life-sized sculptures of soldiers. Can you believe it? 8000 soldiers and some horses and chariots all buried under a farm. It was so impressive and reminded us of when we went to Egypt and saw the pyramids because the warriors were buried with the dead emperor and meant to protect him in the afterlife, like pharaohs in Egypt were buried with servants and riches.

We're excited about our Yangtze River cruise in a few days. We can't wait. We're having fun travelling with lots of other grandparents.

Love you. Miss you. Nonna and Nonno XXX

Text 2: Exploripedia: The free encyclopedia: The Terracotta Army

The Terracotta Army is a collection of more than 8000 life-sized clay sculptures of soldiers as well as 150 cavalry horses and 130 chariots pulled by 520 horses, discovered in 1974 under farmland in Xian in China. The army was buried in 7 m deep pits around 210 BC. The sculptures are examples of funerary art, art made to commemorate the dead.

The warriors were buried with the first Emperor of China, Qin Shi Huang to protect him in the afterlife. As well as soldiers the pits included sculptures of entertainers such as acrobats and musicians. The sculptures were originally brightly painted but the paints have faded or flaked off.

1 What is the purpose and audience of Text 1?

- **A** to persuade a family member to visit Beijing
- **B** to inform the general public about Beijing
- **C** to inform a family member about a holiday
- **D** to tell people about a great holiday

2 What is the purpose and audience of Text 2?

- **A** to persuade people to visit the Terracotta Army
- **B** to provide information for scientists
- **C** to persuade people to travel to China
- **D** to provide general information

3 What sort of people are Nonna and Nonno?

- **A** knowledgeable but judgemental
- **B** grandparents who get lonely
- **C** adventurous and fun-loving
- **D** elderly and cautious travellers

4 What is the tone of the email (Text 1)?

- **A** solemn
- **B** serious
- **C** formal and technical
- **D** informal and playful

5 Which of these is not an example of funerary art?

- **A** tombstone
- **B** coffin
- **C** ice sculpture
- **D** war memorial

6 How might Josh feel as he reads Text 1?

....

....

....

Answers and explanations on p. 122

Mixed questions

Use the **Step-by-step-guide** on page 4 to help you read the text and answer the questions below. Circle the correct answers or write your answers on the lines.

THE DAILY CHRONICLE

LONDON, 31ST JULY

Royal kidnapping thwarted

Palace security is on high alert after a mysterious woman who attended the Royal Gala Ball on Saturday night has now vanished. A number of witnesses report that the unidentified woman, who introduced herself only as Cindy Ella, danced all night with Prince Harry and then vanished into St James Park and has not been seen since midnight.

Palace Security Chief Poly Minions believes the woman may be associated with an international kidnapping gang known as 'The Step-sisters'. Ms Minions said, 'The woman attempted to lure the Prince into the park. We believe he was in grave danger. My people saved the Prince from the kidnappers.' Ms Minions denied accusations of any fault with her security team. 'My staff responded quickly and followed all protocols appropriately. We saved the Prince's life. The fault lies with the invitation process.'

Official spokesperson for Palace Events and Event Organiser Eva Rafter believes the woman gained access to the Ball using a forged invitation. A horrified Ms Rafter claimed, 'Invitations were only sent to the best and richest families. That woman clearly didn't belong here. Heads will roll over this breach of security.'

Lady Camellia attended the ball and commented, 'She seemed like a lovely girl. I can't believe she is a kidnapper. She had a lovely smile. The Prince seemed quite smitten by her. I saw them dancing all night and he couldn't stop smiling.'

Lord Montybaton said, 'I thought she looked shifty. I'm not surprised she is a kidnapper.'

The Queen has offered a reward of £5000 to any person who assists the police in apprehending the evil woman.

Detectives at Scotland Yard have not confirmed allegations of any attempted kidnapping or the existence of a Step-sisters gang.

1 'Cindy Ella was very engaging and fun.'

Judge which character would agree with this statement.

A The Prince **B** Lord Montybaton
C Poly Minions **D** The Queen

2 What does the author want you to think about a character with the name Poly Minions?

A She is head of a hugely important security department.
B She is ambitious and loves to work.
C She likes to be the boss of many devoted underlings.
D She talks like a parrot to all the people who work for her.

3 What kind of person is Lord Montybaton?

A He is a suspicious man.
B He is a kindly man.
C He worries about others.
D He doesn't like to attend balls.

4 Which witness is the most credible?

A Poly Minions **B** Lord Montybaton
C Lady Camellia **D** Eva Rafter

Why? ....

....

5 What does the statement *have not confirmed allegations* imply?

A Detectives will confirm allegations shortly to the press.
B Detectives are worried and concerned about bad publicity.
C Detectives want to keep secrets.
D There might not be a Step-sisters gang or an attempted kidnapping.

6 What references can you find that link this text to other texts you are familiar with?

....

....

....

Answers and explanations on pp. 122–123

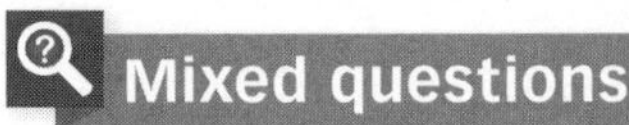

Mixed questions

Use the **Step-by-step-guide** on page 4 to help you read the text and answer the questions below. Circle the correct answers or write your answer on the lines.

Y-o-u-u Tom

"TOM!"

No answer.

"TOM!"

No answer.

"You TOM!"

No answer.

The old lady pulled her spectacles down and looked over them about the room; then she put them up and looked out under them. She seldom or never looked *through* them for so small a thing as a boy; they were her state pair, the pride of her heart, and were built for "style," not service—she could have seen through a pair of stove-lids just as well. She looked perplexed for a moment, and then said, not fiercely, but still loud enough for the furniture to hear:

"Well, I lay if I get hold of you I'll—"

She did not finish, for by this time she was bending down and punching under the bed with the broom, and so she needed breath to punctuate the punches with. She resurrected nothing but the cat.

She went to the open door and stood in it and looked out ... No Tom. So she lifted up her voice at an angle calculated for distance and shouted:

"Y-o-u-u TOM!"

There was a slight noise behind her and she turned just in time to seize a small boy by the slack of his roundabout and arrest his flight.

"There! I might 'a' thought of that closet. What you been doing in there?"

"Nothing."

"Nothing! Look at your hands. And look at your mouth. What *is* that?"

"I don't know, Aunt."

"Well, I know. It's jam—that's what it is. Forty times I've said if you didn't let that jam alone I'd skin you. Hand me that switch."

The switch hovered in the air—the peril was desperate—

"My! Look behind you, Aunt!"

The old lady whirled round, and snatched her skirts out of danger. The lad fled on the instant, scrambled up the high board-fence, and disappeared over it.

Extract from *The Adventures of Tom Sawyer* by Mark Twain, 1876

1 What was under the bed?

A a broom **B** a cat

C Tom **D** nothing

2 Choose all that apply. Aunt's spectacles were

A useless to see with but she loved the look of them.

B useless for anything but looking good.

C useful for searching for Tom.

D good for peering over and under but not through.

3 What does *she turned just in time to seize a small boy by the slack of his roundabout and arrest his flight* mean?

A Aunt seized hold of a boy who'd been about to fly away.

B Aunt grabbed Tom by his clothing and stopped his escape.

C Aunt caught Tom around his waist.

D Aunt held a strange boy by his shirt.

4 What does *the peril was desperate* mean?

A Aunt's skirts almost caught on fire.

B A lad was about to grab Aunt's skirts.

C Tom was about to be hit with the switch.

D Something dangerous lurked behind Aunt.

5 What had Tom been doing in the closet?

A playing **B** looking for the cat

C nothing **D** eating jam

6 Use your own words to explain what happens in the last two paragraphs.

....

....

....

....

Answers and explanations on p. 123

Mixed questions

Use the **Step-by-step-guide** on page 4 to help you read the text and answer the questions below. Circle the correct answers or write your answer on the lines.

News of Ned Kelly

Extract from a letter written by Donald G Sutherland to his parents in Scotland.

Acknowledgement: Donald G Sutherland, author. Source: State Library of Victoria. Biographical/historical note: Donald Sutherland was an employee of the Bank of Victoria at Oxley, near Glenrowan.

8th July 1880

My Dear Parents

... Well since I last wrote you we have had great doings here. The Kellys are annihilated. The gang is completely destroyed. You can read a full and correct account from The Australasian which I send to you along with this letter. They had a long run but were captured at last ... Ned, the leader of the gang being the only one taken alive. He was lying on a stretcher quite calm and collected notwithstanding the great pain he must have been suffering from his wounds. He was wounded in 5 or 6 places. Only on the arms and legs. His body and head being encased in armour. The police thought he was a fiend seeing their rifle bullets sliding off him like hail. The force of the rifle bullets made him stagger when hit but it was only when they got him on the legs and arms that he reluctantly fell exclaiming as he did so "I am done".

Ned does not at all look like a murderer and Bushranger. He is a very powerful man aged about 27 black hair and beard with a soft mild looking face and eyes. After his capture he became very tame and conversed freely with those who knew him.

Ned is now in the Hospital of the Melbourne Gaol treated with every care until he is strong and well enough to be hanged. Such then is Bushranging in Victoria so far.

PS. The hair enclosed is from the Tail of Ned Kelly the famous murderer & Bushranger's mare. His favorite mare who followed him all round the trees during the firing. He said he wouldn't care for himself if he thought his mare was safe.

1 What are *great doings* in the text?

- **A** the writer's excitement at seeing Ned Kelly in person
- **B** the report published in *The Australasian*
- **C** bank robberies and law-breaking
- **D** the end of the Kelly Gang

2 Why did the bullets not kill Ned Kelly?

- **A** He wore armour.
- **B** He was a fiend.
- **C** He was taken alive.
- **D** The force of the rifle bullets made him stagger.

3 What did Ned Kelly mean by "*I am done*"?

- **A** He was worried.
- **B** He was dead.
- **C** He couldn't fight any more.
- **D** He was in extreme pain.

4 Why do you think the writer enclosed hair from the horse's tail in his letter?

- **A** to prove he had been at the scene
- **B** to show off that he had some of a famous horse's tail
- **C** to show how much Ned Kelly valued his horse
- **D** to show the colour of Ned Kelly's mare

5 Which best sums up the writer's opinion of Ned Kelly's character?

- **A** a fiend with black hair and beard
- **B** a murderer and bushranger who became tame when captured
- **C** about 27, powerful and handsome
- **D** fiendish with a soft face and eyes

6 What does the writer mean by *Such then is Bushranging in Victoria so far*?

....

....

....

....

....

Answers and explanations on pp. 123–124

Mixed questions

Use the **Step-by-step-guide** on page 4 to help you read the text and answer the questions below. Circle the correct answers or write your answer on the lines.

TV program: *Live at 10 am*

Compere: Good morning viewers. Welcome to the program. Here with us today are Accredited Nutritionist, Thomas Walters and Certified Personal Trainer, Michelle Bright. Welcome.

Thomas and Michelle: Thanks for having us here.

Compere: Now, you're both here today to promote diabetes awareness because you have concerns about the increase in diabetes in Australia.

Michelle: Yes. Absolutely. We are concerned about the increase in Type 2 Diabetes, a largely preventable condition. And not just in Australia, but globally. Globally, there are more than 10 million new cases of diabetes diagnosed every year.

Compere: Please explain to viewers the problems associated with diabetes.

Thomas: If you have diabetes it means that your body cannot convert the glucose in the foods you eat into energy. Glucose is just another name for sugar and it can be found in processed foods like biscuits and cakes. The glucose stays in your blood causing damage.

Michelle: Having diabetes means you are at increased risk of heart disease, kidney damage, nerve damage, blindness, amputations … It's that serious.

Thomas: Yes and mostly Type 2 Diabetes is preventable through a healthy lifestyle. That's a healthy diet, a healthy weight and regular exercise. And don't smoke, of course.

Compere: What sort of diet would you recommend to our viewers, Thomas?

Thomas: Colourful fruits and vegetables every day. The 2 + 5 rule is a good one to keep in mind. 2 fruits and 5 vegies a day. And French fries are not classified as a healthy vegie! Lean protein such as grilled chicken or fish. Nuts and seeds. Wholegrain breads and rice.

Compere: And exercise, Michelle? What do viewers need to know?

Michelle: People need to be active and not couch potatoes: playing sport, walking, riding a push bike.

Compere: Thank you for your helpful advice.

1 Michelle is most concerned about

- **A** people not eating the correct foods.
- **B** people in Australia who have diabetes.
- **C** people turning into couch potatoes.
- **D** the increasing numbers of people getting diabetes.

2 The compere of the show is most interested in

- **A** how to stay healthy.
- **B** keeping viewers interested.
- **C** preventing diabetes.
- **D** what foods to eat.

3 What is the job of a nutritionist?

- **A** tells people the nutritional value of foods
- **B** tells people what to eat
- **C** advises people about fruit and vegetables
- **D** advises people about diet for health and illness prevention

4 Make a judgement about the trustworthiness of the information in the program.

- **A** It's informative and seems even-handed.
- **B** It's biased about the prevalence of diabetes.
- **C** The experts don't have relevant credentials.
- **D** It lacks factual content.

5 How is diabetes prevented?

- **A** eating healthy foods and exercising
- **B** eating 2 + 5 fruit and veg
- **C** having a healthy lifestyle and not smoking
- **D** having a healthy diet, a healthy weight and getting regular exercise

6 Would this interview influence your behaviour in any way? Explain using evidence from the text.

....

....

....

Answers and explanations on pp. 124–125

Mixed questions

Use the **Step-by-step-guide** on page 4 to help you read the text and answer the questions below. Circle the correct answers or write your answers on the lines.

The rules of this ride

- Persons under 150 cm not allowed on roller-coaster.
- Persons over 151 cm not allowed on roller-coaster.
- *Gameworld* reserves the right to deny entry to any persons deemed unsuitable for ride.
- Wait for the attendant before getting on the ride.
- No hats or shoes allowed on ride.
- No sunglasses, eyeglasses, contact lenses, guide dogs, walking sticks, hearing aids, prosthetic limbs allowed.
- No cameras, binoculars, telescopes, periscopes, stethoscopes allowed.
- Leave all possessions, including wallets, purses, jewellery, limbs and other valuables on the platform.
- No pets allowed on roller-coaster, especially cats.
- Don't stand up while roller-coaster is in motion.
- Keep arms and legs inside carriage.
- Keep head inside carriage.
- Do not dangle any body parts from carriage.
- Do not spit from carriage.
- Do not throw food or money out of roller-coaster.
- Don't vomit while ride is in motion.
- Don't try to get out until ride has fully stopped.

Thank you

Enjoy your ride

Gameworld accepts no responsibility for illness, accidents, injury, death, lost or stolen items or dissatisfaction with ride.

NO REFUNDS under any circumstances.

1 What is the purpose of the text?

A to instruct people what to do

B to keep people safe on a ride at *Gameworld*

C to provide a list of rules for a ride

D to make fun of rules for a ride

2 *Leave all possessions, including wallets, purses, jewellery and other valuables on the platform.* What is your judgement of this rule?

A sensible because these things fall out of rides

B not sensible as things could get stolen

C useful advice before getting on a roller-coaster

D should be obeyed, as it is a rule

3 Choose a word from the text to add to the lexical chain *sunglasses, eyeglasses.*

A guide dogs **B** hearing aids

C prosthetic limbs **D** contact lenses

4 Who would be *deemed unsuitable* for the ride? Choose all that apply.

A a person of 150 cm

B a person eating a sandwich

C a person of 152 cm

D a person with a prosthetic limb

5 Why might the rules say *especially cats*?

....

....

6 Which is the odd one out in this list and why? *cameras, binoculars, telescopes, periscopes, stethoscopes*

....

....

....

....

Answers and explanations on p. 125

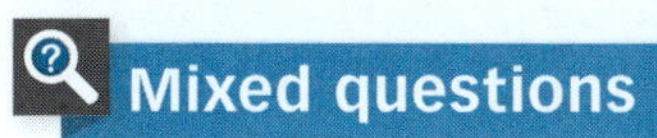

Mixed questions

Use the **Step-by-step-guide** on page 4 to help you read the text and answer the questions below. Circle the correct answers or write your answers on the lines.

Resistance

After the arrival of the First Fleet, European settlers spread throughout the continent of Australia. They invaded the traditional lands of the original inhabitants without asking for permission to use their land, or establishing treaties or making payment of any kind. Settlers took control of land that the First Nations people had lived on for more than 40 000 years, declaring Australia terra nullius, meaning that the land belonged to no-one. They believed that terra nullius gave them the right to take the land.

The invaders cleared land for cities, townships and farming, depriving the Indigenous inhabitants of access to their traditional hunting and gathering lands and water holes, as well as their sacred sites. The British government of the time had no understanding of the complexity of First Nations society or heritage or the relationship of First Nations people to 'country'. In most cases the traditional owners were driven off their lands and only allowed to remain if they became employees of the settlers.

First Nations warriors used guerrilla tactics to resist the invasion. Small bands of warriors used mobility, stealth and surprise to attack larger, stronger forces that had superior weaponry. However, whenever Europeans were killed, the settlers were quick to instigate reprisals. The Myall Creek massacre is one such tragedy. Two European settlers were killed by First Nations warriors so a group of stockmen rounded up 28 men, women and children from a nearby First Nations camp at Myall Creek, tied them together, beat them to death and then burned their bodies. Seven of the stockmen were eventually convicted of murder and hanged. This was the first time that settlers were successfully prosecuted for First Nations deaths. In prior cases the Europeans were not found guilty in spite of evidence to the contrary.

The First Nations history of Australia includes accounts of many tragedies but also stories of the amazing resilience of Aboriginal and Torres Strait Islander peoples.

1 Why did First Nations warriors use guerrilla warfare?

- **A** because guerrillas are strong
- **B** because guerrilla units are small, mobile and surprise the enemy
- **C** to outnumber and overpower the enemy
- **D** to instigate retaliation

2 We recognise now that First Nations warriors were resistance fighters. What would the majority of colonists have called them in 1802?

- **A** a noble and proud race
- **B** clever warriors
- **C** murderous savages
- **D** well-organised soldiers

3 Write a sentence that sums up the point of view of the early settlers.

4 Write a sentence that sums up the point of view of First Nations Australians towards European settlers at that time.

5 Why was the Myall Creek massacre an important event in terms of the law?

6 What is the point of view of the text's writer and how do you know?

Answers and explanations on pp. 125–126

Mixed questions

Use the **Step-by-step-guide** on page 4 to help you read the text and answer the questions below. Circle the correct answers or write your answer on the lines.

Why sea levels are rising

Climate change is causing sea levels to rise at a faster rate than previously predicted by scientists.

Sea levels rise in two ways

1 Land-based ice melts into the sea.

a In Greenland warmer weather is causing the ice sheet to melt at the surface and the melted water is running off the top of the ice sheet and into the sea.

b In Antarctica warmer seas are undermining the ice shelf from below, causing large masses of ice to break off. As soon as these chunks of ice hit the sea they cause the sea level to rise in the same way that a chunk of ice added to a glass of water will make the water level in the glass rise. These icebergs float in the sea until they melt. If the West Antarctic ice sheet fully breaks up, the sea is predicted to rise by 6 m.

c The world's glaciers are melting and contributing to sea-level rise. Diminishing glaciers will also result in water shortages for millions of people because glaciers are fresh water storehouses.

2 Warm water expands.

Water expands as it heats so sea levels are rising because oceans are taking up more space.

Major consequences

A rise in sea levels has two major consequences.

Inundation of low-lying coastal areas. Seawater floods agricultural land contaminating it with salt. It is estimated that for every 2.5 cm of sea-level rise there is a corresponding 2.4 m horizontal shoreline loss due to erosion.

Some Pacific Islands will be completely submerged during this century.

1 Why is the Antarctic ice shelf melting?
- **A** The sunshine is melting surface ice.
- **B** Chucks of ice are falling into the warm sea and melting.
- **C** Warmer water below causes ice to break off into the sea.
- **D** The ice is melting into the sea.

2 Why is the Greenland ice sheet melting?
- **A** The ice is melting into the sea.
- **B** People are using too much water.
- **C** Warmer weather is melting surface ice.
- **D** The sunshine heats the ocean.

3 Give one reason why sea levels are rising.
- **A** Icebergs are melting.
- **B** Warm water expands.
- **C** Sea levels rise in two ways.
- **D** Melting glaciers are causing water shortages.

4 How does a rising sea level impact on food production?
- **A** More fish are carried inland.
- **B** Salt water ruins soil.
- **C** Animals drown.
- **D** Low-lying coastal areas are inundated.

5 What is the purpose of the text?
- **A** to provide information about glaciers
- **B** to give information about Antarctica
- **C** to explain some causes of climate change
- **D** to convince people that climate change is a problem

6 What conclusions can you draw about the impact of climate change from the text?

....

....

....

Answers and explanations on p. 126

Mixed questions

Use the **Step-by-step-guide** on page 4 to help you read the text and answer the questions below. Circle the correct answers or write your answer on the lines.

The Day of Scrapes

Mrs. Knight's school was a low, one-storey building and had a yard behind it, in which the girls played at recess. Unfortunately, next door to it was Miss Miller's school, equally large and popular, and with a yard behind it also. Only a high board fence separated the two playgrounds. Mrs. Knight was a stout, gentle woman, who moved slowly, and had a face which made you think of an amiable and well-disposed cow. Miss Miller, on the contrary, had black eyes, with black corkscrew curls waving about them, and was generally brisk and snappy. A constant feud raged between the two schools as to the respective merits of the teachers and the instruction. The Knight girls for some unknown reason, considered themselves genteel and the Miller girls vulgar, and took no pains to conceal this opinion; while the Miller girls, on the other hand, retaliated by being as aggravating as they knew how. They spent their recesses and intermissions mostly in making faces through the knot-holes in the fence, and over the top of it when they could get there, which wasn't an easy thing to do, as the fence was pretty high. The Knight girls could make faces too, for all their gentility. Their yard had one great advantage over the other: it possessed a wood-shed, with a climbable roof, which commanded Miss Miller's premises, and upon this the girls used to sit in rows, turning up their noses at the next yard, and irritating the foe by jeering remarks. "Knights" and "Millerites," the two schools called each other; and the feud raged so high, that sometimes it was hardly safe for a Knight to meet a Millerite in the street.

Extract from *What Katy Did* by Susan Coolidge*, 1872, Chapter III

*Sarah Chauncey Woolsey (1835–1905) wrote under the pen name Susan Coolidge.

1 In the text *feud* means

- **A** a comparison.
- **B** a fight.
- **C** a competition.
- **D** a discussion.

2 In the text *genteel* means

- **A** pretty.
- **B** naughty.
- **C** well-mannered.
- **D** gentle.

3 What does *turning up their noses* mean in the text?

- **A** acting like they were better
- **B** feeling inferior
- **C** making annoying faces
- **D** being mean

4 In the text *aggravating* means

- **A** passive.
- **B** unassuming.
- **C** adorable.
- **D** annoying.

5 How did the girls use the wood-shed?

- **A** All the girls jumped on it.
- **B** The Millerites sat on it to look down upon the Knights.
- **C** The Knights sat on it to look down upon the Millerites.
- **D** They stored firewood in it.

6 What did the Knight and Miller girls think of their own schools?

....

....

....

....

....

....

....

Answers and explanations on pp. 126–127

ANSWERS

Fact-finding questions

The Eureka Stockade (page 30)

1 B **2** B **3** A **4** B **5** A and D
6 See below

Explanations

1 This is a **fact-finding** question. **B** is correct. You read *on the Victorian goldfields during the 1850s … The name given to a miner was 'digger'* (see lines 2–3). The answer is stated directly in the text. The other answers do not relate to information in the text, which is about the Victorian goldfields.

2 This is a **fact-finding** question. **B** is correct. You read *The worst thing about being a digger was the requirement to pay for a mining licence* (see line 6). (This is what led to the rebellion of the Eureka Stockade.) The answer is stated directly in the text. **A** and **C** are incorrect. The weather and living conditions were often harsh but these were not the biggest problems for miners. **D** is incorrect because the mining tax replaced, and was an improvement on, the mining licence fee.

3 This is a **fact-finding** question. **A** is correct. You read *Without a licence a digger could be fined and arrested* (see line 7). **B**, **C** and **D** are not what happened when a digger was caught without a licence.

4 This is a **fact-finding** question. **B** is correct. You read *In 1855, the Victorian Government implemented a mining tax, as a tax on gold found, to replace the unfair miner's licence which had to be paid regardless of whether the miner found any gold* (see lines 18–19). **A** is a fact in the text but does not answer the question. **C** is not correct, because even though miners thought the tax was fairer than the licence, there is nothing in the text to tell readers it was popular. **D** does not answer the question and doesn't make sense in the text.

5 This is a **fact-finding** question. **A** and **D** are correct. You read *the diggers … burned their unfair licences* (**D**) *as a form of protest* (see line 13) (**A**). **B** is not why they burned their licences. **C** is incorrect and not a fact in the text.

6 This is a **fact-finding** question. You read *In Australia's history, the Eureka Rebellion is the only time armed rebellion has been used to change unfair laws. The Eureka Stockade Rebellion is considered the birthplace of Australian democracy* (see lines 20–21). Your answer needs to paraphrase, or be a copy of, these facts from the text.

Huntsman spiders (page 31)

1 B **2** A **3** A **4** D **5** D **6** See below

Explanations

1 This is a **fact-finding** question. **B** is correct. You read *A huntsman spider's legs are jointed so that their legs twist forwards and sideways* (see lines 10–11). **A**, that the spider can run backwards, is not a fact in the text. **C** is about a crab and not a spider. **D** is a fact in the text but is not the answer to the question.

2 This is a **fact-finding** question. **A** is correct. You read *Huntsman spiders … hide … under rocks or under loose tree bark* (see lines 13–14). **B** and **D** do not make sense. Notice the preposition *on* in **C**, on tree bark. **C** is incorrect because the spider does not hide on tree bark but under it.

3 This is a **fact-finding** question. **A** is correct. You read *A spider sucks its liquid meal up through a tube-like mouth* (see lines 17–18). **B** and **C** are not facts in the text and are inaccurate because the spider sucks and does not chew or swallow food whole. **D** is not an answer to the question, which asks how. **D** tells what the spider eats.

4 This is a **fact-finding** question. **D** is correct. You read *Birds, geckoes and wasps eat huntsman spiders* (see line 24). **A**, **B** and **C** are not facts in the text.

5 This is a **fact-finding** question. **D** is correct. You read *The venom paralyses the prey and begins the chemical breakdown of the prey's tissues* (see lines 16–17). The term *chemical breakdown* means that the prey starts to dissolve. **A** is a fact in the text but not the answer to the question. **B** is not a fact in the text as the venom paralyses rather than kills prey. **C** is only partially correct, as it does not include the fact that the venom firstly *paralyses the prey* (see line 16).

6 This is a **fact-finding** question. You read *the huntsman prefers to run away from humans rather than chase or attack them* (see line 22). Your answer needs to state or paraphrase this fact from the text.

Australian bush tucker (page 32)

1 B **2** D **3** C **4** B **5** C **6** See below

Explanations

1 This is a **fact-finding** question. **B** is correct. You read *Bush tucker is food that is native to Australia* (see line 2). **A** is incorrect because it only lists plants and does not include animals, or specify that the food is native to Australia. **C** and **D** are incorrect because they do not specify food that is native to Australia.

2 This is a **fact-finding** question. **D** is correct. You read that the fruit *can be eaten raw or dried while quandong leaves can be made into a medicinal ointment* (see lines 8–10). **A**, **B** and **C** are incorrect as the text states that the fruit is eaten.

3 This is a **fact-finding** question. **C** is correct. You read *The nuts are actually toxic to dogs* (see line 15). *Toxic* means harmful or poisonous. **A** and **B** are incorrect because you read the fact in the text: *The delicious and healthy macadamia nut* (see line 13). **D** is incorrect because you read the fact in the text: *The macadamia tree is indigenous to Australia but is now grown commercially in other parts of the world* (see lines 14–15).

4 This is a **fact-finding** question. **B** is correct. You read *Witchetty grubs are the larvae stage of a few kinds of moth* (see lines 17–18). This means that witchetty grubs turn into moths. **A** and **D** are incorrect because you read *The grubs can be eaten raw or cooked* (see line 18). **C** is incorrect. You read *Some people say the raw grubs taste like almonds* (see line 18).

5 This is a **fact-finding** question. **C** is correct. You read *A honey ant's abdomen is used to store food for the ant colony. The food is in the form of a sweet liquid* (see lines 20–21). **A**, **B** and **D** are facts in the text but not the answers to the question which asks why.

6 This is a **fact-finding** question. You read *The highly nutritious fruit is bright red and can be eaten raw or dried while quandong leaves can be made into a medicinal ointment to treat skin sores* (see lines 8–10). Your answer needs to state that quondong fruit can be eaten and the leaves made into a medicine to treat skin sores.

Day for Children (page 33)

1 B **2** C **3** C **4** B **5** A and B
6 See below

Explanations

1 This is a **fact-finding** question. **B** is correct. You read *The school has recently participated in UNICEF Australia's Day for Children, announcing at a school assembly that $1680 has been raised as a donation towards the education of children in Timor-Leste* (see lines 4–8). ... *Every year Bridport school has a fund raising activity to help educate children in other countries* (see lines 25–26). **A** is incorrect. Raising awareness of the work of UNICEF is an outcome of the Day for Children but not the reason the school participated. **C** is incorrect because it was not given as a reason why the school became involved in the Day for Children. **D** is incorrect because it does not answer the question.

2 This is a **fact-finding** question. **C** is correct. You read in paragraph 3 that *Year 6 recited poems* (see line 20). Check to confirm that the other options are incorrect. There is no information in the text about singing (**A**), a dramatic performance (**B**) or a debate (**D**).

3 This is a **fact-finding** question. **C** is correct. You read *Principal Ms Julia Wong explained the Day for Children using a PowerPoint presentation of materials provided by UNICEF* (see lines 19–20). Check to confirm that the other options are not facts in the text.

4 This is a **fact-finding** question. **B** is correct. You read *AusAID funding helps children attend school and stay at school for longer so that they have a better education and improved prospects for their future* (see lines 24–25). Check to confirm that the other options are not facts in the text.

5 This is a **fact-finding** question. **A** and **B** are correct. You read *Timor-Leste is only 450 km from Australia, off the coast of Western Australia and the Northern Territory. Australian Aid (AusAID) is given to Timor-Leste to improve educational outcomes for children* (see lines 21–23). **C** and **D** are inaccurate and contradict facts in the text.

6 This is a **fact-finding** question. The answer is stated directly in the text. People who attended the launch are included in paragraph 3. You read

that there was *an assembly of the whole school, parents and other community members* (see line 18). You might list the Principal, teachers and students separately but they can be summarised as *the whole school* along with parents and other community members.

Synthesis questions

Book Review: *Home and Away* (page 38)

1 D **2** C **3** A **4** See below **5** See below **6** See below

Explanations

1 This is a **synthesis** question. **D** is correct. To work out the function of paragraph 2 you need to re-read the paragraph, synthesise the information it contains and think about why this is included in the text. Paragraph 2 introduces readers to the characters in the picture book. **A**, **B** and **C** are incorrect. The paragraph does not summarise the plot, tell readers about journal writing or summarise the main events in the story.

2 This is a **synthesis** question. **C** is correct. To work out the function of paragraph 4 you need to think about the whole paragraph and the information it contains. Paragraph 4 makes a recommendation to readers. It sums up the writer's point of view or judgement about the book. **A**, **B** and **D** are incorrect. The paragraph does not function to tell about the Award, give Marsden's point of view or summarise the story's conclusion.

3 This is a **synthesis** question. **A** is correct. To work out the purpose of the text you need to think about the whole text and what it tells you. You read the opening sentence *Home and Away is a picture book for mature readers* (see line 2). You can connect information from across the text to work out that the text tells you about a picture book and makes a recommendation that *it should be read and discussed in upper primary and secondary classrooms* (see lines 23–24). **B**, **C** and **D** are incorrect because the text reviews a book about asylum seekers but is not itself about asylum seekers.

4 This is a **synthesis** question. To work out the answer you need to think about the ideas expressed by the reviewer across the whole text. You can tell that the reviewer is sympathetic to the plight of refugees because of the use of emotive language such as *desperate struggle for survival* (see lines 3–4); *they hope to find sanctuary and begin new lives* (see line 19); *weeks at sea on a small, leaky, ill-equipped boat* (see lines 19–20); *a detention centre behind razor wire fences, labelled illegal immigrants by a country that does not want them* (see lines 20–21). The reviewer suggests that readers *put themselves in the shoes of people who become asylum seekers* (see lines 6–7). Your answer should state that the reviewer cares about refugees and hopes that the book will help readers understand the difficulties faced by people who become refugees.

5 This is a **synthesis** question. To make a decision whether you'd like to read the book you need to synthesise all the information given in the review. You might decide that the book is too *confronting and sad* (see line 5) and choose not to read it. Or you might decide that you should read it because the reviewer recommended it as a *thought-provoking picture book* and because it *was a Children's Book Council of Australia Honour Book in 2009* (see line 22).

6 This is a **synthesis** question. A sequel is a story that continues after a previous story ends. In order to suggest ideas for a sequel you need to have read and understood what the text tells you about the original story *Home and Away*. You read that at the conclusion of the story *when the children finally reach Hollania they are placed in a detention centre* (see line 20). In your answer, you could suggest a sequel where Hollania changes its rules about asylum seekers; the children are released from the detention centre to be fostered by a family; that they attend school in their new country; that they face language difficulties and cultural differences but eventually settle into their new home with hope for their future. This storyline would provide a resolution for the children's problems.

The woylie (page 39)

1 D **2** C **3** A and C **4** C **5** See below

Explanations

1 This is a **synthesis** question. **D** is correct. To work out the purpose of the text you need to read and understand the whole text. The text is a radio interview that informs people about woylies. **A** and **B** might occur as a result of the radio interview but are not its purpose. **C** is incorrect. There is no point of view presented about endangered animals.

2 This is a **synthesis** question. **C** is correct. To work out the answer you need to think about the information across the whole text. Look at the pattern of questions asked by the interviewer/radio host. Nerida is asked what a woylie is, what the woylie looks like, why it is endangered, and how it is being helped. **A**, **B** and **D** are each only partly correct.

3 This is a **synthesis** question. **A** and **C** are correct. To work out the answer you need to think about the information provided in the text and then draw conclusions about information that has not been given but that might be relevant to radio listeners. You would expect listeners to want to know about the captive breeding program and ways to donate to help woylies. These topics expand on information already provided. **B** has already been covered in the text. **D** is irrelevant because the text says that foxes are predators of the woylie and you would understand they kill woylies for food.

4 This is a **synthesis** question. **C** is correct. To draw a conclusion about the future of woylies you need to understand the information in the text. You read *Radio host: Are you confident the woylies will breed in captivity? Nerida: Yes, we currently have three females with joeys in their pouches* (see lines 38–41). You also read (Nerida) *We've instigated a captive breeding program to ensure their survival* (see line 35–37). Nerida is optimistic and confident that the captive breeding program will be a success. There is no evidence to support **A**. **B** and **D** are facts in the text but do not answer the question.

5 This is a **synthesis** question. To be able to draw an impression of a woylie you need to think about the information in the text and visualise a woylie. You read *Nerida: It looks a bit like a miniature kangaroo but with a pointier nose and smaller ears. It's cute, furry, nocturnal, about 30 cm tall and has a long tail. It uses its tail to carry nesting materials* (see lines 17–21). To draw it to scale you need to include an item 30 cm in length. The best item would be a 30 cm ruler.

John Macarthur (page 40)

1 C **2** D **3** A **4** D **5** B **6** See below

Explanations

1 This is a **synthesis** question. **C** is correct. To work out the answer you need to read and understand the text as a whole and connect ideas from across the text. The text presents a point of view about John Macarthur and each paragraph supports the point of view. **A** is incorrect. An autobiography provides detailed information about events in a person's life written by the person. **B** is incorrect. The text does not provide a factual report of the events. It gives a biased account of events. **D** is incorrect. The text does not describe the history of the wool industry.

2 This is a **synthesis** question. **D** is correct. To work out the answer you need to think about the ideas in paragraph 1 in relation to the rest of the text. Paragraph 1 is the thesis statement. It presents the writer's point of view, which is expanded upon in subsequent paragraphs, then restated in the concluding paragraph. **A** is incorrect because the text is not about the wool industry. **B** is incorrect because the function of the text is not to describe Macarthur but to state a point of view about him. **C** is incorrect as the paragraph does not describe the early colony of NSW.

3 This is a **synthesis** question. **A** is correct. To work out the answer you need to synthesise all the information in paragraph 2 and summarise it in one statement. The summary of the paragraph is that Macarthur was given a lot of land for free. **B**, **C** and **D** are facts in the paragraph but each is only a part of the paragraph and not its key point.

4 This is a **synthesis** question. **D** is correct. To work out the answer you need to synthesise all the information in the text. Macarthur had powerful friends and allies. The information in the text is about Macarthur's ambition and ability to use allies to defeat opponents. **A** and **B** are incorrect. They are facts in the text but each is only part of the information in the paragraph. **C** is incorrect because Macarthur plotted against Governors Hunter, King, Bligh and Macquarie. The text does not state that Macarthur used those particular Governors.

5 This is a **synthesis** question. **B** is correct. To work out the answer you need to synthesise all the information in the paragraph and condense it down to one statement. Macarthur was involved in illegal activities such as profiteering and plotting

the take-over of a government. **A** and **D** are facts in the paragraph but each answer is only part of what the paragraph is about. **C** is incorrect. The text does not state that Macarthur started the Rum Rebellion.

6 This is a **synthesis** question. To write the answer you need to synthesise the positive information given about Macarthur in the text into one statement. You read *John Macarthur holds an honoured place ... for ... co-founding the Australian wool industry* (see lines 2–3) and that *Macarthur is a man held in high regard in Australian history for his work with merino sheep* (see line 23). You might also state that Macarthur was honoured on the $2 note. Your answer needs to recognise the importance of Macarthur to the Australian wool industry.

The Chinese on the goldfields (page 41)

1 C **2** C **3** C **4** B **5** C and D **6** See below

Explanations

1 This is a **synthesis** question. **C** is correct. To work out which headline could have been printed in a Chinese newspaper you need to have read and understood the points of view of Chinese miners and European miners presented across the whole text. **C** is the only headline that represents a Chinese point of view, suitable for a Chinese newspaper. The headlines in **A**, **B** and **D** represent the European point of view at the time.

2 This is a **synthesis** question. **C** is correct. You read *The Chinese miners were generally peaceful and industrious. Many European miners were distrustful of ... their different clothing, habits, customs and traditions* (see lines 10–13). To work out the answer you need to connect ideas from across the text and recognise the anti-Chinese perspective. **A** is incorrect as many European miners did not want to accept the legal rights of the Chinese. **B** is incorrect. This is an opinion stated by the writer of the text but it was not an opinion held by anti-Chinese miners. **D** is only partially correct. The miners accused the Chinese of wasting water. The text does not say that the Chinese used all the water.

3 This is a **synthesis** question. **C** is correct. To work out the answer to this question you need to connect ideas from across the text and draw conclusions. Mostly the text describes life on the goldfields at that time as difficult. **A**, **B** and **D** are incorrect. A synthesis of information in the text should not lead you to the conclusion that life was exciting, boring or profitable for the majority of miners.

4 This is a **synthesis** question. **B** is correct. To work out the purpose of the text you need to connect ideas from across the text and think about their meaning and function. The text provides information about racism against the Chinese on the goldfields. **A** is incorrect. The text doesn't complain about racism. It presents the facts. **C** and **D** are incorrect. The text doesn't justify or deny that there was racism.

5 This is a **synthesis** question. **C** and **D** are correct. To work out what extra information would be relevant in the report you need to consider firstly the information that has been included. What happened during the riots and how the troops quelled the riots would be relevant information in the report. **A** is incorrect. The text includes information specific to the NSW goldfields so information about gold in China would be irrelevant. **B** is incorrect. How water is used in mining is irrelevant to a report that gives information about racism against the Chinese on the NSW goldfields.

6 This is a **synthesis** question. To draw conclusions about being Chinese in NSW at that time you need to connect information about treatment of the Chinese on the goldfields with information about changes to the law. Your answer would need to mention that people in the colony of NSW held largely racist attitudes towards the Chinese. Proof of this was the government's *Chinese Immigration Restriction and Regulation Act* of 1861 designed to restrict the numbers of Chinese immigrants to NSW.

Inferring questions

The finals (page 46)

1 B **2** D **3** D **4** C **5** See below
6 See below

Explanations

1 This is an **inferring** question. **B** is correct. You read *"Will you be home for dinner?" asked Dad from the kitchen. "I'm defrosting some chicken."* (See lines 2–3) You have to work out the answer by reading between the lines. Scan the text to look for the key word *dinner*. To work out what Dad is cooking for dinner you need to connect *dinner* with *chicken*. You can infer that Dad will cook the chicken for dinner. **A**, **C** and **D** are incorrect. Sam was having noodles (**C**) for dinner that night but Dad was not cooking them. You read *Sometimes they had sushi (see lines 8–9)* (**A**) but sushi wasn't planned for that night.

2 This is an **inferring** question. **D** is correct. You read that Sam says *I have soccer practice* and *we're having noodles afterwards (see lines 4–5)*. You read *Sam loved having something to eat with her teammates after practice. They did it every Friday night (see lines 7–8)*. You can work out the answer using the clues in the text. You can infer that the day is Friday. **A** and **B** are incorrect by a process of elimination. **C** tells a time of day and not a day of the week.

3 This is an **inferring** question. **D** is correct. You should infer that it is NOT true. There is nothing in the text to support an inference that Sam trains harder than any other team member. You read *The team had trained hard three afternoons this week (see line 11)*, so you can infer that **A** is true because people who train hard like to do well. You read *Sam loved having something to eat with her teammates … It was a time when the team could relax and have fun … (see lines 7–10)* You can work out that **B** is true, Sam's team has fun together. The text says that *They had a semi-final game the next day. The competition was tough but they expected to win (see lines 12–13)* so you can infer that **C** is true, Sam plays in a good soccer team. Use a process of elimination to work out which answer is unlikely to be true (**D**).

4 This is an **inferring** question. **C** is correct. You read *He attended all the games he could, depending on his shifts (see lines 20–21)*. Sometimes work prevented Dad from attending Sam's game. **A** and **D** are not the reasons he didn't attend all Sam's games. There's nothing in the text to imply **B** that Sam's dad didn't like soccer.

5 This is an **inferring** question. The question is asking you to use information in the text to make an inference about Sam's attitude to soccer. You can infer from the text that Sam enjoys soccer. You read *They are keen to do well, working hard but having fun too (see lines 14–15)*. You can infer that Sam is keen to do well, she works hard but she has fun too.

6 This is an **inferring** question. To work out the answer you need to think about information that is implied in the text. Scan or re-read the text to look for key words from the question, such as *night shift (see line 19)*. You read *Sam's dad was currently on night shift* so you can infer that he is not always on night shift and that his shifts change. You know from the text that he sometimes has to work during the day on Saturday because he sometimes misses Sam's game. Your answer should explain as follows: Sam's dad doesn't always work night shift. We know he sometimes works day shifts because that's when he misses out on watching Sam play soccer.

Robogal a winner! (page 47)

1 C **2** B **3** B **4** B **5** D **6** See below

Explanations

1 This is an **inferring** question. **C** is correct. You read *The Young Australian of the Year Award is presented* for *outstanding contributions to the community* or for *excellence* in a *chosen field (see lines 37–41)*. Marita won the award while she was still a university student. You can infer that she won the award because of her encouragement of girls to study engineering. **A** and **B** are incorrect. You should infer that studying engineering and making engineering fun will not qualify a person for the Young Australian Award. **D** is incorrect because it doesn't make sense.

2 This is an **inferring** question. **B** is correct. You read *Ms Cheng realised that males outnumbered females in engineering courses and careers by 10 to 1 … so she decided to do something about that (see lines 12–15)*. You can infer that Marita started Robogals when she realised there weren't many female engineers in Australia. **A**, **C** and **D** are facts in the text but are not the reasons she started Robogals.

3 This is an **inferring** question. **B** is correct. You can infer that Marita would disagree with a statement that boys make better engineers than girls. You can infer from the text that Marita would agree with **A**, **C** and **D**.

4 This is an **inferring** question. **B** is correct. You read *Engineers design, invent and build everything from buildings and bridges to aeroplanes and bicycles, appliances and the millions of devices that improve lives (see lines 16–19)*. You can infer that engineering is part of everyone's life as we use engineered products daily. **A** is incorrect because the text is all about girls becoming engineers. Prior to Marita's efforts many people mistakenly believed that engineering was a boy's subject. That perception is changing. **C** contradicts facts in the text. **D** is incorrect because the Award is not given for engineering.

5 This is an **inferring** question. **D** is correct. You read *Ms Cheng founded Robogals ... to visit schools and talk to girls about careers in engineering and technology* (see lines 27–30). You can infer the aim of Robogals is to encourage girls to study engineering. **A** and **B** are what Robogals does to encourage girls to study engineering but are not the aims of Robogals. **C** is incorrect as it doesn't specify engineering.

6 This is an **inferring** question. To infer what Marita will achieve in her life you need to think about her interests as described in the text. You could infer that she will design robots to do household chores or improve people's lives in other ways. You might also predict she could teach engineering to others.

My grandmother (page 48)

1 D **2** D **3** A **4** B **5** B **6** See below

Explanations

1 This is an **inferring** question. **D** is correct. To work out where the writer's grandmother was born you need to read between the lines. You read *My grandmother migrated from Romania in 1948, after World War II* (see lines 2–3). You can infer that the grandmother was born in Romania. **A** tells when the grandmother left Romania. **B** and **C** tell where the grandmother moved to after World War II.

2 This is an **inferring** question. **D** is correct. You read that the grandmother was always telling the writer's mother *to work hard at school* (see lines 9–10) and *This is advice my grandmother took* (see lines 10–11). You can infer that the advice was to get a good education. **A** is what the grandmother became with her good education. **B** and **C** are not the advice given by the great grandmother.

3 This is an **inferring** question. **A** is correct. To infer what makes the writer's grandmother proud of Romania you read *grandmother also says proudly that Romania has the some of the best-preserved forest areas in all of Europe, with brown bears, wolves and hundreds of animal species unique to Romania* (see lines 22–23). The grandmother is proud of Romania's forests and animals. **B** is incorrect as the grandmother only jokes about Count Dracula and Nadia Comaneci. **C** is not a reason the grandmother is proud of Romania. **D** is only about the animals and does not mention the forests.

4 This is an **inferring** question. **B** is correct. You can infer that the writer's grandmother feels she is doing something worthwhile when you read *I think it sounds very depressing but when my grandmother talks about it her eyes sparkle* (see lines 15–16). **A** is incorrect. The grandmother would not volunteer if she felt it was a waste of time. **C** is incorrect because only the writer finds the idea of palliative care depressing. **D** is incorrect. There is nothing in the text to infer that It's too hard.

5 This is an **inferring** question. **B** is correct. You can infer that the volunteer does not deliver lots of babies. You can infer what a palliative care volunteer doesn't do by understanding what they do. You read *My grandmother no longer works as a nurse but is a palliative care volunteer. Palliative care is given to people who are dying* (see lines 13–15). **A**, **C** and **D** are incorrect because these are things a palliative care volunteer would do, based on clues in the text.

6 This is an **inferring** question. You need to read the whole text to be able to infer why the writer refers to Bunica as *my hero* (see line 2). Your answer should include some of the following ideas: Bunica was a refugee from Romania after WWII and migrated to Australia as a little girl, studied hard at school, became a nurse and now volunteers to help dying people. Bunica is a good community member. She is smart, kind and helps others. She has a good sense of humour.

Halloween (page 49)

1 C **2** D **3** C **4** C **5** B **6** See below

Explanations

1 This is an **inferring** question. **C** is correct. To answer the question you need to understand that Rhonda does not enjoy any aspect of Halloween. You read where Rhonda says *greedy children revolt me* (see lines 17–18). From the strongly expressed emotive term *revolt* you can infer that Rhonda thinks greedy children are the worst thing about Halloween. **A** is true but not the worst thing. **B** and **D** are incorrect because you can infer from the text that Rhonda finds these aspects of Halloween interesting.

2 This is an **inferring** question. **D** is correct. To answer the question you need to realise that Rhonda's email to Bill is friendly and personal. You read that Rhonda signs her email *See you at work tomorrow. Regards, Rhonda* (see lines 21–23). You should work out that Rhonda and Billy are

friends from work. You can infer that they are more friendly than **B** (work associates) but not **A** (boyfriend and girlfriend). You can infer that they are not neighbours, **C** because Rhonda says *I hope you don't get too many door-knockers at your place tonight* (see lines 20–21). If they had been neighbours, she might have said "I hope we both don't get too many door-knockers in our street tonight."

3 This is an **inferring** question. **C** is correct. You can infer from the text that Matt's dad is Doug when you read Justin's mum's SMS text *Justin, do not go out tonight unless Matt's dad goes too. I will email Doug to check his plans* (see lines 24–26). This makes the other answers incorrect.

4 This is an **inferring** question. **C** is correct. You can infer that Justin's mother is concerned about Justin's safety when she states that he is not allowed to go trick-or-treating unless Matt's dad goes too. **A**, **B** and **D** are not supported by information in the text.

5 This is an **inferring** question. **B** is correct. You can infer that Ava doesn't care about trick-or-treating when she says that she agrees with her parents about giving money to UNICEF rather than spending it on sweets for neighbourhood children. There is no evidence in the text to support an inference that **A**, **C** or **D** are correct.

6 This is an **inferring** question. You can infer that Matt is excited about trick-or-treating. You read that he has been corresponding with Justin and Ava about Halloween arrangements. You can infer that his dad had agreed to supervise the children. Matt's friend, Justin is excited. You read Justin's email to Matt *I hope we score heaps of loot. My sister's helping me with my costume. It's a surprise. See you soon* (see lines 32–34). You can infer that Matt is likely to be as excited as Justin.

Landcare (page 50)

1 A **2** D **3** C **4** A **5** See below

Explanations

1 This is an **inferring** question. **A** is correct. You can infer that Hebe joined Landcare to 'help the environment' when you read *Landcare Australia is a not-for-profit organisation that aims to protect and restore the natural environment* (see lines 4–6). **B** is mentioned as a Landcare project but not as Hebe's reason for joining. **C** is incorrect. Hebe says she has made friends but she didn't join Landcare to make friends. It is a result of joining Landcare but not the reason. **D** is incorrect because awards are not mentioned in the text.

2 This is an **inferring** question. **D** is correct. You can infer that Hebe is trying to share her enthusiasm when you read *Now I hope to inspire other students to join Landcare and get involved too* (see lines 8–10); and statements such as *There's so much you can do* (see line 25); and *It's actually really easy to get involved and be part of something wonderful—helping nature* (see lines 28–29). There is no evidence in the text that Hebe is trying to annoy everyone (**A**), show off (**B**) or be bossy (**C**).

3 This is an **inferring** question. **C** is correct. You read *My parents joined Landcare five years ago* (see lines 15–16). You can infer that it's most likely Hebe became involved in Landcare through her parents. There is nothing in the text to support an inference that Hebe joined Landcare through school, her teachers or a friend.

4 This is an **inferring** question. **A** is correct. You read *You can get involved in bush regeneration, restoring wild life habitats and corridors so that they are returned to their natural state* (see lines 24–25). You can infer from the text that *restoring wildlife habitats* involves planting native bushes and trees. There is no evidence in the text to support inferences that Landcare volunteers create animal parks (**B**), build homes for wildlife (**C**) or pull down sheds (**D**).

5 This is an **inferring** question. You read *My parents joined Landcare five years ago* (see lines 15–16). You can infer that Hebe's parents are supportive of Hebe's involvement in Landcare and proud of her because they volunteer for Landcare too.

Missing person (page 51)

1 B **2** A, B, C and D **3** D **4** B **5** B
6 See below

Explanations

1 This is an **inferring** question. **B** is correct. You can infer that police might think the female running in St James Park after midnight was Cindy because the female was in a ball gown and she was running awkwardly. You would infer that someone with only one shoe would run awkwardly. **A** does not answer the question. **C** is inaccurate in the text because the witnesses were out that late. **D** could be correct if Cindy had taken off her shoe in order to run swiftly. However, **D** does not mention a ball gown so the best answer is **B**.

2 This is an **inferring** question. All answers are correct. You read *she was last seen dancing with a happy Prince Harry* (see lines 13–14) and you can infer that Prince Harry ran after Cindy because he had enjoyed dancing with her (**A**) and that he liked her and wanted her to stay (**C**). You read that the *Prince picked up her shoe and ran after her* (see lines 17–18) so you can infer that the Prince was keen to return the lost shoe to its owner (**B**). You could infer that the Prince didn't understand why she was running away (**D**) because he ran after her.

3 This is an **inferring** question. **D** is correct. You can infer that the guards forced Prince Harry to stop chasing Cindy because they were concerned for his safety. They are security guards and the safety of the Prince and other royal family members is their job. **A** is incorrect. You can infer that the Prince would know his way around the park adjacent to the palace and not get lost in the dark. **B** is incorrect because it would be unreasonable not to allow a Prince to run anywhere. **C** is incorrect because you should infer that the security guards would not control who the Prince danced with.

4 This is an **inferring** question. **B** is correct. You can infer that the witness statements might be important to police because they confirm Cindy's last known whereabouts which could provide clues to what had happened to her. **A** is incorrect because it's unlikely a criminal will come forward as a witness. **C** is true but not why police would be interested in witness statements. **D** is incorrect. Police would not expect the witnesses to know what happened to Cindy.

5 This is an **inferring** question. **B** is correct. You read *Missing Person … Last seen: Saturday, 12th July* (see lines 1–4) and *Updated 15th July* (see line 26). You can infer that local police are concerned because Cindy has been missing for 3 days. **A** and **D** are irrelevant to police concerns. There is no evidence in the text to imply **C** that St James Park is a dangerous place.

6 This is an **inferring** question. If you are familiar with the Cinderella fairy tale you will recognise this Missing Person text as a parody of the tale. You can make several inferences about what might happen next in the story based on the fairy tale. The prince will search for Cindy and find her and they will marry and live happily ever after. Or, you can continue with the parody: the prince will find Cindy but perhaps she will not want anything to do with him, perhaps she thought he was boring or a poor dancer or had bad breath or she didn't enjoy his company. If you are not familiar with the Cinderella fairy tale, you might still infer the same endings.

Invader (page 52)

1 C **2** C **3** D **4** B **5** D **6** See below

Explanations

1 This is an **inferring** question. **C** is correct. The poet says *You don't belong in this wilderness*! (see line 5) because the pig is a feral animal and not native to the landscape. **A** is incorrect as you cannot infer that the poet dislikes pigs, only the problems they cause in the environment. There is nothing in the text to imply that any particular pig escaped from a farm. **B** and **D** are not the reasons the poet says *You don't belong in this wilderness*.

2 This is an **inferring** question. **C** is correct. You read *Conqueror* (see line 10) and *Breeder* (see line 14). You can infer that the pig colonised the landscape by invading it and by breeding successfully. **A** is incorrect. There's no evidence that the pig killed all other creatures, only that it trampled the earth. **B** is incorrect because the pig is not an alien. The term *alien* in this context means 'foreign' rather than 'extra-terrestrial'. The poet uses the term metaphorically. **D** is inaccurate and not the answer to the question.

3 This is an **inferring** question. **D** is correct. You can infer that the poet means the pig has no natural predator. There is no animal in the Australian bush that preys on pigs. The only way to defeat the feral pig is for people to shoot it. **A**, **B** and **C** are incorrect. They do not answer the question.

4 This is an **inferring** question. **B** is correct. You read *My heart weeps for the damage done* (see line 17) and can infer that the poet is upset about damage done to the environment. **A**, **C** and **D** are not supported by evidence in the text.

5 This is an **inferring** question. **D** is correct. You can infer that the poet is concerned and wants readers to feel concerned about feral pigs. The poet uses emotive words and phrases such as *trampling the fragile earth* (see line 12) to influence the reader's feelings. There is no evidence in the text to infer that the poet wants readers to feel shocked, amazed or happy.

6 This is an **inferring** question. You should be able to infer that the poet would feel the same about feral foxes as she does about feral pigs. They don't belong in the native landscape. They have no

natural predators. You might also infer that the poet would not like feral foxes because they kill native animals.

The jungle above (page 53)

1 B **2** A **3** D **4** C **5** C **6** See below

Explanations

1 This is an **inferring** question. **B** is correct. You read that the creature *sat looking down into the pit … its face and shoulders sagging. Min followed its gaze and knew instantly why it was sad* (see lines 17–19). Min observed the situation. **A** is incorrect because the smaller creature was not trapped. **C** is incorrect because the creature did not talk. **D** is true, the creature wanted the children to help but that is not why it looked sad.

2 This is an **inferring** question. **A** is correct. You read [the creature] *dropped Ben's arm and sat looking down into the pit and then back at the children, from one to the other, its face and shoulders sagging* (see lines 16–19). You can infer that the creatures used body language to communicate. There is no evidence in the text to be able to infer **B**, **C** or **D**.

3 This is an **inferring** question. **D** is correct. You can infer that the children are equals in the story. You read that the children work together throughout the text. Neither is given greater prominence in the story and neither seems to be in charge of the other. Ben is grabbed and Min follows. Min works out why the creature is sad. Ben spots the fallen trunk. Both children manoeuvre it to the hole. Both children agree when it's time to depart and they leave together. There is no evidence in the text to support **A**, **B** or **C**.

4 This is an **inferring** question. **C** is correct. You read *By then it was nightfall and there were strange noises the children couldn't identify. The children looked at each other. It was time to go home* (see lines 23–24). You can infer that the children thought the wild noises were scary and it was dark in the jungle. There is nothing in the text to support **A** or **B**. **D** is only partially correct because it only mentions what the children heard and misses the fact that it was dark (*nightfall*).

5 This is an **inferring** question. **C** is correct. You read *The children looked at each other. It was time to go home. The creatures seemed to understand. They led the children back to the tree* (see lines 23–25). You can infer that the creatures seemed to understand that the children wanted to leave. This is why they lead the children to the tree with the rope ladder attached. There is nothing in the text to support **A**, **B** or **D**.

6 This is an **inferring** question. You read *The children waved goodbye, vowing to return* (see line 25). You can infer from this statement that the children will return to the jungle. You might infer that they are interested in the welfare of the creatures they befriended and want to return to check that they are well and safe. You might infer that the children wonder how or why the pit was made, and by whom, and if further dangers are ahead for the creatures. You might infer that the children are fascinated by the other world they discovered above the tree.

Language questions

A dog (page 58)

1 B **2** C **3** D **4** B **5** C **6** See below

Explanations

1 This is a **language** question. **B** is correct. An opinion is a point of view. Both writers share the same opinion about the birds being disturbed. Neither writer likes it. The writer of Text 1 says that the dog loves to *terrify any birds she spies* (see line 7) and the writer of Text 2 says *poor birds* (see line 15). **A** is not an opinion. **C** and **D** are incorrect because only the writer of Text 1 recognises that the dog loves attention and to be patted and thinks the dog is cute.

2 This is a **language** question. **C** is correct. Read how the term is used in the context of Text 2: *My neighbour's labradoodle is a loose cannon. It runs around madly and creates chaos* (see lines 12–13). You can work out that a *loose cannon* is a term that means 'out of control and likely to cause problems'. You should visualise a large cannon crashing into things and causing damage. Calling the dog *a loose cannon* is a metaphor (one thing is said to be another). **A** and **D** are facts about the dog but not the meaning of the expression *loose cannon*. **B** is the literal meaning of *cannon*.

3 This is a **language** question. **D** is correct. Read how the term is used in the context of Text 1: *She likes to bark but she's all bark and no bite* (see lines 10–11). The expression *all bark and no bite* means it sounds fierce but it won't hurt you. You can work out that **A**, **B** and **C** don't make sense in the text.

4 This is a **language** question. **B** is correct. Read how the term is used by the writer of Text 2 in the context of the text: *It does not know how to come when it is called. Once in a blue moon it will obey a command* (see lines 13–14). *Once in a blue moon* is an idiomatic expression that means 'very rarely'. You should work out that the other answers are not accurate in the context of the text.

5 This is a **language** question. **C** is correct. Read how the term is used in the context of the Text 2: *It is a stupid-looking dog with zero brains and no common sense. I'm afraid it is a waste of space* (see lines 18–20). The idiomatic expression *a waste of space* means 'something of no value'. You can tell that the writer of Text 2 does not think the dog is of any value or use. The other answers are incorrect.

6 This is a **language** question. The only thing the letter can rightfully complain about is the barking. You need to express this in a non-emotive sentence: The dog barks all day when its owners are out.

Bella's party (page 59)

1 A **2** C **3** B **4** B **5** B **6** See below

Explanations

1 This is a **language** question. **A** is correct. Scan the text and read how the sentence *I said no, she sighed wearily* (see line 7) is used in context. It comes after a series of arguments and before the sentence, *Liam had been trying to persuade his mum to allow him to go to a party* (see line 8). *Wearily* means 'tiredly'. You can tell that when Liam's mum sighs *wearily* it means she is tired of arguing, and not annoyed with Liam (**B**), or tired from having too little sleep (**C**) or because she's busy in the kitchen (**D**).

2 This is a **language** question. **C** is correct. *Now he sat brooding* (see line 11) follows a series of failed arguments Liam had tried on his mum to get his way. Liam is now sulky and deep in thought. Other answers are incorrect. Liam is not crying (**A**) or angry (**D**). Liam is pushing his cereal around in the bowl because he is deep in thought rather than because he is not hungry (**B**).

3 This is a **language** question. **B** is correct. Scan the text and read *He absently pushed his cereal around in the bowl* (see line 11) in the context of the text. *Absently* is an adverb that tells readers how Liam stirred his food. It's used to tell readers that Liam's mind was focused on other things and he stirred his food without thinking about it. **A** does not make sense as the text says he stirred the food so there is cereal in his bowl. **C** and **D** are not supported by evidence in the text.

4 This is a **language** question. **B** is correct. Scan the text and read how the expression is used in context. You read *Liam thought about asking his stepdad for permission to go to the party. Sure as eggs his stepdad would say yes* (see lines 16–17). *Sure as eggs* is a high modality idiomatic expression that shows certainty. It implies 'as sure as eggs crack' something will certainly happen. You can tell that Liam is convinced that his stepdad would agree with his request to attend the party. The other answers are lower modality, or less certain, and therefore incorrect.

5 This is a **language** question. **B** is correct. You read *Sure as eggs his stepdad would say yes but he decided against it as his mum would go ballistic and he'd just get his stepdad into trouble* (see lines 16–17). *To go ballistic* is idiom or slang for getting very angry. The term *ballistic* is most often used to refer to a weapon, the ballistic missile. You can work out that if the stepdad is in trouble then Liam's mum is angry. **A**, **C** and **D** do not make sense in the context of the text.

6 This is a **language** question. Scan the text for the sentence *His mum looked at him sideways* (see line 20). This expression means that his mum was suspicious of Liam's motives. She guessed he was up to something. The clues are that he offered to do the dishes and tidy the kitchen. When his mum looked at Liam *sideways* it was to acknowledge that she knew he was up to something and that he was trying to manipulate her.

The neighbours (page 60)

1 B **2** A **3** C **4** B **5** D **6** See below

Explanations

1 This is a **language** question. **B** is correct. You read *Sometimes problems with neighbours escalate but mostly issues with neighbours can be resolved amicably when people just consider the needs of others* (see lines 8–11). You can work out from the context that *escalate* means get worse. **A** and **C** do not make sense in the text. You can work out that **D** is incorrect because the sentence means that when problems DON'T resolve by themselves they escalate.

2 This is a **language** question. **A** is correct. You read that *mostly issues with neighbours can be resolved*

amicably (see lines 9–10). You can work out that *amicably* means in 'a friendly way' because the dad's problem was resolved when the neighbour agreed to help. It was an amicable conversation. **B** and **C** are the opposite of *amicably*. **D** does not make sense in the text.

3 This is a **language** question. **C** is correct. Examine the way *She* is used in the text. You read *Her neighbour complained about the noise. She sleeps in the day because she works at night* (see lines 22–23). You can work out that the pronoun *She* refers to *Her* (Amira's) *neighbour* in the previous sentence. **A**, **B** and **D** do not make sense in the text.

4 This is a **language** question. **B** is correct. The writer's neighbour is *The man who lives in the unit below …* (see lines 13–14) You read *Dad told our neighbour that we were worried about breathing in the toxic smoke. Our neighbour apologised. He said he hadn't realised the smoke was coming into our unit* (see lines 17–18). The neighbour was apologetic. He is depicted as a reasonable person. He is not described as forceful (**A**), having strong opinions (**C**) or disagreeable (**D**).

5 This is a **language** question. **D** is correct. You read *Amira felt really bad for being so thoughtless. She now puts a bark control collar on Foxy before she goes to school* (see lines 23–24). Amira is depicted as kind but unthinking. Based on information in the text she cannot be described as (**A**) lonely or (**C**) inconsiderate of others. There is no evidence in the text to support **B**.

6 This is a **language** question. You need to accurately represent Dad's feelings as he is described at the end of the conversation: *Dad was so happy* (see line 20). For example, Dad said "Thank you so much. I appreciate your help and understanding." Or "Thank you for your understanding and cooperation."

Pets (page 61)

1 B **2** A **3** D **4** B **5** C **6** See below

Explanations

1 This is a **language** question. **B** is correct. Scan the text to find the key words *barking up the wrong tree* (see lines 11–12). You read *Animal Lover needs to find another cause as he/she is barking up the wrong tree with this one* (see lines 10–12). You can work out by the way the expression is used in the text that the writer thinks *Animal Lover* is making a mistake. **A**, **C** and **D** do not make sense in the context of the text.

2 This is a **language** question. **A** is correct. You read *Walk-by shoppers buy pets on impulse when they get their groceries. This is why we have so many unwanted cats and dogs needing to be rehomed by RSPCA and other animal welfare groups* (see lines 21–25). The pronoun *This* refers to the action of buying pets on impulse. **B** and **D** are not what causes so many unwanted dogs and cats needing to be rehomed. **C** is incorrect as you cannot buy pets at a grocery store, rather at pet stores near grocery stores.

3 This is a **language** question. **D** is correct. You read *Pet shops have regulations, enforced by law and all the managers and staff I deal with have the utmost integrity in caring for their animals* (see lines 7–10). You can work out by the tone of the text that *Shop Owner* is defensive of pet shops and wants readers to believe that pet shops operate responsibly. **A** is not the specific point of view expressed in the letter. **B** and **C** are statements made in the letter but do not best represent the writer's point of view.

4 This is a **language** question. **B** is correct. The answers are all expressed as commands. You need to work out which command is in accord with *Animal Righter*'s opinion. You read *Buying a pet is something that should be thoroughly researched and planned for* (see lines 19–20). You can work out that *Animal Righter* wants readers to take the decision to buy a pet seriously. **A** and **D** are incorrect. They contradict the writer's position on the topic. **C** is incorrect, however you could infer that this is what *Animal Righter* would want people to do IF the decision to buy a pet was NOT taken seriously.

5 This is a **language** question. **C** is correct. You read where *Shop Owner* says *As an owner of a pet shop I was insulted to read 'Puppy Factories and Kitten Farms' (Animal Lover, April 9th)* (see lines 3–5) and Text 2, *I agree with Animal Lover ('Puppy Factories and Kitten Farms', April 9th)* (see lines 15–16). You can work out that both of the letters were written in response to a previously published letter, titled 'Puppy Factories and Kitten Farms'.

6 This is a **language** question. You can agree or disagree with the point of view expressed in either letter. You need to write your opinion and your reasons. Use thinking and feeling verbs. You might start with:

I agree/ disagree with the opinions expressed by_________________. I think that …

Another day in Parliament (page 62)

1 D **2** B **3** A **4** D **5** C **6** See below

Explanations

1 This is a **language** question. **D** is correct. You read *5 minutes later* (see line 8) *... and later ...* (see line 11) *and later still* (see line 14). These are adverbs and phrases that tell readers how time has passed between one frame and the next. **A** is incorrect as the frames are linked in a chronological sequence and not through cause and effect. **B** is incorrect as the images do not show the passage of time (i.e. images of morning and night). **C** is incorrect as the comic strip is not a narrative. There is no complication, climax or resolution.

2 This is a **language** question. **B** is correct. It is an example of political satire. Satire is a type of humour that makes fun of human failings or society's weaknesses. Political satire makes fun of the failings or weaknesses of politicians. **A** is partially correct. The comic strip does make fun of people but the particular people in political satire are politicians. Political cartoonists often use the news of the day to make social or political comments. They use caricature and exaggeration to make a point. **C** and **D** miss the point of the text, which is to make a joke.

3 This is a **language** question. **A** is correct. You can recognise from the context of the text that the character saying *I'm glad he's opposed to sledging* (see lines 14–16) is being sarcastic or using irony because the main character in the comic is actually *sledging*. Irony is when you say the opposite of what you mean. Irony is meant to be humorous or to exaggerate a point. The character in the comic strip is being ironic. **B** and **D** are incorrect. The character is not making a truthful or honest statement. **C** is incorrect because the character isn't lying—the character is being sarcastic.

4 This is a **language** question. **D** is correct. A *sandwich short of a picnic* (see line 13) is an example of an idiom. It means 'not that smart'. It is used to put somebody down. It infers that there's something missing mentally (i.e. that the person is foolish). You can tell this from the way the expression is used negatively in the text. **A** is a muddled translation of *a sandwich short of a picnic* and is incorrect. **B** and **C** are positive statements so you should work out that they would be incorrect in the context of the text.

5 This is a **language** question. **C** is correct. The main character has called other politicians negative names using alliteration: *mangy maggot* (see line 9), *diminutive donkey* (see line 11), *a sandwich short of a picnic* (see line 13). The only negative suggestion in the answers is **C**, despicable worm. **A**, **B** and **D** are all positive noun groups and so are incorrect. The frame would look like this:

The storyboard frame would show the speaker's right arm pointed out. The heading would need to indicate the passage of time, e.g. *and still later ...* or *later on ...* or *that night*.

6 This is a **language** question. You should read the text and realise that *sledging* means insulting someone, putting them down or calling them names. Your answer should define sledging as a put-down. The cartoonist is attempting to use humour to make a point that sledging is inappropriate behaviour for Members of Parliament in Parliament House.

The life of Herman (page 63)

1 B **2** C **3** C **4** A **5** D **6** See below

Explanations

1 This is a **language** question. **B** is correct. The first frame shows a close up of the ant's face to introduce readers to a main character or an important character. Subsequent frames show events from that first ant character's point of view. Other answers are incorrect because the first frame does not show readers any of the setting (**A**), or what the ants are doing (**C**) or build suspense (**D**).

2 This is a **language** question. **C** is correct. The frame shows the main ant character nearly being stepped on by a human foot. Readers are shown this image so that we can see the ant's point of view and empathise with it. **B** and **D** are incorrect. The person's face is not shown and so readers are not meant to feel concern for the human. **A** is incorrect because the point of the shot is to focus viewers' attention on the ant rather than the foot.

3 This is a **language** question. **C** is correct. The view in the frame is drawn to show the size of the ants in relation to the human. This puts the size of the ants in perspective in the shot/frame. Tip! Perspective here means showing the size of the ants in relation to other elements in the shot. The type of drawing of the human is called foreshortening. It is a way to get a whole body into a frame. **A** is incorrect. This frame does not show how the ants feel. **B** and **D** are incorrect. Readers are not shown the human's point of view or any of the background in the scene.

4 This is a **language** question. **A** is correct. You need to read the visual language to work out the answer. Frames 1 to 3 show a happy ant. Frame 4 shows a frightened ant. Frame 5 shows a brave ant facing a larger foe. The sequences of emotions listed in the other answers are not the same as in the storyboard's sequence of images.

5 This is a **language** question. **D** is correct. The human's point of view is not shown. Readers are not shown the human's feelings. To show what the human is feeling readers would need to see the human's facial expressions, body language and/or gestures. None of these are given for the human so **B** and **C** are incorrect. **A** is incorrect because readers are not shown even that the human is oblivious to the ants. We would only be able to tell this if we saw the human looking in the opposite direction and obviously being unaware of the ants on the ground below. The ant is the main character and the storyboard only shows the ant's feelings.

6 This is a **language** question. Frame 5 shows the main character shaking a finger at the human foot. Your answer should include exclamations or sentences such as "Watch where you're going!" or "Be careful! You nearly squished me."

A foiled plan (page 64)

1 C **2** A **3** C **4** B **5** B **6** See below

Explanations

1 This is a **language** question. **C** is correct. You read *'You scratch my back and I'll scratch yours,' I entreated, quoting my mum and using one of her favourite sayings; one she used whenever she wanted me to do something* (see lines 11–14). You can work out by the way the expression is used in the text that it means do something for me and I'll do something for you. **A** and **B** might be the literal translations of the expression but are not what it means figuratively in the text. **D** is also a more literal translation of the expression and not correct in the context of the text.

2 This is a **language** question. **A** is correct. You read *Mel ignored that; steely eyed; impervious to my mum's sayings* (see lines 15–16). You can work out by the way the expression is used in the text that it means not influenced or not persuaded. **B** is incorrect. You can work out in the context of the text that Mel IS listening to her friend. **C** is incorrect. It is a fact in the text: *She'd heard them all before* (see line 16), but it is not the meaning of *impervious*. You can work out by the use of *impervious* in context in the text that **D** (impressed) is incorrect.

3 This is a **language** question. **C** is correct. You read *I shrugged sheepishly. Worth a try, I thought* (see line 17). This occurs in the text after Mel had ignored Abigail's nagging. You can work out by the way the word is used in the text that Mel is a bit embarrassed to have been trying so hard, even resorting to using one of her mum's sayings. **A**, **B** and **D** do not make sense in the context of the text.

4 This is a **language** question. **B** is correct. You can tell by the narrator's attitude to events and in her interactions with Mel that she expects Mel to do what she wants. She can't believe that Mel says no. **A** and **C** are incorrect. There is nothing in the text to imply that the narrator is a bully or that she cries and whines. **D** is incorrect because, although you could say that the narrator is argumentative, she is not very persuasive as Mel has not been persuaded to go along with her wishes.

5 This is a **language** question. **B** is correct. Readers learn about Mel's character through what the narrator tells you. The first-person narrator, Abigail, says that *Mel's face was inscrutable* (see line 2). Mel was *steely-eyed; impervious* (see line 15). Readers are told that Mel usually agreed with the narrator. You read *She always agrees. She's like putty—very malleable. I didn't understand. What was happening here? She always, always does what I say. Mel and Abigail, peas in a pod* (see lines 23–26). **A** is incorrect because Mel's facial expression is *inscrutable* (see line 2), meaning that you can't tell what she is thinking from her facial expressions.

C is incorrect as Mel only speaks twice and that is to say *No* (see lines 19 and 21). **D** is incorrect as the text does not include anyone's thoughts except the narrator's.

6 This is a **language** question. When you read *'You're driving me up the wall!' I stormed off* (see line 29) you know that the narrator, Abigail, is feeling annoyed and frustrated because she can't get her own way with Mel. You read that Mel is *like putty* (see line 23). This is a simile. It means that Mel is usually very agreeable and easy to manoeuver or manipulate. Your answer needs to suggest any of the following: Abigail feels angry, frustrated, annoyed, disappointed and puzzled (or use synonyms for these words).

Feral animals in Australia (page 65)

1 See below **2** A **3** D **4** C **5** A
6 See below

Explanations

1 This is a **language** question. You read the thesis statement for the text, *Feral animals are an environmental disaster* (see lines 4–5). *Disaster* is the emotive term that sums up the writer's opinion of feral animals. The statement is followed by all the problems caused by feral animals that prove they are a *disaster*.

2 This is a **language** question. **A** is correct. You can work out the meaning of the word *endeavour* by reading it in context. You read *Government agencies endeavour to clear feral animals from specific limited areas* (see lines 12–13). To *endeavour* means to 'try, strive or work at something'. You can insert 'try' to replace *endeavour* and the sentence still makes sense. **B** (forget), **C** (disregard) and **D** (hate) do not make sense in the text because the text describes efforts being made to rid the environment of feral animals.

3 This is a **language** question. **D** is correct. You need to work out the meaning of the term 'rights' as it is used in the question and relate this to your understanding of the text. You read *any methods used must … comply with government guidelines on the humane treatment of feral animals* (see lines 25–26). You can work out that feral animals have the right under law to be treated humanely. **A**, **B** and **C** are not supported by the meaning of the text and are incorrect.

4 This is a **language** question. **C** is correct. You read *Western Australian native animals seem to have developed a tolerance for this poison* [the West Australian native pea] *so are not harmed* (see lines 18–19). The conjunction *so* tells you that the two parts of the sentence show cause and effect. *Developed a tolerance* means that they can eat it without being harmed. Other answers do not make sense in the context of the text.

5 This is a **language** question. **A** is correct. The writer does not give an opinion about shooting feral animals. The writer factually lists the possible methods of dealing with feral animals but does not give a personal preference. There is nothing in the text to suggest that the writer doesn't like shooting as a means of controlling feral animals. You read *The federal government department responsible for the environment believes that shooting, by professional licenced shooters, is the most humane method of dealing with larger feral animals like horses, pigs and buffalo* (see lines 21–23), but the writer does not mention a personal preference for this method, nor does the writer use emotive language. For example, instead of *shooting*, a more emotive term such as *slaughtering* would have indicated writer bias.

6 This is a **language** question. You can tell that the word *humane* in the context of this text means to kill the animals, in as quick and painless a way as possible, without unnecessary cruelty.

Judgement questions

Targeting Maths Year 5 app (page 70)

1 C **2** A and D **3** B, C and D **4** B
5 See below **6** See below

Explanations

1 This is a **judgement** question. **C** is correct. You read *Within this app, students can access a huge range of activities* (see line 6) and *With the ability to make multiple accounts, each student's individual progress is tracked and recorded* (see lines 18–19) and *all we know about how children learn maths* (see lines 20–21). You can judge that the advertisement is talking to teachers. **B** is incorrect because parents would not need to *make multiple accounts* (see line 8) to track each student's individual progress. **A** and **D** are incorrect as the advertisement talks about students rather than to them.

2 This is a **judgement** question. **A** and **D** are correct. You read the questions and judge what they claim based on your understanding of the advertisement. You can judge that the app seems

fun (**A**). Notice the low modality term *seems*. You read *81 question sets that cover the 9 big topics of Year 5 Mathematics* (see line 9) and you can judge that **D** is correct. Answers **B** and **C** are incorrect. They are high modality statements typical of advertisements. You cannot read the advertisement and accept that the app will *definitely help children learn maths* or that students will be *happy to do the maths activities*. These claims are only possibly true for some children.

3 This is a **judgement** question. **B**, **C** and **D** are correct. You read *we have brought together all we know about how children learn maths* (see lines 20–21) and you can recognise that the product developer is claiming expertise (**C**). You read *a huge range of activities that make learning maths facts fun, motivating and very rewarding!* (see lines 6–7) and *powerful interactivity … irresistible combination of engagement and learning* (see lines 21–22) and you can recognise the high modality evaluative words and phrases (**B** and **D**). **A** is incorrect as the advertisement does not make claims based on scientific evidence.

4 This is a **judgement** question. **B** is correct. You can judge that students would find the inclusion of *a Dictionary of terms* (see lines 10–11) to be the least motivating reason to buy the product. **A**, **C** and **D** are incorrect because they sound more fun and enjoyable and therefore would be more important to a Year 5 student.

5 This is a **judgement** question. You need to use evidence in the text to make your judgement. The emphasis of the ad is on learning. You can highlight the claims in the ad that you judge relate to learning then use a different colour and highlight claims that you judge relate to fun.

These claims relate to learning:

- *an amazing new way to learn mathematics* (see line 5)
- *the 9 big topics of Year 5 Mathematics* (see line 9)
- *81 question sets* (see line 9)
- *a scratch board for working out problems* (see line 10)
- *a Dictionary of terms* (see lines 10–11)
- *Timed—increase speed in essential addition, subtraction, word and mixed mathematic facts* (see lines 14–15)
- *we have brought together all we know about how children learn maths* (see lines 20–21)
- *irresistible combination of engagement and learning will switch on all students, even those who don't think that they are good at maths* (see lines 22–23).

These claims relate to fun:

- *activities that make learning maths facts fun, motivating and very rewarding* (see lines 6–7)
- *Multiplayer—up to 4 players can play against each other in this game of speed and fun* (see lines 12–13)
- *Badges—220 badges* (see line 16)
- *Games—tokens to spend on fun games in the circus area* (see line 17).

6 This is a **judgement** question. You need to judge the ad and decide for yourself whether you would choose to try this app. Use evidence from the ad to support your judgement.

The shark debate (page 71)

1 B **2** C **3** B **4** D **5** B **6** See below

Explanations

1 This is a **judgement** question. **B** is correct. The most commonly held point of view is against the use of shark nets so that harmless animals are not inadvertently killed. **A** is incorrect because only Speaker 2 is in favour of nets. **C** is incorrect as shark nets do not protect harmless animals, they are responsible for their deaths. **D** is incorrect because no speaker is against shark nets in order to protect people. This does not make sense.

2 This is a **judgement** question. **C** is correct. You can judge that Speaker 2 wants to protect people and specifically mentions the importance of tourism therefore could be a member of Sydney City Tourism Board. **A**, **B** and **D** would most likely represent people who want to protect sharks and by-catch from nets or culling.

3 This is a **judgement** question. **B** is correct. You can judge that Speaker 3 could be a representative from an organisation called Save the Shark Alliance. Speaker 3 speaks in defence of sharks. You can judge that **A** and **C** would most likely be for people in favour of culling sharks in order to protect people. You can judge that **D** is a website for an organisation to support dogs and is irrelevant to the question.

4 This is a **judgement** question. **D** is correct. You read Speaker 1: *People: Don't swim or surf in shark territory or at shark feeding times* (see lines 8–11). You read Speaker 4: *when people trespass in the marine environment they should do so at their own risk* (see lines 36–37). Both speakers advise common sense and are against netting. **A** and **C** are incorrect because they point out differences when the question asks for similarities. Also **A** is

incorrect because it states that Speaker 4 is not concerned about by-catch, which is inaccurate. **C** is incorrect because Speaker 4 is not against people swimming in the ocean. **B** is incorrect as both speakers are against netting.

5 This is a **judgement** question. **B** is correct. It is the most emotive statement. It uses the emotive words 'saved' and 'horrific'. The words used by the speaker are dramatic and extreme. **A**, **C** and **D** are high-modality statements but they do not make use of such emotive words or phrases.

6 This is a **judgement** question. You can agree with any of the speakers but you must explain your reasons using evidence from the text. Start your answer by stating 'I agree with Speaker … because …'

Teacher trouble (page 72)

1 B **2** D **3** C **4** D **5** See below
6 See below

Explanations

1 This is a **judgement** question. **B** is correct. You read that George admits *I muck around a little bit and have a joke* *(see lines 14–15)*. You can judge that George gets into trouble in class. **A** is what George complains is happening but you should realise that this is not true. **C** is true in the text but it is not the answer to the question. **D** George complains about everything does not explain George's problem with his teacher.

2 This is a **judgement** question. **D** is correct. You can judge that Nikolas is a good listener and George's friend. You can tell from the text that Nikolas listens to George without argument or disagreement and doesn't challenge George or tell him to stop complaining. You might judge that he is too nice to say anything negative to George or that by saying nothing he is hoping George manages to see that his problems are of his own making. **A** and **B** are incorrect. There is no evidence in the text to say that they are true. **C** is incorrect. There is nothing in the text to suggest that Nikolas does his homework or works hard in class.

3 This is a **judgement** question. **C** is correct. By George's own admission the teacher thinks George *can do better* *(see line 33)* and has *"unfulfilled potential"* *(see line 40)*. **A** is incorrect. You can judge that the teacher expects more of George and is disappointed in his lack of effort. **B** is incorrect. It is unlikely that the teacher thinks George should move to another school. He just wants George to apply himself in class. **D** is incorrect. While it may be true, there is no evidence in the text to support a judgement that this answer is correct. The teacher might think that Nikolas is a good friend for George but the text doesn't tell us that.

4 This is a **judgement** question. **D** is correct. Nikolas's character does not say very much in the text. His character listens and does not offer any opinions. In Nikolas's position the reader might want to tell George **A**, **B** and **C** but you can judge that the character of Nikolas would not say these things or speak at all in the situation described in the text.

5 This is a **judgement** question. George admits he mucks up in class, is loud and doesn't always do his homework. You read that the teacher thinks he makes as little effort as possible in class. You read that he complains when the teacher suggests he could do better and that he expects more of him. You might judge George to be an annoying and complaining boy. You might judge George to be immature because he accuses the teacher of picking on him rather than accepting responsibility for his own actions and behaving responsibly. You might judge that George must be fun because he has a friend like Nikolas and George says he likes to *have a joke* *(see line 15)*. You must support your judgement of George's character using evidence from the text.

6 This is a **judgement** question. You may or may not know someone like George but you should recognise the type of person he is because the text is realistic in its portrayal of his character. Have you known children who muck around in class when they could be doing better but they don't make the effort? Explain the reasons for your judgements using evidence from the text and your own knowledge and understanding.

Endangered languages (page 73)

1 D **2** B **3** C **4** D **5** See below
6 See below

Explanations

1 This is a **judgement** question. **D** is correct. You read *An open letter to the Australian business community* *(see lines 4–5)* and recognise that it is a letter addressed to that audience. You can judge the purpose of the text is to persuade business leaders to support Indigenous language programs. The text is in the form of an open letter. An open letter is a letter addressed to a specific audience but published for a wider audience to read.

This letter offers ways for businesses to contribute to its cause. **A** is incorrect because even though it does raise awareness of the problem that is not the main purpose of the letter. **B** is incorrect because the letter is not a newspaper report. **C** is incorrect because the letter does not attempt to persuade people to learn to speak any of the endangered languages.

2 This is a **judgement** question. **B** is correct. You can judge that this text would not be useful in compiling a government agency report about the status of endangered languages. You can judge that the letter is from an organisation with an agenda. You might agree with the assertions in the letter but you can't make a judgement that it is a trustworthy source of information. **A** and **C** are incorrect because you can't judge the information in the letter as reliable or accurate. **D** is incorrect because the letter is not an advertisement.

3 This is a **judgement** question. **C** is correct. You can judge that the exclamation *Isn't that amazing!* (see lines 25–26) is an attempt to engage the reader. It addresses the reader to try to connect with the reader. **A** is incorrect. The exclamation starts like a question with *Isn't* but is not punctuated or intended as a question. **B** is incorrect because the exclamation does not express surprise but rather appreciation, wonderment and praise. **D** is incorrect because *Isn't that amazing!* is not a fact.

4 This is a **judgement** question. **D** is correct. You can judge the writer values culture because of the sentiments expressed in the text: *Language carries cultural identity, ancestral knowledge and tradition. Our world is richer for the variety of languages that are maintained and used* (see lines 20–23). There is no evidence in the text to support **A** or **B**. The writer could be Indigenous or non-Indigenous but the writer's ethnicity is irrelevant to the requests made in the letter. **C** is incorrect. There is no evidence to suggest that the writer works for the government. The web address for the writer's organisation does not have *.gov.au* in it.

5 This is a **judgement** question. The text infers that many Indigenous Australian languages are already extinct and tells you that many are critically endangered. The text should make you feel that it would be a terrible shame to lose any more Indigenous Australian languages. The writer presents a persuasive point of view. You read *Our world is richer for the variety of languages that are maintained and used* (see lines 21–23) and *Australian Indigenous languages are the oldest surviving languages in the world* (see lines 24–25). So your judgement should state that the writer believes preserving Indigenous languages is important and worthwhile for the benefit of all Australians as part of Australia's heritage, history and culture.

6 This is a **judgement** question. You can judge that First Nations languages have not been considered important in the past because they were allowed to become extinct. Now people are trying to save the critically endangered ones from extinction, so attitudes have changed considerably.

Longline fishing (page 74)

1 B **2** A **3** D **4** B **5** See below
6 See below

Explanations

1 This is a **judgement** question. **B** is correct. The point of view in the text is that longline fishing is inhumane and wasteful. The writer uses emotive words and phrases such as *dragging them … drowning them* (see line 6). … *It is a tragedy that these animals die needlessly* (see line 11). **A**, **C** and **D** are statements of facts from the text. They do not give the writer's opinion.

2 This is a **judgement** question. **A** is correct. The text makes readers think about the problems with a fishing method. **B** is incorrect because the text does not say longline fishing is useful in catching turtles. The word 'useful' implies a positive attitude towards this practice whereas the text is very negative about the death of turtles caught on longlines. **C** is incorrect. The text mentions Humane Society statistics on by-catch but does not encourage readers to find out more about the Society. **D** is incorrect because the text only describes one method of fishing, not the plural methods of fishing.

3 This is a **judgement** question. **D** is correct. Reading Text 1 could be helpful if you were creating a petition to help ban longline fishing because you could quote the numbers of animals killed as by-catch. **A**, **B** and **C** are incorrect because the text does not provide enough information to support any of these uses.

4 This is a **judgement** question. **B** is correct. The writer's overall point of view in Text 2 is positive as the writer describes longline fishing as a very successful fishing method. You read *Longline fishing is a highly productive, cost-effective, commercial fishing method* (see lines 14–15). **A** is one opinion stated in the text to justify longline

fishing but not the overall point of view. **C** is an opinion about the reputation of longline fishing whereas the writer's opinion in the text refers to the reputation of the fish not the method of fishing. You read *longline caught fish have a reputation for freshness* (see line 23). **D** is incorrect because the writer's point of view is evident in the use of evaluative terms (*highly productive, cost-effective* (see line ??)).

5 This is a **judgement** question. Text 1 would probably be considered the most effective at influencing opinions. It uses emotive words to sound convincing and appeal to the reader's emotions. In general, readers would be upset to read about turtles and sea birds drowning. Text 1 also uses logic and reasoning. It does not make sense to needlessly waste animals' lives when the text asserts there are alternative fishing methods that do not result in by-catch. You might choose Text 2 as the most persuasive especially if you are involved in the longline fishing industry because you would read the text from your own perspective on the issues.

6 This is a **judgement** question. Your answer needs to state your opinion and cite evidence in the texts that enabled you to reach a decision.

Book review: *The One and Only Ivan* (page 75)

1 B **2** A **3** B **4** See below **5** See below **6** See below

Explanations

1 This is a **judgement** question. **B** is correct. You can judge the reviewer thinks Ivan is a believable narrator when you read *The author uses Ivan's voice to give readers a very credible insight into the life of a captive animal* (see lines 3–4). The word *credible* in the text means 'believable'. **A** and **C** don't reflect the opinions of the reviewer. **D** does not describe the way the story is narrated or told.

2 This is a **judgement** question. **A** is correct. You read *The story is beautifully told* (see line 12) and you read *This is a moving story* (see line 16) and you can judge the reviewer thinks the author is talented. **B** is incorrect. Although the book did win a Newbery Medal the reviewer doesn't use this fact to praise the author's ability to tell a story. **C** might be true but the reviewer isn't concerned about this in the text. **D** is incorrect. There is no evidence in the text to suggest that the reviewer thinks the author takes the subject matter too seriously.

3 This is a **judgement** question. **B** is correct. You read *This story highlights the underlying immorality of keeping exotic animals as pets and in cages for human entertainment* (see lines 10–11). You can judge that the reviewer thinks circuses with exotic animals are immoral. **A** is incorrect because, even though you could judge that the reviewer would agree with the comment it is not an opinion about circuses. **C** and **D** are incorrect because you can judge that the reviewer would disagree with these descriptions.

4 This is a **judgement** question. You read what the reviewer says about the language of the story: [It] *is beautifully told using poetic language* (see line 2). You can judge that the reviewer thinks poetic language enhances the storytelling of Ivan, the narrator. You can work out why by reading the example of poetic language quoted by the reviewer: *Gorillas are as patient as stones* (see line 12).

5 This is a **judgement** question. You can judge the reviewer uses this quote in the review to give readers an example of the way Ivan tells his story. It expresses very clearly that Ivan was born in the wild and he looks like a true wild gorilla but he was just a baby when he was captured and has never associated with gorillas so he does not know how to behave like a gorilla. The quote compares the outside of Ivan, his wild gorilla appearance, to what he is now on the inside, a captive and tame gorilla, not wild at all.

6 This is a **judgement** question. You need to express your opinion about the review and give reasons. You can decide that you would not want to read the book because the reviewer has made the subject seem too sad or boring, or given away the ending. In this case the review was useful because it helped you decide not to read the book. Or you can state that you would like to read the book because it sounds interesting. You can quote the reviewer to explain your reasoning. In either case the reviewer has presented enough information about the book for you to be able to form a judgement.

Slaves for sugar (page 76)

1 B **2** A and D **3** B **4** A, B, C and D **5** See below **6** See below

Explanations

1 This is a **judgement** question. **B** is correct. You read Pacific Islanders *were either kidnapped or tricked into coming to Australia. … Indentured*

labour was really just another name for slavery … It was hard, dirty work in the heat and dust … Most indentured labourers were badly treated … [and deportation] … *was devastating for many families* (see lines 12–23). You can judge that the writer believes that Pacific Islander people, whether they were indentured or free labourers, were treated very badly. **A** and **C** are incorrect because the writer's point of view is evident in the text in the choice of wording. **D** is incorrect because it is a statement of fact and doesn't answer the question.

2 This is a **judgement** question. **A** and **D** are correct. You can judge that the writer wants you to think that blackbirding was a common practice on sugar plantations. Paragraph 3 describes the impact of the White Australia Policy on Pacific Islander people living in Australia in 1906 and you can judge that many Australians held racist attitudes at that time. There is nothing in the text to support a judgement that **B** is correct. **C** is inaccurate as you read *'Blackbird' was a term used instead of slave* (see line 8).

3 This is a **judgement** question. **B** is correct. You read *Free labourers were also badly exploited* (see line 18) and you can judge that exploitation means taking advantage of someone or treating them unfairly. You can judge from your understanding of the whole text that Pacific Islanders were exploited. **A** is somewhat correct. You can infer that greed for high profits made blackbirding a common practice on the cane fields but the text is more concerned with the exploitation of the labourers than the implied greed of the farm owners. **C** is incorrect. Jealousy is not referred to in the text. **D** breaking the law is discussed in paragraphs 1 and 3 but this is not as important a theme as exploitation.

4 This is a **judgement** question. **A**, **B**, **C** and **D** could all be judged correct. As a plantation owner in 1890 you would want to make money using good cheap labour for higher profits. You would have recognised that Pacific Islanders are hard workers, that employees are difficult to get because of the terrible, hot and dirty conditions. You would most likely have a racist attitude to Pacific Islanders and believe that they must be happier living in Australia than back home.

5 This is a **judgement** question. You might mention that you are concerned about being deported as you've lived in Australia for a long time. You might mention that you have friends and family members in Australia and that you are concerned about finding anyone you know, either friends or family on your home island, if deported. You would be concerned about where you would live and whether you could get a job.

6 This is a **judgement** question. You should judge that indentured labourers were generally treated very badly by their employers on the sugar cane farms as well as by the government when they were deported. You should recognise that indentured labour was a way to exploit workers. It was legal but it was unjust.

The Hunt (page 77)

1 C **2** C **3** See below **4** See below
5 See below **6** See below

Explanations

1 This is a **judgement** question. **C** is correct. You can judge that the narrator is a colt (a young male horse). He is bewildered by events that he had never witnessed before. It is the first time he has seen a hunt and he is so *astonished* (see line 14) that he didn't notice that a horse had fallen. Other answers are incorrect. The narrator wasn't worried (**A**), excited (**B**) or jealous (**D**).

2 This is a **judgement** question. **C** is correct. You read *My mother said, "I never yet could make out why men are so fond of this sport."* (see line 16) And later the narrator says, *My mother seemed much troubled … She never would go to that part of the field afterward* (see lines 21–22). The mother horse is puzzled about the popularity of the hunt and sad for her friend. **A** is only partially correct. The text says the mother is *troubled* so you can judge that she might be (**A**) sad but there's nothing in the text to suggest that she accepts that accidents happen during the hunt. **B** and **D** are true in the context of the text. You can judge that the mother is powerless to change things and that she is worried about the colts getting hurt but these are not answers to the question.

3 This is a **judgement** question. You read *Just then a hare wild with fright rushed by and made for the woods* (see line 6) and later *the dogs were upon her with their wild cries; we heard one shriek, and that was the end of her* (see lines 11–13). The text implies that the hare was torn apart by the dogs but because the narrator moves on to talk about the horse that has fallen, the reader doesn't have time to be too concerned about cruelty to

the hare. You read *As for me, I was so astonished that I did not at first see what was going on by the brook; but when I did look there was a sad sight; a fine horse lay groaning on the grass* (see lines 14–15). The narrator doesn't give the hare a second thought before referring to the *sad sight* of a *fine horse* that had fallen, and so the reader isn't expected to dwell on the hare either.

4 This is a **judgement** question. The story of *Black Beauty* was published in 1877. It is an anthropomorphic story in that the horses are given human feelings and concerns. It has a first-person narrator, the colt. You should judge that an animal narrator gives an animal's point of view of events and this would have helped readers empathise with horses and perhaps view animals more humanely than was usual at that time in history.

5 This is a **judgement** question. The main protagonists in the text are males: Black Beauty (the narrator), the men on horseback, Mr Bond, the farrier who shoots the horse, the horse that was shot. The only two females represented in the story are the colt's mother and the hare. You might make a judgement that most stories written in those times had males as heroes or protagonists. Females were usually mothers or sisters or were defenceless and helpless like the hare.

6 This is a **judgement** question. The hunt described in the text is not a sport in the dictionary sense of the meaning of *sport* because the hare as an individual cannot compete against a team of dogs and riders on horseback. You could suggest that physical exertion is involved. You might suggest that the riders need skill to stay upon their horses while leaping streams and racing through woods. You might suggest that the dogs enjoy themselves and the men find the activity entertaining. But you need to explain that six to eight men on horseback and a large number of dogs competing against one *hare wild with fright* (see line 6) does not fit in with the dictionary definition of *sport*.

Note: the type of hunting activity described in the book *Black Beauty* was popular in a number of countries for hundreds of years but the law now specifies that the hunted animal be killed humanely. Most countries have laws that state the dogs used for hunting must not be permitted to worry, maim or injure animals.

Mixed questions

Extremes (page 78)

1 C **2** C **3** D **4** A **5** D **6** See below

Explanations

1 This is a **synthesis** question. **C** is correct. You need to read the whole poem and think about meaning across the stanzas. The poem describes contrasts between *extremes* of weather as gentle or destructive. For example, you read *Rain: gentle drips feed the earth* (see line 6) and *scorching drought cracks open the earth and dries up all life* (see lines 14–15). The poem doesn't talk about predicting the weather (**A**). The poem doesn't give instructions about what to do in extreme weather (**B**). The poem does imply that people are unable to control the weather (**D**) but that is not what the poem is about.

2 This is a **fact-finding** question. **C** is correct. The answer is stated directly in the text. You read *but bullying gusts tear at my shirt; rip off my hat* (see line 3). **A**, **B** and **D** are incorrect. **A** is about fluttery breezes. **B** and **D** are about the wind affecting rain and dust rather than bullying people.

3 This is an **inferring** question. **D** is correct. The poet infers that extreme weather can be dangerous. You read *raging storms snatch branches off trees and roofs off the houses* (see lines 4–5) and *flooding rain blocks off the roads and isolates people* (see lines 9–10). **A** is incorrect. The poem does not imply that climate change is to blame. **B** is incorrect because the poem doesn't make the weather sound like fun. **C** is incorrect because the poem does not imply that dams will be filled.

4 This is a **judgement** question. **A** is correct. You can judge the tone of the text to determine the poet's attitude to the subject. The poet is inspired enough by the weather to write a poem about it. **B** is incorrect. The focus of the poem is to contrast the extremes of weather rather than to express any feelings of concern about harm caused by weather events. **C** is incorrect. The poet does not seem thrilled about the weather's unpredictability. **D** is incorrect. You could not judge the poet to be bored by the weather.

5 This is a **judgement** question. **D** is correct. You read *scorching drought cracks open the earth and dries up all life* (see lines 14–15) and can judge that the poet thinks drought is the worst. The poet does not accuse rain, wind or flood of drying up all life so **A**, **B** and **C** are incorrect.

6 This is a **judgement** question. Your answer will depend on your own experiences of extreme weather and the ways you have connected with the poem. For example, a person who has experienced the terror of bush fires will judge them differently from a person has not experienced that kind of extreme event. You may have experienced flooding, tropical storms, tidal surges, and so on. Make sure you explain why you judge that particular kind of weather as the worst.

Waltzing Matilda (page 79)

1 D **2** B **3** C **4** A **5** D **6** See below

Explanations

1 This is a **synthesis** question. **D** is correct. The song tells a story. It begins with an orientation to set the scene and to introduce the main character. It provides a complication when the swagman steals a sheep. The consequence is that the squatter brings the police to arrest the swagman. The resolution is the outcome or the way the story is resolved, as the swagman jumps into the billabong and dies. A coda is a final concluding statement or moral, *And his ghost may be heard as it sings by the billabong* (see lines 27–28). The other answers are incorrect. **A** is incorrect because a song is written in verses rather than stanzas. *Waltzing Matilda* has extra structural components not listed in **B** and **C**.

2 This is a **synthesis** question. **B** is correct. The function of an orientation is to introduce characters and set the scene. The orientation to *Waltzing Matilda* introduces the homeless man and the setting, by the billabongs under the shade of the tree. **A** omits the relevance of the setting. **C** implies that *Matilda* is a person rather than a swag or bedroll. **D** omits the introduction of the protagonist or main character, the swagman.

3 This is a **synthesis** question. **C** is correct. The function of a complication in a narrative is to introduce a problem for the main character. The swagman's problem was created when he stole the sheep. **A** is incorrect because the problem was not that he *camped in the billabongs* (see lines 2–3). **B** is incorrect because the sheep having a drink did not cause a problem for the swagman. **D** is incorrect because it is a consequence of the problem. The squatter arrives as a result of the sheep being stolen.

4 This is a **language** question. **A** is correct. The swagman viewed the sheep as food, and was gleeful (happy) to stash the food in his tucker bag. (*Tucker* is a word for food.) The other answers are incorrect. The use of *with glee* (see line 13) does not imply that the swagman was excited about stealing things (**B**). **C** is incorrect because *with glee* is not used to describe the sheep's emotions. **D** is incorrect because the swagman did not dance.

5 This is a **language** question. **D** is correct. The Footnotes to the text provide definitions for terms used in the song. To go *waltzing Matilda* (see line 9) is to go on the road (as swagmen did in those times) looking for work, with your bedroll as your backpack. It does not mean to go to jail (**A**), dance with a sheep (**B**) or dance with a swag (**C**).

6 This is a **judgement** question. You need to include your own thoughts and reasons to explain why this song has remained so popular in Australia. Perhaps you can judge it is because it was written by a famous poet, AB 'Banjo' Paterson. Perhaps Australians like the idea that the swagman avoided police. Perhaps some Australians like the use of historical terms such as *jumbuck* and *swagman* (see lines 11–12). Perhaps some people like the fact that the song has been around for a long time. Others might like the fact that it represents an era in Australia's history where people did go on the road looking for work. Or it might be that people like the idea of the jolly swagman's freedom in travelling the countryside and camping by billabongs. Make sure you justify your judgement.

Kaili Valley Wetlands (page 80)

1 D **2** B **3** C **4** D **5** B **6** See below

Explanations

1 This is a **judgement** question. **D** is correct. The report was commissioned by the government. You read *Summary of a Queensland Government Report* (see line 2) so you would expect it to be factual and trustworthy. You can also judge that there are no emotive terms or persuasive devices used in the text to influence opinions so other answers are incorrect.

2 This is a **synthesis** question. **B** is correct. You read *Development activities and resulting habitat degradation, including human interference with the area's natural water cycle pose similar potential risks to animal life at Kaili Valley Wetlands* (see lines 29–33). This conclusion can be summarised or paraphrased as human activity threatens fauna that use the area. **A** is a fact in the text but not a conclusion of the report. **C** and **D** are threats to the wetlands but not the full conclusion.

3 This is a **fact-finding** question. **C** is correct. You can find the answer stated directly in the text. You read that the report was commissioned to describe the '*environmental values of the Wetlands and the threats to these values*' *(see lines 3–5)*. The purpose of the report is to list everything valuable about the wetlands ie its fauna, and to assess any threats to those values. **A** and **D** mentions birdlife or fauna but not the potential risks. **B** only mentions threats and risks so is not the full answer.

4 This is a **fact-finding** question. **D** is correct. You read *human interference with the area's natural water cycle pose similar potential risks to animal life at Kaili Valley Wetlands. Sea-level rise is considered a long-term risk (see lines 30–34)*. **D** is not a fact in the text. **A**, **B** and **C** are facts that that are stated directly in the text.

5 This is a **fact-finding** question. **B** is correct. The answer is stated directly in the text. Migratory birds live part of the year in the wetlands and then leave. **A** is not a fact because you read that the Northern Quoll is a threatened species not an extinct species. **C** is incorrect because resident birds live in the wetlands all of the time not some of the time. **D** is incorrect because foraging animals use the wetlands as a corridor. They do not migrate to the wetlands.

6 This is a **judgement** question. You have to judge for yourself the value of the wetlands to Australia based on the evidence in the text. Explain your reasons using the values mentioned in the text to support your arguments. For example, you might state that saving endangered fauna from extinction is an important reason to protect the wetlands from development and human interference.

Monarch butterflies (page 81)

1 B **2** B, C and D **3** B **4** C **5** D
6 See below

Explanations

1 This is a **judgement** question. **B** is correct. You can judge the writer's feelings about the subject by the use of an evaluative adjective *amazing*. You read *Monarch butterflies … are amazing … because …* *(see lines 2–3)* **A** is incorrect because the writer does not express an opinion about the threats to the Monarch. **C** is incorrect because the writer does use an evaluative word, *amazing*. **D** is a fact in the text and does not answer the question.

2 This is a **judgement** question. **B**, **C** and **D** are all correct. You can judge that the writer included distances from real-life places (*Melbourne to Darwin* and *Sydney to Perth*) *(see line 11)* to put the distances into perspective for readers and make them relevant to an Australian audience. **A** is incorrect because including the distances will not tell readers how long it would take the Monarch to fly the distance as the text does not state how fast the Monarch flies.

3 This is a **synthesis** question. **B** is correct. You can connect the ideas in the text to work out that the purpose of the text is to provide information about a butterfly species. **A**, **C** and **D** are all only partially correct because the report includes this information but each of these is not the purpose of the report as a whole.

4 This is a **judgement** question. **C** is correct. You can judge that the main idea in the text is that Monarchs are different from other butterflies. Paragraph 1 outlines the structure of the report with a thesis statement that Monarchs are interesting for a number of reasons. These reasons are then explained in subsequent paragraphs. Paragraph 2 is about the migration. Paragraph 3 is about milkweed. Paragraph 3 is about the life cycle. All of these things make the Monarch different from other butterflies. **A**, **B** and **D** are facts in the text but each one is not the most important idea in the text.

5 This is a **language** question. **D** is correct. You read *a build-up of the milkweed chemical in the Monarch's body mean the insect is distasteful to predators (see lines 16–17)*. Examine the use of the negative prefix *dis* in *distasteful*. *Distasteful* means 'an unpleasant taste'. You can work out that insect eating animals do not like the taste of Monarchs. **A** is incorrect because milkweed is not poisonous to adult Monarchs. **B** is incorrect because this is not the meaning of the word *distasteful*. **C** is the opposite of the meaning in the text.

6 This is a **synthesis** question. Think about the information included in the report and the kind of information that you still do not know about the Monarch butterfly. Decide for yourself what further information might be of interest to readers that connects with the ideas already in the text or expands on them. For example, where Monarchs/Wanderers can be found in Australia. Whether anything is being done to protect them in the wild in North America and Mexico. Whether they are at risk of becoming a threatened species in Australia.

Film review: *The Lost Thing* (page 82)

1 B **2** C **3** D **4** C **5** See below
6 See below

Explanations

1 This is a **fact-finding** question. **B** is correct. The answer is stated directly in the text. You read *Each group's task was to share opinions ... then present a group consensus* (see lines 2–3). **A** and **D** are incorrect because, although the group discussed character and plot, these were not the only purpose of the discussion. **C** is incorrect because the purpose of the discussion was to share ideas rather than argue points of view.

2 This is a **judgement** question. **C** is correct. You read Molly's contributions to the discussion *I think it's the best film, just awesome* (see lines 8–9) and you can judge that Molly is the most enthusiastic about the film. She loved the characters, the setting and the film as a whole. Stephanie (**A**) liked the story but not the ending. Jonah (**B**) liked the animation, the sound effects and the music. Luca (**D**) liked plot, characterisation and setting.

3 This is a **fact-finding** question. **D** is correct. The answer is stated directly in the text. You read *the Thing ... only communicated with body language and bells* (see lines 5–6) and [it] *started jiggling on the beach, excited* (see line 7) and [it] *turned around to say goodbye with its bells* (see line 18). **A** is incorrect because the Thing does not talk. **B** is partially correct because the Thing jumps and jiggles to show excitement. **C** is partially correct because the Thing uses bells but there is no evidence in the text that it makes cute noises.

4 This is a **fact-finding** question. **C** is correct. The answer is stated directly in the text. You read that Molly says *I think the themes are belonging and being different* (see line 9). You read that Jonah says *I think another theme is responsibility* (see line 10). You read that Stephanie says *I guess one of the themes of the story is growing up* (see lines 22–23). Other answers are incorrect. **A** is incorrect because sadness is not mentioned as a theme, only as an aspect of the film towards its end related to the theme of growing up. **B** is the structure of the film's narrative as described by Stephanie. **D** is a description of the film provided by Luca.

5 This is a **synthesis** question. You need to draw together ideas from across the text to work out what the group's consensus about the film would be.

The group would report along the following lines: We enjoyed the film. It was a good story with a solid plot and well-developed characterisation and settings. We thought the animation was really clever and that the sound effects and music matched the film really well. The film covered important themes such as belonging and being different.

6 This is a **judgement** question. You have to decide for yourself, based on evidence in the text, whether children your age would enjoy the film *The Lost Thing.* You should judge that they would enjoy the film and cite the opinions of the children in the text to support your judgement, noting that the discussion group consisted of students in Year 5.

Geoffrey Gurrumul Yunupingu (page 83)

1 B **2** A **3** A, B, C and D **4** A, C and D
5 B **6** See below

Explanations

1 This is a **judgement** question. **B** is correct. Your read *His music is hauntingly beautiful and evocative* (see line 16). You need to judge the descriptions of Gurrumul's music and decide which answer is the best fit. You can judge that soulful and lyrical are appropriate descriptions of his music based on descriptions in the text. You read *He also played the didgeridoo* (see line 16) so you can decide that **A** is incorrect as the didgeridoo is only part of his music. Yothu Yindi was a rock band so **C** is incorrect for Gurrumul's solo performing. You read *Audiences around the world were spellbound* (see lines 16–17) and paragraph 3 lists well-known people who have been in his audience, so you can judge that **D** is incorrect because his music doesn't just appeal to young people.

2 This is a **synthesis** question. **A** is correct. You need to interpret and connect ideas across the text to answer this question. You can tell that the writer respects Gurrumul's remarkable abilities. There is nothing in the text to imply **B** and **C** although they are probably true. There is no evidence in the text to support **D**.

3 This is a **synthesis** question. You need to connect information from across the text to work out the correct answers are **A**, **B**, **C** and **D**. There is evidence in the text to support each statement.

4 This is an **inferring** question. **A**, **C** and **D** are correct. You read *He sang in the First Nations languages … His music speaks of his heritage* (see lines 15–17) and *sings the music of his ancestry* (see line 18) and you can infer that he valued his First Nations heritage. **B** is incorrect because the fact that his music can be described as *hauntingly beautiful and evocative* (see line 16) is not evidence that he valued his heritage.

5 This is a **judgement** question. **B** is correct. Every answer is true in the text but you need to judge how Gurrumul would have felt. You can judge from evidence in the text that family, heritage and culture were the most important things in his life, rather than fame (**A**) or that he played for the Queen (**D**) or that his uncle was Australian of the Year (**C**).

6 This is a **language** question. You need to use emotive and persuasive words to create an advertisement. You should use *hauntingly beautiful and evocative* (see line 16); *audiences … are spellbound* (see lines 16–17); *lyrical voice and musicianship* (see line 17); *numerous awards, including Best World Music Album at 2011 ARIA Artisan Awards* (see lines 11–12).

Pieces of Eight (page 84)

1 B **2** C **3** D **4** A **5** B
6 See below

Explanations

1 This is a **fact-finding** question. **B** is correct. The answer is stated directly in the text. The narrator could distinguish (see or make out) nothing. You read *All was dark within, so that I could distinguish nothing by the eye* (see line 2). **A** and **C** are incorrect. The narrator knew men were sleeping on the floor because he could hear their snores but he couldn't see them. **D** is incorrect. The narrator could not see his arms in the dark. You read *With my arms before me I walked steadily in* (see line 6). The narrator's arms are held in front as protection from bumping into things.

2 This is a **fact-finding** question. **C** is correct. You read *"Pieces of eight!" … Silver's green parrot, Captain Flint! It was she … who thus announced my arrival with her wearisome refrain* (see lines 13–17). The answer is stated directly in the text. This makes **A**, **B** and **D** incorrect.

3 This is a **language** question. **D** is correct. You read *"Pieces of eight! Pieces of eight! Pieces of eight! Pieces of eight! Pieces of eight!" and so forth, without pause or change* (see lines 12–13). You can work out the meaning of the expression *wearisome refrain* (see line 17) from the way it is used in the text. A refrain is something that's continually repeated. The word *wearisome* means 'tiresome or boring, continuous, repetitive'. **A** is incorrect. A refrain is not an announcement although Captain Flint did announce the narrator's arrival. **B** is incorrect although the bird's refrain is described as being *a shrill voice* (see line 11). **C** is incorrect although the bird's pecking sounds like *the clacking of a tiny mill* (see lines 13–14).

4 This is an **inferring** question. **A** is correct. You need to work out the answer by reading between the lines in the text. It is Silver who commands Dick to bring a torch. You can infer that Silver is in charge. Dick is commanded to bring a torch so you can tell he is not in charge (**B**). Captain Flint is the green parrot so it is not in charge (**C**). The narrator tried to sneak in but now he has been detained, so he is not in charge (**D**).

5 This is a **language** question. **B** is correct. *Torch* and *lighted brand* are synonyms in the text. You read *"Bring a torch, Dick," said Silver when my capture was thus assured. And one of the men left the log-house and presently returned with a lighted brand* (see lines 22–23). You can work out the meaning of the term *torch* the way it is used. You should realise that **A** and **C** are incorrect because of the historical context of the extract. **D** could be correct but it is not used as a synonym for *torch* in the text.

6 This is a **synthesis** question. You need to consider ideas across the text and imagine them visually in a sequence of images that can carry the important moments in the story. Your storyboard could have the following sequence:

Frame 1: the narrator with arms stretched before him.

Frame 2: the narrator's foot hits a sleeper's leg.

Frame 3: the parrot shouts "Pieces of Eight".

Frame 4: the sleepers wake up and Silver cries out "Who goes?"

Frame 5: someone grabs the narrator while Silver calls for a torch.

Frame 6: a lighted brand illuminates the narrator.

Remember that you do not need to be an artist to create a storyboard. You just need to get the meaning across visually.

Coral reefs (page 85)

1 B **2** B **3** D **4** C **5** See below
6 See below

Explanations

1. This is a **fact-finding** question. **B** is correct. You read *The coral polyp and the algae have a symbiotic relationship. This means they are of mutual benefit to each other* (see lines 12–13). The answer is stated directly in the text. *Symbiosis* means that both benefit. **A** and **C** are incorrect because they only mention one species benefitting another and omit the concept of mutual benefit. **D** is incorrect because it is not accurate or factual in the text.
2. This is a **fact-finding** question. **B** is correct. You read *The calcium carbonate skeletons of coral-forming polyps are the structures left behind as polyps die* (see lines 2–3). The answer is stated directly in the text. **A**, **C** and **D** are incorrect because coral is not made of these things.
3. This is a **synthesis** question. **D** is correct. You read *Warmer water stresses coral polyps and they expel the algae. This is referred to as coral bleaching because the algae give coral its colour* (see lines 13–14). You need to connect the ideas in the text. The answer paraphrases the information in the text. Coral bleaching occurs because the oceans become warmer. **A** refers to acidification and not coral bleaching. **B** and **C** are inaccurate.
4. This is a **fact-finding** question. **C** is correct. You read that *Ocean acidification* is when *Oceans absorb carbon dioxide* and this *dissolves coral skeletons* (see lines 5–7). The answer is stated directly in the text. **A** and **B** are incorrect because they tell what happens but not how acidification harms coral. **D** is incorrect because it's a statement about air pollution and it doesn't answer the question.
5. This is an **inferring** question. The answer is not stated directly in the text. You need to read between the lines. You read the paragraph with the subheading *Erosion* (see line 19). You should infer that *construction* (see line 21) includes a coastal building project. Your answer should state that loose soil is washed into the ocean when it rains. The soil smothers reefs and blocks out their sunlight.
6. This is an **inferring** question. The answer is not stated directly in the text. You need to read between the lines. You read that *pesticide and fertiliser contamination caused by agricultural run-off* (see line 16) is a threat to coral reefs. You can infer that agricultural run-off is due to farming practices.

Heroism (page 86)

1 D **2** C **3** B **4** See below **5** See below
6 See below

Explanations

1. This is a **judgement** question. **D** is correct. You need to find the reference to *ordinary people* in paragraph 1 and judge what is meant by the phrase. Paragraph 1 tells you that a hero might be from the military or the public service where people are trained to do their jobs. An ordinary person from the local community (i.e. someone's neighbour) is not trained to be heroic. They just step into that role if they are needed.
2. This is a **judgement** question. **C** is correct. You need to read the text and judge that the writer thinks a hero is person who helps others. The writer would not agree with **A**, **B** or **D**; a person doesn't have to be famous or a soldier or in a war to be her hero.
3. This is a **judgement** question. **B** is correct. The purpose of the text is for the writer to reflect on the topic of heroism. You read the whole text and you can judge that the writer is writing her own thoughts about heroes. She does not attempt to write persuasive arguments on the importance of heroism (**D**) or persuade others to agree with her opinions (**A**). She does not define the concept of a hero (**C**).
4. This is a **language** question. When Pa says that Nan is a brick he is using a metaphor. A metaphor is when one thing is said to be another. Pa doesn't mean that Nan is literally a brick. Pa means that Nan has the qualities of a brick. Think for yourself about what this could mean about Nan. The implication of the metaphor is that Pa thinks Nan is dependable, solid, reliable and strong—you build houses with bricks. Bricks are the foundations of buildings and so Nan is a foundation for the family with her strength and dependability.
5. This is a **judgement** question. You need to make a judgement about the writer, Chloe. The text tells you that she values helping others and admires people who do help others, such as her grandparents and Corporal Roberts-Smith. She likes working as a member of a team and lists this as one reason for believing she would enjoy being in the navy. You can tell she is adventurous because she wants to work overseas in disaster relief areas. You can also judge that she is brave because even though she admits that she would not want to fight in a war she does think she

would like to be involved in peace-keeping missions and these can be dangerous.

6 This is a **synthesis** question. You need to take into account everything that Chloe has stated in the text and then connect this to your own ideas about heroes. Your answer cannot be wrong if you have thought clearly about the topic and included personal reflections on the concept of heroes.

The Terracotta Army (page 87)

1 C **2** D **3** C **4** D **5** C **6** See below

Explanations

1 This is a **synthesis** question. **C** is correct. You read *We're having fun travelling with lots of other grandparents* (see line 22). The text is an email from grandparents (Nonna and Nonno) to a family member (Joshua), telling him about a holiday. **A** is incorrect as the text is not persuasive. **B** is incorrect because the text is for a specific familiar audience and not for the general public. **D** doesn't take into account the familiar audience.

2 This is a **synthesis** question. **D** is correct. You read the heading *Exploripedia: The free encyclopedia* (see line 24) and then the information included in the text and you can work out that the text provides general information for the public. The other answers are incorrect. It is not a persuasive text (**A** and **C**). There is not enough technical or detailed information to conclude that the text is for scientists (**B**).

3 This is a **judgement** question. **C** is correct. You can judge that Josh's grandparents are adventurous because they are currently travelling in China and have previously been to Egypt. You can judge that they are fun-loving because they talk excitedly about their trip and mention having fun. **A** and **D** are incorrect. There is no evidence in the text to show that the grandparents are judgemental or cautious. **B** contradicts the evidence in the text.

4 This is a **judgement** question. **D** is correct. The email has an informal and playful tone. The grandparents are happy, and impressed by their trip. **A**, **B** and **C** are incorrect because the tone of the email is not formal, serious or solemn.

5 This is a **language** question. **C** is correct. You read that the Terracotta Army is a collection of sculptures and *examples of funerary art, art made to commemorate the dead* (see line 29). You can work out in the context of the text that an ice sculpture is not an example of funerary art. **A**, **B** and **D** are incorrect. Tombstones, coffins and war memorials are all made to commemorate the dead.

6 This is a **judgement** question. You need to place yourself in Josh's shoes and think about how you would feel as you read the email from your grandparents. You should judge that he would feel pleased and happy that his grandparents are having a lovely trip but he might also feel a little envious and wish that he could see the Terracotta Army, too.

Royal kidnapping thwarted (page 88)

1 A **2** C **3** A **4** C **5** D **6** See below

Explanations

1 This is a **judgement** question. **A** is correct. You need to read the text and think about what the text reveals about each character to judge who would agree with the statement. You read that Cindy Ella danced all night with Prince Harry so the Prince might have considered her very engaging and fun. **B** is incorrect because Lord Montybaton didn't like Cindy Ella. He said, '*I thought she looked shifty. I'm not surprised she is a kidnapper.*' (see lines 37–38). **C** is incorrect because Poly Minions believed Cindy to be a kidnapper. **D** is incorrect as the Queen called Cindy an *evil woman* (see line 41).

2 This is a **language** question. **C** is correct. If you are familiar with the words *poly* and *minions* you have clues about why the writer chose this name for the character in charge of palace security. *Poly* is a word that means 'many'. *Minions* is a word that means 'underlings'. The name implies that the character likes to be the boss and have people doing her bidding. **A** is a fact in the text but does not represent the full implications of the name. **B** is probably correct but there's no evidence in the text to support the claim. There is no evidence in the text to suggest **D** is correct.

3 This is a **judgement** question. **A** is correct. You can judge characters based on what they say to or about others. You can judge that Lord Montybaton is a suspicious man by his comment '*I thought she looked shifty. I'm not surprised she is a kidnapper.*' (see lines 37–38).There is no evidence in the text to support **B**, **C** or **D**.

4 This is a **judgement** question. **C** is correct. You can judge that Lady Camellia is the most credible witness because she tells what we know to be a fact. You read '*I saw them dancing all night and he couldn't stop smiling*' (see lines 34–36). The other answers are incorrect because Poly Minions, Eva Rafter and Lord Montybaton only give their

opinions and their opinions are not confirmed by events in the text.

5 This is a **language** question. **D** is correct. The words *have not confirmed* (see lines 42–43) tell you that allegations of a Step-sisters gang and kidnapping attempt are probably exaggerated and sensationalised by the newspaper and not accurate. The statement doesn't imply that the allegations will be confirmed (**A**). There is no evidence to suggest that detectives are concerned about bad publicity (**B**) or that they want to keep secrets. The report was not a secret because it was in the newspaper (**C**).

6 This is a **language** question. *Royal kidnapping thwarted* (see line 3) is based on a fairy tale, *Cinderella*. There is word play in *Cindy Ella* (Cinderella) (see line 9) and *Eva Rafter* (Ever After) (see line 24) to give you clues. The text is a parody of a newspaper article with interview quotes and sensationalism.

Y-o-u-u Tom (page 89)

1 B **2** A and B, D **3** B **4** C **5** D
6 See below

Explanations

1 This is a **fact-finding** question. **B** is correct. You read Aunt was *punching under the bed with the broom, and so she needed breath to punctuate the punches with. She resurrected nothing but the cat* (see lines 20–23). The answer is stated directly in the text. The narrator uses the term *resurrected* to indicate that the cat rose from under the bed. **A** is incorrect. Aunt poked a broom under the bed to locate Tom. **C** is incorrect because Tom was in the closet. **D** is incorrect because the cat had been under the bed.

2 This is a **synthesis** question. Answers **A**, **B** and **D** are correct. Visualise the paragraph that begins *The old lady pulled her spectacles down* (see line 8). You can see how Aunt wears her spectacles. You need to synthesise the information across the paragraph to work out that the glasses *were built for "style," not service* (see lines 13–14) but Aunt loved them. They were the *pride of her heart* (see line 13). **C** is incorrect because the glasses were not used to see through.

3 This is a **language** question. **B** is correct. You need to think about the meaning of the term *slack of his roundabout* (see line 30). You can work out that a *roundabout* must be an article of clothing. The *slack* part of it would be an area of loose fabric that Aunt could seize or grab hold of. To *arrest his flight* (see line 30) means to stop him getting away. The narrator introduces Tom to readers as *a small boy* (see line 29) in this part of the text as this is the first time we 'see' him. We know the *small boy* is Tom because Aunt has been searching for him. **A** is incorrect because it doesn't name Tom as the small boy. **C** is incorrect as it doesn't mention that Aunt stops Tom's escape. **D** is incorrect because it refers to a strange boy instead of Tom.

4 This is an **inferring** question. **C** is correct. *Peril* means danger. *The peril was desperate* (see lines 40–41) means immediate danger or imminent danger. You have to read between the lines to work out what was happening in the scene. Aunt was about to hit Tom with the switch (a thin cane). **A**, **B** and **D** are incorrect. There was no fire, or lad about to grab Aunt's skirts or anything dangerous lurking behind Aunt.

5 This is an **inferring** question. **D** is correct. You read the part of the text that says Aunt identified that Tom had been eating jam: *"Look at your hands. And look at your mouth. What is that?" "I don't know, Aunt." "Well, I know. It's jam—that's what it is."* (see lines 34–37) Tom had been hiding in the closet and eating jam that he'd been told *forty times* (see lines 37–38) not to take. **A**, **B** and **C** are incorrect. Tom was not looking for the cat or playing in the closet, and even though he answers *"Nothing"* (see line 33) when Aunt asks what he'd been doing in the closet, this is not true.

6 This is an **inferring** question. Read between the lines to work out that Tom tricked Aunt into thinking that there was something behind her that she needed to be fearful of and while she was distracted he quickly escaped outside and climbed over a high fence to get away.

News of Ned Kelly (page 90)

1 D **2** A **3** C **4** C **5** B **6** See below

Explanations

1 This is a **language** question. **D** is correct. *Great doings* (see line 7) include the wounding and capture of Ned Kelly and the end of the Kelly Gang. **A** is true in the text but not the correct answer. The writer seems excited about seeing Ned Kelly in person but this is not the *great doings* discussed in the letter. **B** is incorrect because the newspaper is not the *great doings*. **C** is incorrect as the letter doesn't describe bank robberies and law-breaking.

2 This is a **fact-finding** question. **A** is correct. You read *His body and head being encased in armour. The police thought he was a fiend seeing their rifle bullets were sliding off him like hail* (see lines 12–13). The answer is stated directly in the text. **B** is an opinion expressed by police and not the reason bullets did not kill Ned Kelly. **C** is a fact in the text but not the answer to the question. **D** is what happened when the bullets hit the armour but this doesn't answer the question.

3 This is a **judgement** question. **C** is correct. You read *it was only when they got him on the legs and arms that he reluctantly fell exclaiming as he did so "I am done"* (see lines 13–14). You can judge that Kelly would have kept fighting in spite of pain until he couldn't fight anymore. **B** is incorrect as it doesn't make sense. **A** and **D** are incorrect because there is no evidence in the text that being worried or in pain would have deterred Ned Kelly from continuing to fight.

4 This is an **inferring** question. **C** is correct. You read *He said he wouldn't care for himself if he thought his mare was safe* (see lines 21–22). You can infer that the writer found it fascinating that Ned Kelly was more concerned about the welfare of his horse than himself. You can infer that the writer wanted to convey this idea to his parents. **A** is incorrect because the writer would not have felt he needed proof for his parents to believe him. **B** and **D** are incorrect because there's no evidence in the text that the writer was a show-off.

5 This is a **judgement** question. **B** is correct. The writer's opinion of Ned Kelly is that he was a murderer and bushranger who became tame when captured. **A** is incorrect because it was the police who briefly thought Kelly was a fiend and not the writer. **C** and **D** are incorrect because they are physical descriptions of Kelly rather than opinions about his character.

6 This is an **inferring** question. You need to infer what the writer means by *Such then is Bushranging in Victoria so far* (see line 19) at the conclusion of his letter. You can infer the writer means that bushrangers are killed, or captured and executed in prison. *Such then* means 'this is what happens'. *So far* means that the writer expects to have further news in the next letter—the next instalment of great doings about bushranging in Victoria.

TV program: *Live at 10 am* (page 91)

1 D **2** B **3** D **4** A **5** C **6** See below

Explanations

1 This is a **synthesis** question. **D** is correct. Michelle states at the beginning of the interview, in response to the compere's first question, *We are concerned about the increase in Type 2 Diabetes* (see lines 14–16) but you need to read the whole text to confirm this is what is of most concern to her. Michelle is also concerned about the information listed in **A**, **B** and **C** but not most concerned.

2 This is a **synthesis** question. **B** is correct. You need to read all the compere's dialogue to determine the answer. The compere's role is to move the interview along at a pace that will keep viewers interested. The compere does not express any point of view or particular concern about the topic. **A**, **C** and **D** are topics mentioned but not the compere's priority.

3 This is an **inferring** question. **D** is correct. You need to read the whole text to be able to infer what it is that a nutritionist does. Thomas Walters is introduced on the program as an *Accredited Nutritionist* (see line 4). His responses to the compere's questions are all about what to eat for health and to prevent illness. **A**, **B** and **C** are each only part of his job.

4 This is a **judgement** question. **A** is correct. You need to judge the content of the program. The program seems informative and even-handed. It presents factual information about Type 2 Diabetes. **B** is incorrect because you can judge that the number of people disclosed as having diabetes is accurate and not biased. **C** is incorrect. You read *Accredited Nutritionist, Thomas Walters and Certified Personal Trainer, Michelle Bright* (see lines 4–6) so you can judge that the experts have relevant credentials. **D** is incorrect because you can judge that there is enough relevant factual content to convince a viewer about the importance of the information.

5 This is a **fact-finding** question. **C** is correct. You read *Type 2 Diabetes is preventable through a healthy lifestyle. That's a healthy diet, a healthy weight and regular exercise. And don't smoke, of course* (see lines 35–39). **A** is incorrect because it leaves out *a healthy weight* and *no smoking*. **B** is incorrect because fruit and vegetables are only part of a healthy lifestyle. **D** is incorrect because it leaves out *no smoking*.

6 This is a **judgement** question. You need to judge the evidence in the interview and its relevance to your life or your family. You might, for example, state that you already have a healthy lifestyle, with a good diet and exercise so the interview would not have any influence on you. Or you might say that after reading the interview you have concerns about lifestyle choices your family members make and you will try to make a difference. Make sure you explain the reasons for your judgement.

The rules of this ride (page 92)

1 D **2** B **3** D **4** C **5** See below
6 See below

Explanations

1 This is a **judgement** question. **D** is correct. You can judge that the rules are not real. They are a send-up or parody. They make fun of the rules for rides at theme parks. **A**, **B** and **C** are incorrect because the rules are a parody.

2 This is a **judgement** question. **B** is correct. On a real ride a rule such as this would be impractical as all the items left behind on a platform could get stolen. You can judge that people getting on a ride would never be told to take off their jewellery or leave their wallets and purses behind. Also you read *Gameworld accepts no responsibility for illness, accidents, injury, death, lost or stolen items* (see lines 34–35) and you understand that leaving items on the platform risks theft. **A**, **C** and **D** are incorrect.

3 This is a **language** question. **D** is correct. The two items are aids to use for vision. **A**, **B** and **C** are incorrect because you don't wear them on your eyes. **A** is also incorrect because it is for vision impairment, whereas sunglasses in the question are not for vision impairment.

4 This is an **inferring** question. **C** is correct. You read *Persons over 151 cm not allowed on roller-coaster* (see lines 4–5). A person 152 cm tall would be deemed unsuitable for the ride. **A** is incorrect. You read *Persons under 150 cm not allowed on roller-coaster* (see lines 2–3) so you know that a person of 150 cm would be deemed suitable. **B** is incorrect. You read *Do not throw food or money out of roller-coaster* (see lines 27–28) so you can infer that people are allowed to eat on the roller-coaster. **D** is incorrect. You read *No sunglasses ... prosthetic limbs allowed* (see lines 11–13) and *Leave all possessions, including ... limbs and other valuables on the platform* (see lines 16–18). You can infer that people can use the ride if they take off their prosthetic limbs.

5 This is an **inferring** question. You need to think about cats and a reason for them to be *especially* (see line 20) not allowed on the ride. You can infer that any pet could be dangerous on the ride. They could fall out and get hurt or hurt someone. You could infer that cats are banned because they might climb and damage equipment. Cats also have claws and might scratch people if frightened.

6 This is a **language** question. The odd one out is *stethoscopes* because this device is used by a doctor to listen to your chest and heartbeat. The other devices are all used to see through.

Resistance (page 93)

1 B **2** C **3** See below **4** See below
5 See below **6** See below

Explanations

1 This is a **fact-finding** question. **B** is correct. You read *... used guerrilla tactics .... Small bands of warriors used mobility, stealth and surprise to attack larger, stronger forces that had superior weaponry* (see lines 12–13). First Nations warriors were outnumbered and had inferior weaponry so they needed to rely on *mobility, stealth and surprise*. **A** is incorrect. There is nothing in the text to say that guerrillas are strong. **C** is untrue in the text because First Nations warriors were the ones who were outnumbered. **D** is incorrect as retaliation is the last thing the First Nations warriors would have wanted to instigate.

2 This is a **judgement** question. **C** is correct. In order to judge what the majority of colonists in 1802 would have called First Nations warriors you need to think about the information and ideas in the text and what the text says about life in the colonies at that time. None of the European colonists were happy about the deaths of white settlers. You should recognise that the colonists would have viewed First Nations Australian resistance fighters as murderers and savages. **A**, **B** and **D** would not represent the opinions of the majority of white settlers in 1802.

3 This is a **judgement** question. To answer this question you need to judge the information in the text. The early settlers felt they had a legal right to the land because it had been declared terra nullius. They felt justified in defending their land and themselves.

4 This is a **judgement** question. To answer this question you need to make a judgement about First Nations Australians' point of view at the time of the First Fleet. Your answer should include these concepts: 'We have a right to use our traditional lands for water, and for hunting and gathering, and to access our sacred sites.'

5 This is a **judgement** question. You need to re-read paragraph 4 and understand the consequences of the massacre. You read that *Seven of the stockmen were eventually convicted of murder and hanged. This was the first time that settlers were successfully prosecuted for First Nations deaths* (see lines 17–19). Your answer needs to reflect your understanding that white settlers, guilty of murdering First Nations people, had never before been found guilty in an Australian court and punished for their offences. You might consider that the judges in the courts were European settlers too and so would have been fearful for their own lives and interested in protecting their own property. They might also have held racist attitudes towards First Nations Australians.

6 This is a **judgement** question. To work out the answer to this question you need to have read and understood the whole text and judge that the text is supportive of First Nations Australians. It uses emotive terms such as *invaded, invaders, depriving, reprisals, tragedy* and *massacre* to describe the treatment of First Nations Australians.

Why sea levels are rising (page 94)

1 C **2** C **3** B **4** B **5** D **6** See below

Explanations

1 This is a **fact-finding** question. **C** is correct. You read *In Antarctica warmer seas are undermining the ice shelf from below, causing large masses of ice to break off. As soon as these chucks of ice hit the sea they cause the sea level to rise* (see lines 8–11). The answer is stated directly in the text.

A is incorrect. Surface melt only causes sea levels to rise if it runs off land into the sea. **B** and **D** are incorrect because they don't answer why the ice shelf is melting.

2 This is a **fact-finding** question. **C** is correct. You read *In Greenland warmer weather is causing the ice sheet to melt at the surface* (see lines 5–6). **A** and **D** are facts in the text but do not answer the question. **B** is not a fact in the text and does not relate to the question.

3 This is a **fact-finding** question. **B** is correct. It is the only accurate answer available. **A** is incorrect because melting icebergs do not cause sea levels to rise. Answers **C** and **D** are statements of fact that do not answer the question.

4 This is an **inferring** question. **B** is correct. You read *Seawater floods agricultural land contaminating it with salt* (see lines 19–20). From this, you can infer that food crops can't be grown on soil ruined by salt. **A** and **C** are incorrect as this will not have an impact on food production. **D** is a fact in the text but does not explain how sea-level rise impacts on food production.

5 This is a **synthesis** question. **D** is correct. When you synthesise the information from across the text you can work out that the purpose of the text is to explain about some impacts of climate change. The text connects climate change to rising sea levels and the problems this causes. **A**, **B** and **C** are topics discussed in the text but not the purpose of the text as a whole. Note that you can tell the writer of the text has a point of view because of the subtly emotive claims such as *water shortages* (see line 15) and *completely submerged* (see line 28).

6 This is a **synthesis** question. To draw a conclusion from the text you need to have read and understood the meaning of the whole text and be able to summarise it. You could draw the conclusion that climate change is contributing to sea-level rise through melting surface ice running into the sea, through warmer oceans undermining the Antarctic ice shelf and because warmer oceans expand and rise.

The Day of Scrapes (page 95)

1 B **2** C **3** A **4** D **5** C **6** See below

Explanations

1 This is a **language** question. **B** is correct. You read *A constant feud raged between the two schools as to the respective merits of the teachers and the instruction* (see lines 7–8) and *the feud raged so high, that sometimes it was hardly safe for a Knight to meet a Millerite in the street* (see lines 18–20). You can work out the meaning of the word *feud* by examining the way it is used in the text. You can tell that *feud* in this context means 'fight'. It does not mean 'comparison' (**A**) or 'competition' (**C**). Although the girls did compete over who had the better school, the text provides evidence that the competition was more aggressive than simply a competition. **D** is incorrect because there is no discussion referred to in the text.

2 This is a **language** question. **C** is correct. You read *The Knight girls could make faces too, for all their gentility* (see lines 13–14). You can work out the meaning of the word *genteel* by examining the way *gentility* is used in the text. You can work

out that *genteel* girls would not usually pull faces, meaning they must be polite and well mannered. The antonym for *genteel* used in the text is *vulgar*. *Vulgar* means 'badly mannered or rude'. **A**, **B** and **D** are incorrect because they are not the meaning of the word as it is used in the text.

3 This is a **language** question. **A** is correct. You read *the girls used to sit in rows, turning up their noses at the next yard, and irritating the foe by jeering remarks (see lines 16–17)*. You can work out the meaning of *turning up their noses* by examining the way it is used in the text. When you turn up your nose you act as if you are better than others or superior to them. Feeling inferior (**B**) is the opposite in meaning. You can work out that *turning up their noses* does not mean 'making annoying faces' (**C**) or 'being mean' (**D**).

4 This is a **language** question. **D** is correct. You read *the Miller girls, on the other hand, retaliated by being as aggravating as they knew how (see lines 9–10)*. You can work out the meaning of *aggravating* by examining the way it is used in the text. *Aggravating* means 'annoying'. You can work out that being aggravating is a negative behaviour and so it is not **A**, **B** or **C**.

5 This is a **fact-finding** question. **C** is correct. You read *The Knight girls … Their yard … possessed a wood-shed, with a climbable roof, which commanded Miss Miller's premises, and upon this the girls used to sit in rows … (see lines 13–16)*. The answer is stated directly in the text. You can visualise the Knight girls sitting on the roof of the wood-shed in their yard looking down upon the Miller girls. The Miller yard did not have a wood-shed so **A** and **B** are incorrect. **D** is incorrect. The wood-shed would have stored wood but this is not how the girls used the wood-shed.

6 This is a **fact-finding** question. You read *Miss Miller's school, equally large and popular (see line 3)* and *A constant feud raged between the two schools as to the respective merits of the teachers and the instruction (see lines 7–8)*. The answer is stated directly in the text. You can work out that the girls were very competitive. Each set of girls strongly believed that their teacher and school was the better of the two.

TEXT OVERVIEW GRID

Page no.	Title	Type of text	Additional teaching points	Writing activity
		Fact-finding questions		
26	An emergency	Informative—recount	Dialling 000; paramedics; first person narrator	Write a recount of an event in your life.
30	The Eureka Stockade	Informative—report	The Victorian goldfields; colonial Australia	Research a historical event and write a report, or do further research and write an account of the Eureka Stockade event for a newspaper of the day.
31	Huntsman spiders	Informative—report	Subjective language; paragraphing	Research and then write a report about a living thing.
32	Australian bush tucker	Informative—report	Indigenous foods; paragraphing	Research other kinds of Australian bush tucker and write a report, or research foods from another country and write a report.
33	Day for children	Informative—newspaper article	UNICEF; Global issues; Australia's neighbours	Research and then write a report about a country in Asia or the work of UNICEF.
		Synthesis questions		
34	The Grey Cub	Imaginative—narrative	*White Fang* by Jack London; classic literature; third-person narrator; topic sentences; foreshadowing	Write a book review for a novel.
38	Book review: *Home and Away*	Persuasive—book review	*Home and Away*—a picture book by John Marsden and Matt Ottley; asylum seekers and refugees	Create a picture book based on a topic in the news such as climate change or a natural disaster. Or write a report about a refugee organisation such as the Refugee Council of Australia.
39	The woylie	Informative—interview	Radio interview transcript; endangered native animals	Research an endangered species. Write an interview transcript to present the information on radio or TV.
40	John Macarthur	Persuasive—argument	John and Elizabeth Macarthur; the wool industry; the colony of NSW; point of view	Write an argument text that gives your point of view about a historical figure, a current celebrity or a character from a novel.
41	The Chinese on the goldfields	Informative—report	Lambing Flats riots; immigration; racist attitudes in colonial Australia	Research Australia's current anti-discrimination laws. Write a report. Or write a persuasive text about aspects of racism.
		Inferring questions		
42	Someone's been eating my porridge	Imaginative—narrative	Folktale; parody: *Goldilocks and the Three Bears*; third-person narrator	Write a parody of a traditional tale. Change the gender of a character, change the resolution or make the setting present day.

Page no.	Title	Type of text	Additional teaching points	Writing activity
		Inferring questions *(continued)*		
46	The finals	Imaginative—narrative	Realism genre; third-person narrative; female protagonist	Write a realistic narrative.
47	Robogal a winner!	Informative—newspaper article	Gender equity; Australia Day Awards	Write a newspaper article about a Young Australian of the Year Award winner.
48	My grandmother	Informative—description	Multicultural families; grandparents; immigration; refugees; Romania	Write a description of a family member. Include information about his or her culture and/or history.
49	Halloween	Persuasive—correspondence	Informal digital communication—email, SMS; point of view	Choose a topic and write opposing points of view about it.
50	Landcare	Persuasive—speech	Volunteering; the environment; sustainability; the structure of a persuasive speech	Write a persuasive speech. Include thesis, arguments and supporting evidence, and a conclusion.
51	Missing person	Imaginative—report	Poster; parody of Cinderella fairy tale	Create a missing person report for a story character.
52	Invader	Imaginative—poem	Introduced species; feral pigs	Write a poem that deals with a social or environmental issue.
53	The jungle above	Imaginative—narrative	Fantasy genre—entering 'other' worlds; third-person narrator; setting; narrative structure	Write a narrative where characters enter a fantasy world.
		Language questions		
54	Royal kidnapping thwarted	Informative—newspaper article	Sensationalism; parody; interview quotes	Write a sensationalised news article based on a fairy tale (e.g. *Little Red Riding Hood*).
58	A dog	Persuasive—description	Point of view; idiom; emotive language	Write an emotive description.
59	Bella's party	Imaginative—narrative	Third-person narrative; conversation; point of view	Write a playscript that uses dialogue to present characters' points of view.
60	The neighbours	Informative—recount	First-person narrator; conflict resolution	Write a formal letter of complaint or appreciation to your local council.
61	Pets	Persuasive—Letters to the Editor	Point of view; modality	Write a letter to the Editor of a newspaper in response to a letter published there.
62	Another day in Parliament	Imaginative—comic strip	Satire; irony; idiom	Draw a comic strip send-up of something or someone in the news.
63	The life of Herman	Imaginative—narrative storyboard	Film-making; shot types; point of view; visual language	Create a storyboard for a scene from a novel you are reading.
64	A foiled plan	Imaginative—narrative	First-person narrator; conversation; dialogue; idiom; point of view	Write a narrative. Include yourself as a character and first-person narrator.
65	Feral animals in Australia	Informative—report	Objectivity in factual writing; paragraphing	Write an objective account of a local issue or write your point of view on the topic of feral animals and how to eradicate them.

Page no.	Title	Type of text	Additional teaching points	Writing activity
		Judgement questions		
66	Joose	Persuasive—advertisement	Evaluative and emotive words and phrases; modality; persuasive devices	Write an advertisement for the same Joose product but your target audience is people your own age, or write a poster ad for a shop that sells healthy food and/or beverages.
70	Targeting Maths Year 5 app	Persuasive—advertisement	Evaluative and emotive words and phrases; modality; persuasive devices	Choose an app or a game that you enjoy playing. Create an advertisement for it. Target children your age.
71	The shark debate	Persuasive—debate	Argument; point of view; modality; persuasive devices	Write an argument text to present your point of view on an environmental issue.
72	Teacher trouble	Imaginative—playscript	Dialogue; point of view; body language; characterisation	Work with a partner to role-play a conversation between two friends; then write your dialogue as a play script.
73	Endangered languages	Persuasive—argument	Indigenous languages; endangered languages; point of view	Write a letter asking a particular audience for support on an issue that concerns you.
74	Longline fishing	Persuasive—argument	Point of view	Write two texts that present different points of view on an issue.
75	Book review: *The One and Only Ivan*	Persuasive—book review	*The One and Only Ivan* by Katherine Applegate (a novel with an animal protagonist); point of view	Write a book review.
76	Slaves for sugar	Informative—report	Colonial history; indentured labour in Queensland 1860–1903; point of view	Write a report about an aspect of Australian history.
77	The Hunt	Imaginative—narrative	*Black Beauty* by Anna Sewell, 1877; classic literature; anthropomorphism; gender representation; autobiography	Write a third-person anthropomorphic narrative, written to show the points of view of animal characters.
		Mixed questions		
78	Extremes	Imaginative—poem	The weather; extremes of weather events	Write a poem based on comparisons about aspects of a topic.
79	Waltzing Matilda	Imaginative—song lyrics (narrative)	Song lyrics by AB 'Banjo' Paterson, 1895; historical context; classic literature	Choose a song and explain its historical context (e.g. 'With my swag all on my shoulder' or 'From little things big things grow').
80	Kaili Valley Wetlands	Informative—report	Formal reports; technical terminology	Write a formal report on an area of the environment.
81	Monarch butterflies	Informative—report	Paragraphing; animal migration; adaptation	Write a report about an animal that migrates long distances.
82	Film review: *The Lost Thing*	Persuasive—discussion/film review	*The Lost Thing*, a film by Shaun Tan; point of view; plot; characterisation; setting; film-making concepts (sound effects and music)	Write a review of a film or television show.

Page no.	Title	Type of text	Additional teaching points	Writing activity
Mixed questions *(continued)*				
83	Geoffrey Gurrumul Yunupingu	Informative—biography	Australian musicians; famous Australians; Indigenous Australians; paragraphing	Write a biography of an Aboriginal or Torres Strait Islander person.
84	Pieces of Eight	Imaginative—narrative	Extract from *Treasure Island* by Robert Louis Stevenson; classic literature; adventure genre	Write an adventure story.
85	Coral reefs	Informative—report	Ecosystems; the marine environment; factual, objective writing	Research a particular aspect of marine environments and write a report.
86	Heroism	Informative—personal reflection	Defence force roles in international humanitarian and peace keeping efforts; point of view	Write a reflection on the history of a family member and how you relate to it.
87	Text 1: Terracotta Army Text 2: Exploripedia: The free encyclopedia: The Terracotta Army	Informative—Text 1 email Text 2 report	Formal and informal writing; purpose and audience; tone; register (field tenor mode)	Choose a topic of interest and write a formal text and an informal text covering the same subject matter.
88	Royal kidnapping thwarted	Imaginative—newspaper article	Parody: *Cinderella* fairy tale; point of view; characterisation	Write a playscript based on a fairy tale but use a modern-day setting.
89	Y-o-u-u Tom	Imaginative—narrative	*The Adventures of Tom Sawyer* by Mark Twain, 1876; classic literature; dialogue; characterisation; historical context	Write a humorous description of a real or fictitious person.
90	News of Ned Kelly	Informative—recount letter	Letter; historical document about Ned Kelly's final battle and capture	Research a historical document. Write a report on what it says about its time in history.
91	TV program: *Live at 10 am*	Persuasive—television interview	Nutrition; exercise; diabetes prevention; interview techniques	Write the script for a television current affairs interview.
92	The rules of this ride	Informative—procedure: rules	Send-up/parody	Write a set of rules. They can be sensible or parody.
93	Resistance	Informative—report	First Australian history; point of view; racism; paragraphing	Write a report about an event in history from a minority perspective.
94	Why sea levels are rising	Informative—explanation	Climate change; global warming	Write an explanation of something that happens in nature.
95	The Day of Scrapes	Imaginative—narrative	*What Katy Did* by Susan Coolidge, 1872; classic literature; setting	Interview family members about their school days. Write a narrative using the ideas collected.

Notes

Notes

Notes